BRAZIL

This volume forms part of a series on industry and trade in some developing countries edited by Ian Little, Tibor Scitovsky, and Maurice Scott. The others in the series are on India, Mexico, Pakistan, the Philippines, and Taiwan (the last two in one volume). There is also a comparative volume by the editors.

INDUSTRY AND TRADE
IN SOME DEVELOPING COUNTRIES

BRAZIL
Industrialization and Trade Policies

JOEL BERGSMAN

Published on behalf of the

Development Centre of the
ORGANIZATION FOR ECONOMIC CO-OPERATION
AND DEVELOPMENT
PARIS
by
OXFORD UNIVERSITY PRESS
LONDON   NEW YORK   TORONTO
1970

Oxford University Press, Ely House, London W.1

GLASGOW NEW YORK TORONTO MELBOURNE WELLINGTON
CAPE TOWN SALISBURY IBADAN NAIROBI DAR ES SALAAM LUSAKA ADDIS ABABA
BOMBAY CALCUTTA MADRAS KARACHI LAHORE DACCA
KUALA LUMPUR SINGAPORE HONG KONG TOKYO

Hardback edition SBN 19 215325 0
Paperback edition SBN 19 215336 6

Printed in Great Britain
by Richard Clay (The Chaucer Press), Ltd.,
Bungay, Suffolk

Contents

List of Tables

Miss Prism: That would be delightful. Cecily, you will read your Political Economy in my absence. The chapter on the Fall of the Rupee you may omit. It is somewhat too sensational. . .

OSCAR WILDE, *The Importance of Being Earnest*

Figure 1. Brazilian Exchange Rates 1946–67
(including taxes, bonuses, etc.)

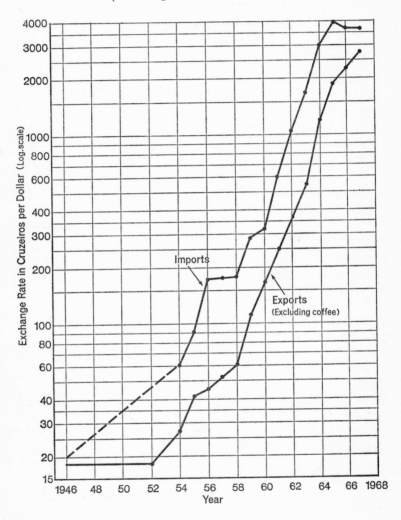

Preface

FROM January 1966 through July 1967 I was one of a group of economists working with the Ministry of Planning of the Government of Brazil, in Rio de Janeiro. We had been sent by the University of California to assist the Office of Applied Economic Research (E.P.E.A.: now known as I.P.E.A.) of the Ministry in its research on economic policy problems in Brazil. I worked with the part of I.P.E.A. concerned with the manufacturing sector.

During that period I was contacted by Dr Ian Little, then Vice-President of the O.E.C.D. Development Centre in Paris. Dr Little was starting a project to study the industrialization and trade policies of a number of less-developed countries (L.D.C.s). Little's research programme was similar to work I had already begun in Brazil, and after some discussion all parties concerned agreed that I would undertake the study of Brazil for the O.E.C.D. project, somewhat expanding the scope of my own programme to approach that of the other O.E.C.D. country studies.

I was very much taken by the idea of the O.E.C.D. project. It seemed to me—as it still does—that economic theory is nowhere more useful to policy-makers than in the areas to be studied: all of today's L.D.C.s are facing the questions of whether to promote industry, what kind of industry, in what time sequence, and with what kinds of instruments. The dilemma of free trade and specialization *v.* self-sufficiency and 'balanced' growth—balanced *vis-à-vis* domestic demand—seems vital to most L.D.C. governments. One more-or-less extreme solution, that of striving to approach free trade and perfect competition, had been coming under a new round of criticism since the 1940s. Another extreme, protecting domestic industries from foreign competition, is being tried by many L.D.C.s, with remarkably bad results in many cases and real success in few or none.

The differences between the two schools of thought are so fundamental that there are few arguments between them. For the most part, each ignores the other. The free-trade school is concerned principally with how to maximize current income, and uses models which ignore some of the world's most important 'imperfections'. Like most economic theory, trade theory does not take into account that instruments differ in ease of implementation as well as in theoretical efficiency. At least as important, trade theory is unconcerned with the essentially *dynamic* nature of development and structural change. Growth in productivity, which is almost by definition the essence of rising *per capita* income, is a dynamic process about which trade theory has nothing to say. On the other hand, protection as practised often seems to be based on the beliefs that if some protection is good, then more is better and most is best; that civil servants and ministers have perfect information about the present and the future and can make decisions at any speed and with perfect rationality; and that the consumer can take care of himself while the government takes care of the producer.

Since neither theory nor practice shows the solution to these important problems, it seemed to me an excellent idea to examine the actual practices of a number of countries, and the results of those practices, in light of the theory and in light of the other examples. The difficulty of making controlled experiments is always a problem in economics. Perhaps the simultaneous study of the same questions in different instances, by people who communicate among themselves, could take a small step towards increasing the number of variables observed, thus reducing the chance that something not observed was influencing the results. Such a group of studies might increase our understanding of the kinds of results that different policies would produce in different circumstances.

These are grand aims. As far as my own work goes, definitive answers to these questions remain to be found—if indeed they exist. I have not found any new simple key to successful trade and development policies. I have not been able to understand things as completely as I would like, nor to measure things as precisely as would be useful. I raise perhaps more questions than I answer, and those recommendations that I do make seem little more than common sense. I hope, however, that I have made some progress; moreover, if this study stimulates someone else to brave the frustrations of studying the Brazilian economy, and if he comes closer to answers to these important questions, I will be content.

Much of the success I have had is due to help from others. I had, really, four collaborators in Brazil: Arthur Candal and Pedro S. Malan at I.P.E.A., who worked with me and whose ideas and results are found throughout this volume, and Werner Baer and Carlos A. Rocca, who were kind enough to write chapters for this volume based on their own research. Werner Baer also deserves to be listed among my many tutors on Brazil: José Luis de Almeida Bello, Walter Ferri da Silveira Horta, Michel Hartveld, Carlos Frederico Hirsch, Diogenes Machado, Osório Chagas Meirelles, Orlando Menezes, Helder Fernandes Motta, Fabiano Pegurier, and Fernando Sarmento of the Industrial Sector of I.P.E.A.; José de Almeida, Isaac Kerstenetsky, and Mário Henrique Simonsen of the Fundação Getúlio Vargas; Ruy Aguiar da Silva Leme of the University of São Paulo; Maria da Conceição Tavares of E.C.L.A.; Joaquim Ferreira Mangia, Otto Ferreira Neves, and José Sampaio Portela Nunes of the Conselho de Política Aduaneira; and José Maria Vilar de Queiroz of the Ministry of Foreign Affairs. I am also greatly indebted to my colleagues Samuel Morley, Gordon Smith, and Willy van Rijckeghem, and my mentors Bela Balassa, Ian Little, Maurice Scott, and especially Tibor Scitovsky for ideas, useful criticism, helpful discussions, and encouragement. I also received many useful criticisms and new ideas from participants in a working conference at Bellagio in March 1968.

I thank the Superintendent of I.P.E.A., João Paulo dos Reis Velloso, and his deputy David Carneiro Junior, for their support and assistance. Regis Bonelli, Neil Boyle, Marcos Flavio Pires de Carvalho, Dag Ehrenpreis, and Betty Heian deserve much credit for their help as assistants, and Marize Martins de Abreu, Julie Cleland, and especially Janie Prior have my heartfelt appreciation for the many times they typed what follows.

Parts of 'Industrialization: Past Success and Future Problems', which I wrote jointly with Arthur Candal and which will appear in Howard S. Ellis (ed.), *The Economy of Brazil*, University of California Press, 1969, have been repeated here with the permission of the University of California Press. We also gratefully acknowledge permission from the Harvard University Press to reprint parts of *Electric Power in Brazil*, by Judith Tendler.

Last but not least, my appreciation for financial support from

the Agency for International Development, the International Bank
for Reconstruction and Development, and the Development
Centre of the Organization for Economic Co-operation and Development. As always, the responsibility for all analysis, conclusions, and judgements is the author's alone.

JOEL BERGSMAN

Berkeley
February 1969

PART I

Background

I

Introduction

THE purpose of this chapter is to describe the aims of this study, and some of the preconceptions and judgements which affected the way it was done. This description will be in the framework of economic theories about trade and development. This first chapter is thus like one long footnote, and those who do not enjoy footnotes are permitted to turn immediately to Chapter 2.

International trade has a basic role underlying the analysis in this study. This is because of one simple fact: from Brazil's point of view, all the other countries in the world, producing among them virtually every product which Brazilians demand, permit a choice to be made between producing something in Brazil or importing it. This means that there is a net present cost to Brazil of producing anything that can be imported for less. This book is about the steps which Brazil took in order to promote domestic production of things which could be bought more cheaply than they could be made in Brazil. My purpose is not only to describe these steps, but to evaluate them: to what extent were they worth while, and how could they have been improved?

I do not know how to do such an evaluation objectively. Brazilians want their country to 'develop', but the goal is not precisely defined and the means are far from clearly known. Any evaluation of development policies will therefore depend on the evaluator's judgement about the precise definition of the goal, as well as about the best means to reach that goal. My own views on these basic but not objectively settled questions must influence what questions I ask, as well as how I answer them. In this chapter some of the theoretical and empirical views which were in the background of my work will be described.

I. WHY WORRY ABOUT POLICIES FOR TRADE AND DEVELOPMENT?

Trade and development theory

The theory of international trade is a theory about static equilibrium. Given the 'technological' information about what types and quantities of inputs can be used to produce what types and quantities of products, it tells us several interesting things:

1. Assuming (among other things) no restraints on trade or on prices, it tells what inputs will be used to produce what products, and what the various prices (= values) of those inputs and products will be.

2. If there are restrictions on trade, or on the prices of inputs or products, it tells us that the total value of production will be less than it would be without those restrictions. This is essentially because without restrictions no inputs will be used to produce less than $1.00 worth of product if they could produce $1.00 worth of some other product (or of the same product in a different way), and no one will buy something that costs $1.00 if he can buy something else that he likes just as well for less than $1.00.

One very interesting thing that trade theory does not tell us is how the 'technological' state of the world is determined—what determines the technology used in production, and the amount of product that a given set of inputs can produce, in a given country and at a particular time.

The theory of trade has, of course, gone far beyond these simple basics. Two kinds of extensions are important here. The first is what a country should do if it has any degree of monopoly power in international trade: if by controlling the quantity it can affect the price of something that it imports or exports. In that case, the theory shows how to regulate the quantity (or price, which amounts to the same thing) so as to maximize the welfare of the country with the monopoly power. There are only a few cases where a country supplies or uses a large enough share of the total supply of something to be able to affect its price—but these cases are by their nature important to the country concerned. Brazilian coffee is an example: Brazil presently supplies about 40 per cent of world consumption, and used to supply over 75 per cent.

Brazilian coffee policy is not analysed in this study, but what happened can be mentioned here. Brazil in effect did and does tax coffee exports, and this has certainly raised the external price of coffee. From 1946 to 1953, the 'tax' was achieved simply by an overvalued export exchange rate, which taxed all other exports (on which Brazil did *not* have any monopoly power) as well as coffee. This policy was often justified as necessary to maximize export earnings. Whatever its usefulness for coffee, it was certainly disastrous for other products. Starting in 1953 Brazil adopted multiple export exchange rates. Other exports were still 'taxed' (the rate for most exports was still overvalued relative to the free trade rate) but not as much, and without the possibility of justifying the taxes as exploitation of monopoly power on coffee.[1]

The second extension of trade theory takes into account certain restrictions on prices of inputs or products, or what economists call 'imperfections in the market'. Three kinds of restrictions or imperfections seem to be important:

1. There may be minimum levels for wages, set by unions, other social factors, or the simple needs of physical survival. Furthermore, the number of available workers may be so large relative to the other things which the workers use—land, machinery, etc.—that workers are not worth this minimum level. The value of product lost if one worker would be fired may be less than his wage. But if we have a family farm or family business, for example, that worker may not be fired.

This is called 'surplus labour', and the essence of the imperfection is that the cost of a worker to an employer is more than his cost to the economy. Employers who are free to hire and fire, but must pay at least the minimum wage, will not hire a worker whose productivity would be less than the minimum wage, even though his productivity might be more than in his present job. And so the total value of production is less than it could be.[2]

---

[1] Obviously the justification was always silly for non-coffee products, but somehow the alternatives of actual taxes on coffee, or multiple rates, were not raised or were not acceptable.

[2] See W. Arthur Lewis, 'Economic Development with Unlimited Supplies of Labor', *Manchester School*, May 1954.

This distortion does appear to exist in Brazil. Its magnitude is hard to measure, but clearly is large. In Brazil there is a legal minimum wage in industry. This minimum for industrial areas such as Rio and São Paulo is at least five times the average productivity of labour in agriculture.[1] The discrepancy between the minimum wage in industry and the *marginal* productivity in agriculture must be even greater. These estimates are very rough, and an adjustment should be made for the higher cost of living which a worker faces in industrial areas. But without trying here to be precise, one could justify a government subsidy to industry to cover a large part of wage costs.[2] The Government is supposed to contribute about a third of total payments into social security (*previdência social*) funds. This would represent roughly 15 per cent of total wage costs. In fact this contribution has not been made in recent years; even if it had, 15 per cent is probably far below the optimum subsidy.

Similar imperfections may exist for other factors; for example, interest rates may be fixed below what money is really worth. Capital may be rationed and given to those with the right friends, or in favoured industries, rather than to those who will put it to the most profitable use and therefore pay the most for it.

2. The profitability of several activities may depend on each other; none may be worth while by itself but all may be worth while together. For example, a railroad in a certain region might not be profitable unless an iron ore mine were opened at one place and a steel mill at another; not only the mine and the mill, but also many other industries and services along the way might not be profitable without the railroad.[3]

An extension of this concept, beyond purely economic lines,

---

[1] Data on minimum wages from *Anuário Estatistico*, 1963, pp. 280, 281. The average productivity of labour in agriculture is hard to estimate because of widely varying estimates of the number of workers. I have used data from the Agricultural Census of 1960, which give the highest estimates of average productivity of labour in agriculture.

[2] An obvious alternative is to reduce the minimum wage. This would probably remove part of the economic distortion, but would be politically very difficult.

[3] See P. N. Rosenstein-Rodan, 'Problems of Industrialization of Eastern and South-Eastern Europe', *Economic Journal*, September 1943; Ragnar Nurkse, *Problems of Capital Formation in Underdeveloped Countries*, Oxford University Press, 1953; and Tibor Scitovsky, 'Two Concepts of External Economies', *Journal of Political Economy*, April 1954.

is that profitability may not be sufficient to induce needed investment. This is especially likely in government-operated or -regulated activities, such as telephones, highways, etc. Here the existence of users may increase the political pressure to make the desired (and socially profitable) investment.[1] These cases can all be referred to as instances of 'external economies'.

3. An investment may have a high expected payoff, but because of unwillingness to bear risk, or unwillingness to wait a number of years to get the payoff, or inability to raise a large required investment, individuals may fail to do what their country—i.e. the Government—would like done.

All three of these restrictions or imperfections are essentially cases of private costs or profits being perceived differently than social costs or profits, or of imperfect economic motivation. They have nothing directly to do with international trade. The best solution lies in domestic taxes or subsidies to bring private perceptions in line with social perceptions, or in provision of better information or planning, or in Government's undertaking what individuals will not or cannot.

To sum up: Basic trade theory tells us that freedom from restrictions on prices or quantities produced or traded will lead to maximum total production. Two modifications of this basic conclusion have been noted: if a country has monopoly power in international trade, it can increase its own welfare—at the expense of others—by taxing trade on the product in question. If on the other hand there are restrictions or imperfections in the structure of domestic costs, prices, or profits, then welfare can be increased by *domestic* subsidies or taxes to remove these distortions. Moreover, taxing trade to compensate for domestic distortions, or taxing domestic production to exploit international monopoly power, only introduces more distortions and may *not* improve the situation.[2]

Perhaps the most common argument for government intervention is the 'infant industry' concept. Here we pass from the theory of trade alone to what is also the theory of development.

---

[1] See Albert O. Hirschman, *The Strategy of Economic Development*, Yale University Press, 1958.
[2] See Jagdish Bhagwati and V. K. Ramaswami, 'Domestic Distortions, Tariffs, and the Theory of Optimum Subsidy', *Journal of Political Economy*, February 1963.

The 'infant industry' argument starts to get at what determines the technological data which trade theory takes as given. It says that individuals and groups of people learn by doing,[1] and that efficiency in an industry which is new to a country may be low at first, but will increase with experience. This simple statement will be true in most cases, but several questions remain: first, will efficiency increase *enough* so that the once-infant industry will be able to compete with foreign competitors? If not, it will *always* be an inefficient use of resources. Second, if so, why is government intervention necessary to get the industry started? It is socially desirable only if the net present value of all its costs and revenues is positive; if this is so then private entrepreneurs can be expected to undertake it without government intervention. Third, if government intervention is necessary, what form should it take? If private entrepreneurs don't start a socially desired industry, it is presumably because of their different perceptions of costs, revenues, risks, etc. The appropriate action is therefore domestic subsidies, better planning, or public investment; it is *not* protection against imports.[2]

Becoming competitive in today's world

Trade theory analyses static situations, in which conditions of supply (i.e. production cost schedules, quantity and quality of inputs available, and technology) and demand have already been determined. These given data then determine comparative costs: which countries can most efficiently produce which products. In fact, however, tomorrow's structure of comparative costs is affected by today's structure of production. Today, industrial efficiency depends on being industrialized.

What makes a country an efficient industrial producer? Raw materials? Japan produces the lowest cost steel in the world with imported raw materials. Cheap, abundant, perhaps non-unionized labour? India, Pakistan, China, and Brazil should then be the most advanced industrial countries. Industrial efficiency today depends on capital—not only financial resources to build factories

---

[1] See Kenneth J. Arrow, 'The Economic Implications of Learning by Doing', *Review of Economic Studies*, June 1962.

[2] Throughout this study 'tariffs' or 'protection' will be used to mean government intervention which allows domestic prices to be higher, and 'subsidies' in a broad sense to mean intervention which reduces domestic costs. The referent is prices in international trade, or prices or costs in competing countries.

and buy machinery, but also workers who are well-educated, easily trained, and socially adapted to the conditions of industrial work—i.e. workers who have grown up in an industrial society. This capital also consists of experienced engineers and managers, the schools to train them, and the industries in which they can gain experience. It consists of well-developed and efficient transport, communication, and electric power, and government help in the regulation and organization of various markets. It would indeed be lovely to have all these factors appear first, and induce industrial development which would be internationally competitive right from the start. Unfortunately for L.D.C.s, these resources appear today as the *results* of industrialization as much as its *causes*.

This should not be pushed too far. Certain raw materials or other locational factors are crucial for certain activities. It is not easy to compete with French wines, Brazilian coffee, or Kuwaiti oil. In many industries the scale of production is important, and countries with insufficient domestic markets can develop such industries only by forming marketing agreements with other countries, or by subsidizing exports. (Whether scale is a problem or not, efficient export industries seldom appear until initial experience has been gained by supplying the domestic market.)

The most important factors in determining a country's comparative costs in most industries is social, human, and economic capital. For a big, naturally rich country like Brazil, efficiency in most industrial activities appears possible, given this capital. Efficiency *may not* appear as a result of industrialization, but *will not* appear without it. In today's world industrialization is a necessary, but not sufficient, condition for industrial efficiency.

This is analogous to the 'infant industry' argument. Brazil's entire industrial sector can be viewed as an infant. This 'infant economy' argument has four elements:

1. Not only individuals and firms, but the whole society 'learns' by doing. Industry creates skills internally, and also makes demands of society for more appropriate education, physical infrastructure, social organization, and government action in fiscal and monetary policy, market organization and regulation, etc.

2. Growth of the economic, social, and human capital needed

for efficient industry will *not* take place at a satisfactory rate except as a product of growth in industrial activity. That is, 'the quantity and quality of factors of production may change substantially over time, in part as a result of the production process itself'.[1]

3. External economies are important among parts of industry, including physical infrastructure. There are therefore benefits to rapid industrialization on a broad front.

4. A country trying to industrialize today faces advanced competitors. Intervention will therefore be necessary until the 'infant economy' grows up. Again, intervention is necessary but not sufficient—the infant economy may *never* grow up!

II. BRAZIL'S FUTURE AS AN INDUSTRIAL COUNTRY

An old joke in Brazil says, 'Brazil is the land of tomorrow—and always will be'. But what sort of tomorrow? Should Brazil indus-trialize? Can Brazilian industry be internationally competitive, even as a result of optimal policies?

The dilemma of the policy-maker is that these questions are answerable only by history, but policies must be designed in the present. Government intervention to promote industrialization might bear fruit. The infant economy might grow up. If the Government does not act—no tariffs on industrial imports, no subsidies to investments in industry, no highways, railroads, telephones, technical and engineering schools, capital market regulation, etc., beyond what existing producers demand—Brazil would probably not industrialize and one would never know what might have been.

Let us ask the question in reverse. What would Brazil be like without a significant and growing industrial sector? Brazil is exceptionally well endowed for agriculture, and her minerals could be exported. Why force an 'unnatural' industrialization? If we consider only the present—in 1968 as in 1946 or earlier—it seems clear that Brazil should *not* take extraordinary steps to promote industry. Some subsidies to wages might be appropriate,

---

[1] Hollis B. Chenery, 'Comparative Advantage and Development Policy', *American Economic Review*, March 1957, p. 21. This article is the classic review of the reasons which, as Chenery puts it, 'destroy the presumption that perfect competition, even if it could be achieved, would lead to the optimum allocation of resources over time' (p. 22).

to reduce the difference between labour's cost to industry and its opportunity cost to the economy. Physical infrastructure, education, and market organization could all stand some improvement. But the value of current output would clearly be maximized by staying much closer to current comparative costs, which would clearly indicate more exploitation of food and fibres, livestock, and minerals. Such an answer does not imply *no* industry; it probably implies industry growing not much faster than population.

The only trouble with this solution is that the Brazil of the year 2000 would probably look very much like the Brazil of 1968 or of 1946—except that the population would probably have increased almost as fast as the value of output. It is very hard to envision continuing growth in *per capita* income in Brazil without a large and growing industrial sector. Why is this so?

The first reason is simply that, assuming growing *per capita* income, the demand for industrial products grows faster than the demand for primary products. Even if Brazilian labour productivity in terms of quantity of output could grow without much industrial growth, demand for imports would be growing faster than demand for exports. Unless Brazil's terms of trade continually improved (highly unlikely for a producer of primary products), this would require continual devaluation of the currency. If we can judge by the past experience of Brazil and other countries, this in turn would probably lead to continued specialization in exports of primary products. But this specialization is rarely accompanied by growth in income, which is the assumption with which this argument began. In sum, continued devaluation of a unitary exchange rate may suffice to handle changes in the structure of demand *if* income is growing. But it probably will not suffice to *induce* that continued growth in income, at least in Brazil.

Behind this problem is the difficulty of continuously increasing the productivity of labour in agriculture and services, in the absence of enough new jobs in industry so that the labour force in agriculture and services can be reduced (or at least not expand very rapidly). This is partly an *a priori* argument, based on diminishing returns because of limited amounts of good land, high-grade mineral deposits, etc. In the Brazilian case these diminishing returns seem far in the future, especially if the labour force in these activities does not have to grow too fast for too long. But the argument is also based on observation: labour productivity rarely does grow very rapidly in the real world of agriculture and services, unless the number of workers is being rapidly reduced. Without some combination of low population growth and high emigration, rising average labour productivity must imply rapid growth of industrial employment, and hence of industrial production.[1]

There are also reasons for industrialization which have little or nothing to do with economics. The United States has its space programme; France its *force de frappe*. The economist as economist can only deplore these activities, estimate their low benefit-cost ratios and perhaps hope that someone will listen. But—thank God—the world is not made up only of economists. And, of course, not all non-economic motivations lead to such un-economic activities. For example, industrialization will induce changes in the educational system and the social structure which may be highly valued in themselves. These 'external economies' of industrialization—call them, together, 'modernization'—may be tremendously important and valuable, although their value is not measurable.

III. CONCLUSION

The effects of basic knowledge and of my prejudices, within which this study has been done, can now be summarized.

First, I do not believe that Brazil should not have a significant and rapidly growing industrial sector. It is true that Brazil has a clear and significant present comparative advantage in many agricultural and mining activities, and there would be benefits from more promotion—or less dis-promotion—of these. But I cannot envision a Brazil where prosperity is growing continuously without a large reliance for that growth on industry. What is more, I *can* imagine a Brazil with an industrial sector that is not only significant and growing, but also reasonably competitive in terms of comparative costs.

Second, I do not expect that Brazil could have industrialized

[1] This is a not-so-elegant restatement of a basic argument in John C. H. Fei and Gustav Ranis, *Development of the Labor Surplus Economy*, Richard D. Irwin, 1964. One does not, however, have to accept the entire Fei–Ranis thesis in order to see the validity in the argument made here.

without some government intervention; whether protection, subsidies, heavy investments in physical infrastructure and education, market organization and regulation, etc.

Major interest is therefore focused on *how* the Government should have intervened. How useful were actual Brazilian policies affecting international trade and industrialization? How well did they balance the trade-off between exploitation of current comparative advantage for maximum present income, and creation of future comparative advantage along lines promising maximum future growth? How much did policies encourage the infant economy to grow up to be productive and competitive, or how much did they induce it simply to become a bigger and greedier infant?

2

The Background of Post-war Industrialization

Brazil is a large country, rich in natural resources and not seriously overpopulated. In area it is larger than the continental United States. Its population is over 80 million people. Arable land is abundant; much good land lies fallow and much more is used in ways which result in very low productivity per acre ('clear-and-burn' farming and extensive grazing). North-eastern Brazil does present a contrasting picture; population density is relatively high, and recurrent droughts join with social and political problems to complicate the situation. The country as a whole, however, is very far from having trouble feeding itself.

Most commonly-used metallic ores are plentiful and economically exploitable, and Brazil is especially well-endowed with iron and manganese ores. The exceptions are copper and tin; recently discovered copper deposits may change this. Some petroleum has been found, but at present about two-thirds of consumption must be imported. Only a little coal is present, and it is of poor quality, i.e. not economically suited for coking for the steel industry. As to energy, economic sites for hydro-electric power are plentiful.

Per capita income is about $300, with a significant difference between the two major centres of population. The north-east, with about 30 per cent of the people, has very little industry, a backward social and economic structure, and a *per capita* income of about $100. The centre-south, with most of the rest of the population, enjoys an income of almost $400 *per capita*. Virtually all of Brazilian industry is in the centre-south, and agriculture there is much more efficient (both per worker and per acre) than in the north-east. The industry centred around São Paulo, Belo Horizonte, and Rio de Janeiro is as significant, modern, and diversified as any in the less-developed world.

Coffee is, of course, very important in Brazil. It accounts for about half of export receipts, which is equivalent to over 3 per cent of Gross Domestic Product (G.D.P.). Brazil supplies over 40 per cent of world coffee consumption. Other important exports are raw cotton, cocoa, sugar, lumber (mostly pine), tobacco, iron ore, manganese ore, rice, and corn. The most important imports are crude oil, wheat, aluminium, copper, tin ore, various chemicals, and various capital goods. The structure of trade is shown in Table 2.1.

Import substitution has been an important aspect of Brazilian industrialization, both as to impetus, and as to structure and sequence. In most presently developed countries gradual industrialization was the basic element in growth, structural change, and creation of the fabric of modern institutions and individuals. Brazil is an outstanding example of a different form of rapid development through import substitution.

From the second world war until the early 1960s Brazil made remarkable progress in economic growth. All major sectors of the economy grew rapidly and steadily throughout the period. From 1947 (the first year for which most data are available) until 1962 G.D.P. grew at an average annual rate of 6 per cent. Agricultural output grew at 4·6 per cent per year, industry (including mining, construction, and electricity) at 9·5 per cent, and manufacturing at 9·8 per cent. Details are shown in Table 2.2.

It is a little harder to estimate the share of industry or manufacturing in total output. Consistent measures are not available for G.D.P., but only for domestic income. Industry's share of the latter has been roughly constant at 24-25 per cent from 1950 to 1962. If the independent measures of manufacturing value added and G.D.P. are used, value added in manufacturing as a percentage of G.D.P. at current prices rose from 22 per cent in 1949 to 30 per cent in 1959 and to about 34 per cent in 1962. These data are shown in Table 2.3.

Industry's share in total production in 1962 was probably higher than that to be expected of a country of Brazil's population and income level. In a comparison of the industrial structure of Brazil with an international pattern, the share of manufacturing in G.D.P. in 1962 was found to be close to the international pattern.[1]

---

[1] See Joel Bergsman and Arthur Candal, 'Industrialization: Past Success and Future Problems', in Howard S. Ellis (ed.), *The Economy of Brazil*, University of California Press, 1969.

TABLE 2.1
STRUCTURE OF BRAZIL'S FOREIGN TRADE
(per cent by value)

Exports

Item	*1946–8*	*1960–2*
Coffee	38%	53%
Cocoa	4	5
Cotton	15	7
Tobacco	2	2
Iron ore	—	5
Hemp	—	2
Sugar	1	4
Manganese ore	—	2
Lumber	3	3
Miscellaneous primary products	31	14
Miscellaneous manufactures	6	3
	100%	100%
TOTAL as per cent of G.D.P.	13%[a]	7%

Imports

Item	*1948–50[b]*	*1960–2*
Finished goods:		
Consumer durables	8%	2%
Consumer non-durables	7	7
Capital goods	38	29
Intermediate products:		
Metallic	8	7
Non-metallic	} 20 {	21
Construction materials		3
Other:		
Crude oil	—	8
Other fuels and lubricants	13	10
Wheat	6	13
	100%	100%
TOTAL as per cent of G.D.P.	10%	8%

[a] 1947–8 only.
[b] Suitable data on imports are not available for years prior to 1948.
Sources: Exports: S.E.E.F., Ministry of Finance. Imports: Data for 1948–50 from E.C.L.A., 'The Growth and Decline of Import Substitution in Brazil', *Economic Bulletin for Latin America*, March 1964; for 1960–2 from I.B.G.E., *Números Indices Annuais dos Preços e das Quantidades no Comércio Exterior e de Cabotagem*, Rio de Janeiro.

In that study, however, a purchasing-power-parity exchange rate was used. In Chapter 3 of this book a 'free trade' exchange rate is estimated. If this rate had been used in the international comparison, the actual share of manufacturing in G.D.P. in Brazil would have been roughly 50 per cent greater than the share predicted by the international cross-section. This problem of the

TABLE 2.2

GROWTH OF PHYSICAL OUTPUT, 1947-65
(index numbers)

Year	Agriculture	Industry	Manufacturing	G.D.P.
1947	89·5	81·4	80·8	86·5
1948	95·7	90·6	90·4	94·7
1949	100	100	100	100
1950	102	111	112	105
1951	102	119	119	110
1952	112	124	125	117
1953	112	135	137	120
1954	121	147	149	130
1955	130	162	166	138
1956	127	174	177	140
1957	139	183	186	151
1958	141	213	218	161
1959	149	241	245	173
1960	156	265	271	184
1961	168	293	301	197
1962	177	316	326	208
1963	179	318	325	212
1964	181	334	341	218
1965	211	318	326	228

Source: Fundação Getúlio Vargas. Real G.D.P. is estimated as a weighted average of the sectoral real product indices, which themselves are ultimately based almost completely on indices of physical output of various products, and on population. The weights used are mostly prices at the product level, and value added at higher levels of aggregation. For details see the *Revista Brasileira de Economia*, March 1962, or Werner Baer, *Industrialization and Economic Development in Brazil*, Richard D. Irwin, 1965, Appendix 1.

TABLE 2.3

INDUSTRY IN THE ECONOMY, 1947-62

	Per cent of domestic income		Per cent of G.D.P.
Year	Agriculture	Industry	Manufacturing
1947	(31)	(21)	(21)
1949			22
1950	29	24	
1959	27	25	30
1960	28	25	
1962	31	25	34

Sources: Domestic Income (*Renda Interna*), Fundação Getúlio Vargas. My estimates for 1947 made by projecting 1950 estimates backward according to real product indices.

G.D.P. from Fundação Getúlio Vargas; manufacturing value added from censuses for 1949 and 1959; *Registro Industrial* for 1962 (adjusted for non-coverage of industries employing less than 5 persons). My estimates for 1947 made by projecting 1949 estimate backward according to real product indices.

The data are obviously inconsistent, since industry covers manufacturing plus transport, construction, and electrical power, and G.D.P. is larger than domestic income. I am unable to reconcile the inconsistency.

proper exchange rate is only one of many problems in interpreting comparisons with international cross-sections, but it seems safe to conclude that Brazil's manufacturing sector in the early 1960s was significantly larger than the international pattern, based on G.D.P. and population, would have predicted.

Whatever success Brazil has achieved in industrialization was made possible by three basic factors. First, income from export production had already allowed the creation of a modest industrial sector and an urbanized population with some modern institutions and attitudes. Second, the great size of the country partially counteracted the low income level and other 'low-level equilibrium trap' problems, and permitted a more diversified and probably lower cost industrial development than is possible in smaller countries. Third, difficulties with the balance of payments and war-time disruption of international trade furnished strong economic and psychological motivation to take advantage of these favourable factors. The result was the creation of the largest and most diversified industry in the less-developed world. (India and China, each with about six times Brazil's population, have roughly the same total value of industrial production.)

Perhaps the outstanding characteristic of growth led by import substitution is that rapid industrial growth can be independent of over-all growth of income and final consumer demand. Once in motion the process induces its own growth in demand for producer goods, and can thus continue until the structure of imports itself restricts further opportunities for new import-substituting investment.

II. A BRIEF REVIEW OF THE PRE-WAR PERIOD[1]

Brazil's early development, as a Portuguese colony, was typical of other colonies in Latin America and elsewhere. The economy

[1] Throughout this study, 'pre-war' and 'post-war' refer to before or after the second world war (1939–45). For analyses of the pre-war economic history of Brazil, see Baer, op. cit.; Celso Furtado, *The Economic Growth of Brazil*, University of California Press, 1963; Roberto Simonsen, *História Econômica do Brasil*, Companhia Editôria Nacional (São Paulo), 1962; Dorival Teixeira Vieira, 'The Industrialization of Brazil', in T. Lynn Smith and Alexander Marchant (eds.), *Brazil: Portrait of Half a Continent*, The Dryden Press, 1951; various papers on Brazil in Simon Kuznets, Wilbert E. Moore, and Joseph J. Spengler (eds.), *Economic Growth: Brazil, India, Japan*, Duke University Press, 1959.

was dominated by successive booms based on production and export of one primary product: first brazilwood, followed by sugar, gold, diamonds, rubber, cotton, cocoa, and finally coffee. During the colonial period manufacturing activity was prohibited.

The strictly colonial period ended in 1808. In 1807, a French army had entered Portugal. The Regent, Prince João, accepted the protection of the British and fled to Brazil with the entire court. Industries were no longer forbidden in Brazil, but generally free trade policies plus special trading concessions to the British kept the economy concentrated on primary production and export.

Prince João was crowned King João VI in Rio de Janeiro in 1816. In 1821 he returned to Portugal, still under British protection, and left his son Pedro as Regent in Brazil. Pedro was torn between demands from his father and the Portuguese parliament to return to Portugal, and pressure from the Brazilian upper classes to remain and rule an independent Brazil. In 1822 he chose the latter course: he declared Brazil independent, subdued (with British help) the few army units loyal to Portugal, and was crowned Pedro I, 'Emperor of Brazil by the grace of God—not to mention the grace of England'.[1]

The Empire period, which lasted until 1889, saw the beginnings of industrialization. By 1889 Brazil had over 6,000 miles of railroads, over 11,000 miles of telegraph lines, a coastal shipping network, and some manufacturing of food products, construction materials, textiles, iron and iron products, and ships. But these were insignificant compared with agriculture and mining activities. Until 1842, a treaty with the British (signed in 1827) imposed an essentially open economy. In the second half of the nineteenth century Brazil resisted British and other pressures, and imposed some restrictions on trade—notably tariffs on textiles. But Brazil in 1889 was still a feudal, agricultural and mining, low labour productivity economy.

The industries which did appear in this early period reflected Brazil's early comparative advantages. In sectors such as food products and construction materials, most regions tend to be largely self-sufficient because of high transport costs. But early

---

[1] Hubert Herring, *A History of Latin America*, Alfred A. Knopf, 3rd edition, 1968, p. 281.

activity in textiles, and iron and iron products, clearly was based on low real costs of production in those lines.[1]

In 1888, after decades of pressures and disagreement, slavery was abolished in Brazil. This was a serious blow to the cotton and sugar economy of the north-east; it was also probably the *coup de grace* to the Empire. Pedro II had ruled since 1841; by the 1880s he was beset by the army which chafed under his refusal to give it the freedom of action it desired, the Church which disliked his liberalism, and many liberals who wanted a republic. There was also general dissatisfaction with his probable successor: his daughter and heir had married a Frenchman who would not even learn Portuguese. With the abolition of slavery many of the rural oligarchs turned against him; a year later in 1889 Pedro yielded to the army's demands, abdicated, and left Brazil a Republic.

Coffee and cattle now became the leading economic sectors. These activities were located in the centre-south, in the states of Rio de Janeiro, Minas Gerais, São Paulo, and Rio Grande do Sul. Protectionism, and then the disruption of imports caused by the first world war, encouraged domestic industry. By the end of the first world war, roughly half of manufacturing activity was in textiles and food products, but many other activities were also present. The distribution of value added is shown in Table 2.4.

TABLE 2.4
DISTRIBUTION OF VALUE ADDED IN MANUFACTURING, 1919

Sector	Per cent of total
Non-metallic mineral products	4·7
Metallurgy	4·3
Machinery	2·0
Wood products and furniture	7·8
Paper and products	1·5
Rubber products	0·2
Leather products	2·4
Chemicals, pharmaceuticals, etc.	6·0
Textiles	28·6
Clothing	8·6
Food products	22·2
Beverages	5·9
Tobacco	3·9
Miscellaneous	1·9
	100·0

Source: Industrial Census of 1920, cited in Baer, op. cit., p. 17.

[1] This is developed further in Chapter 6.

Why didn't industry develop more rapidly in Brazil? There was a succession of very profitable opportunities in agriculture and mining for export; these not only had their economic effects but also resulted in a society controlled largely by landowners. Political-military dependence on the British until the mid-nineteenth century resulted in free trade policies; Britain's head start on industrialization and Brazil's small domestic market meant that Brazil could not compete. From the 1850s on, some industrial growth did occur. But primary exports remained profitable, the society remained feudal, steps to increase labour productivity were not taken, and policies were largely determined by the agricultural and commercial interests.

The first world war was perhaps the first of a series of external shocks to the Brazilian economy which led to industrialization. 'The interruption of supplies from overseas eliminated foreign competition, and many new industries were created to fill the gap and even to supply overseas markets. Additional elements reinforcing the spread of industrial enterprises were the inflationary effect of wartime financing, which created new purchasing power, and the wartime profits from shipping, trading, and manufacturing . . .'[1] Industrial production in São Paulo grew at over 25 per cent per year between 1914 and 1919.[2]

The Brazilian economy had already experienced several boom-and-bust cycles based on one primary export after another. Around the turn of the century, rubber was the profitable crop. But plantations were started by the British and the Dutch in the East Indies, and when these came into full production during 1910–20, Brazilian rubber, which had to be gathered in the Amazon jungle, could not compete. Between 1910 and 1920 Brazil's share of world rubber exports fell from roughly 90 to less than 10 per cent, and the price she received fell from 34 to 6 cents per pound. This represented a loss of about one-third of the value of exports in 1910.

Coffee was still very profitable. But the very conditions which gave Brazil such an advantage also spelled trouble.[3] The abundant supply of good land and labour meant that supply could be

[1] Baer, op. cit., p. 16.
[2] Alfredo Ellis Junior, *A Evolução da Economia Paulista e Suas Causas*, Companhia Editôria Nacional (São Paulo), 1937, p. 245.
[3] This discussion of coffee problems draws heavily on Chapter 30 of Furtado, op. cit.

expanded beyond the limits of even the entire world market. The planters realized this, and used their political power to institute government price support and supply restriction programmes. The price supports worked better than the supply restrictions— both in Brazil and abroad. Brazil, starting from an almost complete monopoly, kept the world price high enough so that more and more production from other countries entered the market. Even at home, profits were too high for the effective functioning of supply restrictions. Much of the excess purchasing power from the government purchases for stockpiling went into new plantings, thus feeding the cycle. A way to escape from this unstable situation was shown during the first world war, when a shortage of imported goods created many new profitable investment opportunities outside the coffee sector. But actual escape came only with the collapse of the world coffee market in 1929. The price of coffee sold by Brazil fell over 60 per cent in two years. Because of the enormous drop in export earnings—value of all exports fell 60 per cent between 1929 and 1932—severe restrictions were placed on imports. The internal coffee price support programmes declined only slightly, but now new investment in coffee looked doubtful compared with producing the now scarce, high-priced manufactured imports. The low financial capacity to import of the 1930s was followed by the disruption of trade due to the second world war, and industrial production grew about 5 per cent per year from 1930 to 1940,[1] and about 5·5 per cent per year from 1940 to 1945.[2] In all these periods when imports were scarce, domestic demand was kept high, either by export booms, or internal price support programmes for coffee and other main export crops.

Political developments after 1930 were also more favourable to industrialization. From shortly after the founding of the Republic, the presidency had alternated between representatives of the Minas Gerais, São Paulo, and (occasionally) Rio Grande do Sul oligarchies. Policies were generally favourable to landowners, and regionalism was very strong. States were allowed to control imports and exports, both international and inter-state, and in fact many states levied taxes on goods manufactured in other states.

[1] G. F. Loeb, *Industrialization and Balanced Growth: With Special Reference to Brazil*, Groningen (Holland), 1957, p. 90.
[2] *Revista Brasileira de Economia*, March 1962.

In the elections of 1930 the outgoing President Washington Luiz, a *Paulista* (from São Paulo), broke tradition and engineered the election of a fellow *Paulista*.[1] The *Mineiros* (from Minas Gerais) joined with the long-frustrated *Gaúchos* (from Rio Grande do Sul) to support Getúlio Vargas, then Governor of Rio Grande do Sul. There was talk of installing Vargas by force; the assassination of their Vice-Presidential candidate João Pessoa increased

TABLE 2.5
VALUE ADDED IN MANUFACTURING, 1939 AND 1949

	1939		1949	
Sector	Million 1949 Cruzeiros	Per cent of total	Million 1949 Cruzeiros	Per cent of total
Non-metallic mineral products	1,260	5·3	3,411	7·1
Metallurgy	1,815	7·6	4,469	9·3
Machinery	958	4·0	1,018	2·1
Electrical equipment	207	0·9	763	1·6
Transport equipment	141	0·6	1,062	2·2
Wood products	800	3·4	2,009	4·2
Furniture	466	2·0	1,030	2·2
Paper and products	349	1·5	1,072	2·2
Rubber products	152	0·6	902	1·9
Hides and skins	404	1·7	627	1·3
Chemicals	1,365	5·7	2,540	5·3
Pharmaceuticals	650	2·7	1,336	2·8
Perfumes, soaps, etc.	550	2·3	751	1·6
Plastics	nil	0·0	122	0·3
Textiles	514	22·0	9,359	19·6
Clothing	1,145	4·8	2,034	4·3
Food products	5,600	23·5	9,780	20·4
Beverages	1,035	4·3	2,140	4·5
Tobacco	541	2·3	680	1·4
Printing and publishing	850	3·6	1,899	4·0
Miscellaneous	259	1·1	777	1·6
TOTAL manufacturing	19,061	100·0	47,781	100·0

Sources: Industrial Census of 1950. Throughout this study the Brazilian concept of 'Valor da Transformação Industrial' is used for value added; the former includes services performed by contractors. The difference does not seem to be more than 3 per cent in any sector, or more than 1 per cent in any but one sector.

Values for 1939 in current cruzeiros were multiplied by the ratio of total 1949 output divided by twice total 1939 output (= 3·71) to reflect the Fundação Getúlio Vargas estimate that the real quantity of manufacturing production in 1949 was 2·0 times its value in 1939. See *Revista Brasileira de Economia*, March 1962.

[1] This discussion draws heavily on Thomas E. Skidmore, *Politics in Brazil*, Oxford University Press, 1967.

the momentum of the revolt, and army units from Rio Grande do Sul marched on Rio de Janeiro. The military in Rio declined to plunge the country into civil war, forced the still-incumbent Washington Luiz to resign, and in November 1930 installed Vargas as President.

Vargas had a more national viewpoint. He owed much to the army, little to the rich landowners of the centre-south, and nothing to the backward feudal bosses of the north-east. The army elements supporting Vargas were more bourgeois, nationalistic, and interested in modernization. Vargas ended state power in inter-state and international trade, gradually reduced coffee price supports, and was sympathetic to industrial development. During the second world war he created the state-owned integrated steel mill at Volta Redonda, today the largest in Latin America.

The structure of manufacturing production in 1939 and 1949 is shown in Table 2.5. Real growth of output during the decade was about 100 per cent, or 7 per cent per year.[1]

The difficulties of importing manufactured goods caused by the two world wars and by several drastic declines in Brazil's export earnings, abetted by some protection and other state support, especially to textiles, joined with Brazil's now larger market and natural advantages in ferrous metals and metal products to create a significant manufacturing sector. By the end of the second world war, manufacturing already accounted for some 20 per cent of G.D.P.

[1] Estimates of physical production from the *Revista Brasileira de Economia*, March 1962.

PART II

Policies

3

Post-war Commercial Policy[1]

THE purpose of this and the next chapter is to describe the policies which Brazil used to promote industrialization in the post-war period. The present chapter is focused on protection and commercial policy, and Chapter 4 on the other relevant policies.

Following these two chapters, an analysis of the results of these policies is presented in Chapters 5–7.

I. REVIEW OF POLICIES

Significant changes in commercial policy have been frequent in post-war Brazil. In this chapter the entire period will be reviewed, but attention will be focused on more recent developments.

No analysis of policy with respect to coffee will be attempted. Coffee is the only product in which Brazilian policies have a significant effect on world prices. Commercial policy for coffee should thus be different than for other products, and at least since 1953 this has been so. I make no judgement as to the details of this policy; others have studied it closely and evaluating it is not necessary for the puposes of this study.

1946–53: Over-valuation and quantitative control of imports

At the end of the war Brazil had large foreign exchange reserves. The exchange rate of Cr$ 18.50 per dollar, which had been in force throughout the war, remained unchanged until 1953; prices rose 285 per cent from 1945 to 1953.[2] Even in 1945 this rate had overvalued the cruzeiro—in terms of dollars it was approximately

[1] Pedro S. Malan collaborated on the basic empirical work for this chapter.
[2] *Conjuntura Econômica*, index No. 2.

the same as in 1937, while prices in Brazil had risen about 80 per cent more than in the U.S.[1] The progressive over-valuation of the currency was made possible by booming exports and restricted imports caused by the war. Three reasons are commonly suggested for the continuation of this over-valuation immediately following the war. First, restrictions on imports during the war had created a large demand for both producer and consumer goods, and the authorities wanted to facilitate these imports. Second, inflation was seen to be a danger, and a balance of payments deficit financed by the accumulated reserves was seen as one important means of keeping prices down. Third was the old idea of 'protecting' the value of coffee exports by keeping the price up through an over-valued exchange rate. These reasons illustrate the conservative nature of the Dutra Government (1945–50): policies favoured the traditional land-owning interests rather than growth of the newer urban industrial sectors, and at least at first followed economic orthodoxy in eschewing controls, multiple exchange rates, or even devaluation.

When a little over one year of unrestricted imports wiped out Brazil's foreign exchange reserves, controls on imports were chosen as the principal means of balancing the balance of payments. From 1947 to 1953, a licensing system was used to control both the level and the structure of Brazil's imports. Foreign exchange was allocated according to a five-category system of priorities:[2]

1. 'Super-essential': agricultural equipment, fuels, oils, lubricants, metals not domestically available, and needs of government agencies.

2. 'Essential': other raw materials, machinery, spare parts, and producer goods in general; some pharmaceuticals.

3. Transfers of capital and earnings of foreign capital.

4. Other goods.

5. Travel, etc.

Of the total amount of foreign exchange allocated to imports of goods (i.e. priority categories 1, 2, and 4), around 17 to 19 per

[1] See Donald L. Huddle, 'Balanço de Pagamentos e Contrôle de Câmbio no Brasil', *Revista Brasileira de Economia*, March 1964, p. 8.

[2] See Huddle, op. cit., and continuation in the *Revista Brasileira de Economia*, June 1964; I.M.F., *Annual Report on Exchange Restrictions*, various years beginning in 1950.

cent went to the 'super-essential' category and about 65 to 70 per cent to the 'essential'.[1]

The imposition of the licensing system was principally a response to a foreign exchange crisis; total imports were to be reduced, and restrictions on existing domestic production were to be kept to a minimum. Protection of existing consumer goods industries was a secondary goal, and growth of new industries was not an intended result. Around 1949 policy started to move towards more deliberate protectionism, with the gradual revival of the prohibition of imports of products for which domestic substitutes existed. This was under the authority of the 'Law of Similars', which had been on the books in one form or another since 1911. The Dutra Government was economically too orthodox to use this and other means of inducing structural change very aggressively. Deliberate industrialization did not take place until the more pragmatic Vargas (1951–4) and then the enthusiastic Kubitschek (1956–60) first tolerated and then embraced the *desenvolvimentismo* philosophy.[2]

Export policy in the 1945–53 period was characterized by the maintenance of a more and more over-valued currency, as mentioned above. Both the *quantum* and the value of exports declined steadily from 1946 until the Korean War. Starting in 1949, exporters of certain products which were being priced out of the market were allowed to sell foreign exchange directly to importers of non-essential goods. This effective devaluation was at first severely limited as to scope among export products, but became important just before and just after the Korean War boom.

In 1951 and 1952, imports rose to almost twice their previous level. Over 55 per cent of the increase was in capital goods, and other producer goods accounted for another 28 per cent. The boom was directly caused, of course, by the Korean War boom in export earnings. The nature of the increased imports, however, was determined by a number of factors. First was the ascendency of *desenvolvimentismo* under Vargas. Second, both the Korean

---

[1] Estimated from data in E.C.L.A., 'The Growth and Decline of Import Substitution in Brazil', *Economic Bulletin for Latin America*, March 1964.

[2] The *desenvolvimentista* ideals seem to be economic growth, modernization (techniques of production, and structure of production, employment, and political power), and reduced dependence on foreign trade and foreign influence in general. See Thomas E. Skidmore, *Politics in Brazil*, op. cit., 1967, pp. 87–100.

War, which caused the export boom but made many imports difficult to obtain, and the sharp drop in the value of exports in 1952 were seen as further evidence that Brazil should decrease her dependence on imports. A large part of the increased capacity to import was therefore used to create new import-substituting industries. Imports of machinery and equipment for manufacturing industry were about $297 million in 1951, $329 million in 1952, $188 million in 1953, and $224 million in 1954. These levels were higher than in any year preceding 1951. The average for 1948–50 had been $157 million.[1]

1953–7: Multiple rates, taxes, and bonuses in broad categories

In 1953 Brazilian commercial policy was significantly changed.[2] On the export side, different rates were established for different products. Bonuses were also used from time to time, and the system was quite complicated and changeable. The average export exchange rate rose about as fast as the domestic price level, but for individual products the real rate and the administrative set-up changed frequently. This lasted until 1959. Both the quantum and the value of exports were more or less stagnant during this period.

On the import side, control by licensing was replaced by a five-category exchange auction system. The monetary authority (S.U.M.O.C.) allocated available foreign exchange among the categories, and the effective import rates were set in auctions. Minimum premia were also set for each auction.

Some commodities were not subject to the auction system. These included imports for governmental agencies, wheat, newsprint, and petroleum products. The rate for these products was usually equal to the average export rate ('custo de câmbio') plus a tax which amounted to as much as 38 per cent *ad valorem*, but which was often waived. Petroleum products were also subject to licensing. These goods accounted for about one-third of the total value of imports. All other imports were classified among the five categories, as follows:

[1] Calculated from E.C.L.A., 'The Growth and Decline of Import Substitution in Brazil', op. cit.

[2] See I.M.F., *Annual Report on Exchange Restrictions*, 1954 to 1958; Alexander Kafka, 'The Brazilian Exchange Auction System', *Review of Economics and Statistics*, August 1956.

1. Inputs to agriculture, certain pharmaceuticals and inputs to the pharmaceutical industry, and some other 'essential' commodities.

2. 'Essential' raw materials (i.e. those for favoured industries, almost all in the intermediate goods category).

3. Other raw materials and 'essential' spare parts and equipment (again, those for favoured industries).

4. Other spare parts and equipment, and fresh fruits.

5. All other commodities (i.e. most finished consumer goods).

According to Kafka, the first three categories generally absorbed at least 80 per cent of the total foreign exchange available for auctions, and the fifth category absorbed a maximum of three per cent.[1] Disaggregated import data for 1954–7 show finished consumer goods to be about 14 per cent of all auction imports, with the remainder divided equally between capital goods and intermediate producer goods. This indicates that the fifth category was not rationed quite as strictly as Kafka suggests.

TABLE 3.1
IMPORT EXCHANGE RATES AND PROTECTION, 1954 AND 1956

Category	Average rate		Protection	
	1954	1956	1954	1956
	(cruzeiros per dollar)		(per cent)	
'Custo de câmbio'	30	44	−21	−38
1	42	74	10	4
2	45	81	18	14
3	58	103	52	45
4	68	116	80	62
5	111	222	190	210

Notes: 'Protection' is the per cent by which the rate exceeds the free trade rate estimated later in this chapter.

The 'Custo de câmbio' is equal to or slightly above the average export rate, and was usually used for imports of wheat, newsprint, petroleum and products, etc.

Source: Average rates from E.P.E.A., *Diagnóstico Preliminar, Setor de Comércio Internacional*, Ministry of Planning, Rio de Janeiro, March 1967 (mimeo).

A rough idea of the relative price effects of the auction system can be had from the average rates shown in Table 3.1. Because the exchange rate was fixed at Cr$18.50 per dollar, the level of the premia rose to keep pace with inflation; the structure, however, remained quite constant. The distribution of commodities among

[1] Kafka, op. cit., p. 310.

classes also was not changed significantly during the period the system was in effect, which was October 1953 to August 1957, although new domestic availability of some goods did result in imports of those goods no longer being considered 'essential'.

The biases among different types of imports were similar in both the licensing period (1947–53) and the exchange auction period (1953–7). The magnitude of the price effects may have differed, but the ranking was almost identical: most favoured were capital and current inputs to agriculture and some favoured industries; next, other producer goods; and last, finished consumer goods. There were great incentives to import substitution of industrial products, great disincentives to export anything at all, and some compensation to agriculture in the form of cheap inputs.

1957 to present: Tariffs on imports

In August 1957 the system controlling imports was reformed once again. A comprehensive set of *ad valorem* tariffs was introduced and the number of exchange rate categories was reduced from five to two. A few goods (fertilizers, newsprint, wheat, petroleum, and petroleum products) again formed a kind of additional separate category, for which a very low exchange rate, generally equal to the average rate for exports, was used. This new system remained in effect with only gradual changes up to March 1967, when the tariff schedule was revised downward and the multiple rates eliminated. In addition to the multiple rates and the *ad valorem* tariffs, certain restrictions and exemptions were used to reduce or to facilitate certain imports. Across-the-board surcharges, advance deposits, and similar devices were also used from time to time, especially during 1961–5, to raise revenue and to change the effective exchange rate for imports.[1]

Most raw materials and other producer goods were placed in the 'general' category. The exchange rate in this category was set in auctions where supply was controlled by the Government until March 1961, when the auctions were discontinued and a free market allowed to function. Most other goods, considered 'in-

[1] For a quantitative description and analysis of tariff changes over time, see Samuel A. Morley, 'Import Demand and Import Substitution in Brazil', in Howard S. Ellis (ed.), *The Economy of Brazil*, op. cit. Also, Paul Clark and Richard Weisskoff, 'Import Demands and Import Policies in Brazil', February 1967 (mimeo), and Paul Clark, 'Brazilian Import Liberalization', September 1967 (mimeo).

essential', were placed in the 'special' category. These goods were mostly finished consumer goods, plus most producer goods which were domestically available. The exchange rate in the special category was controlled by auctions, in which the rate generally varied between two and three times the general category rate. Total value of 'special' category imports was very small.

To over-simplify quite a bit, to import goods in the general category one bore tariffs up to about 80 per cent, while for goods in the special category one had to buy exchange at a premium of 100 to 200 per cent, and also to pay tariffs ranging up to 150 per cent.

The various exemptions and restrictions form a complex set of modifications to the tariffs. Enforcement is very flexible, varying from time to time as well as among products, and a precise description is somewhat difficult; I will try to summarize here the major characteristics. The exemptions are principally of two types. One type is of the following form. Upon proof of purchase of a given quantity of domestic production, a proportional quantity may be imported at a very low tariff rate. The proportion is set so as to protect the full capacity of a domestic industry which exists but does not produce enough to satisfy all domestic demand. This type of exemption usually also functions as a quantitative restriction: if the domestic product is not purchased, it is difficult to import, even paying the higher tariff. The major function of the higher tariff is to establish a ceiling on the price of the domestic substitute, which generally must be sold at or below the import price plus the higher tariff if the protection is to be furnished. Thus for these products the user pays a weighted average of the import price plus the lower tariff, and the domestic price. This type of policy was important for coal, lead, aluminium, and asbestos.

The second type of exemption is for important inputs (mostly capital equipment) for favoured industries. This depends not only on the type of good, but also on the identity of the user. The exact nature of the policy also varied, at times being limited to exemption from the tariff, and at times including a lower exchange rate, or even dispensation from the obligation to buy exchange in the case of foreign-financed imports. These provisions are discussed in detail in Chapter 4. This exemption was widely used, and for capital goods the ratio of tariff collections to value of imports seldom exceeded 10 per cent, even though the average official tariff, weighted by imports, was about 50 per cent. Note that this 10 per cent is not an accurate measure of over-all protection, or lack of it, because many buyers of capital goods were not eligible for these exemptions and were buying the domestic products.

The restrictions are just as complicated as the exemptions. One type of restriction has already been mentioned: that which functioned jointly with the exemptions on coal, lead, aluminium, and asbestos. Other types are the Law of Similars, and monopoly or government price setting combined with quantitative restrictions.

The Law of Similars has been a very important instrument for restrictions on imports since the mid-1950s. The basic idea is that some or all importers are prohibited from importing a product which is recognized by the Government as being available domestically. The practice was formally instituted as far back as 1911; the scope of application among importers, the criteria for government recognition of domestic availability, and the strictness of enforcement have varied considerably since. To register a product as a similar, the manufacturer applied to the Conselho de Política Aduaneira (C.P.A.). This body is composed of representatives of manufacturers, importers, agriculture, and government, but is dominated by the Government. If the C.P.A. was satisfied that domestic suppliers could furnish the product in sufficient quantity and quality (in 1967 reasonable price and time for delivery were added as elements of the criteria) the product was registered as a similar. Goods for which there are registered similars cannot be imported by most public corporations, mixed (partly owned by the Government) companies, public authorities, or by an importer who receives any special treatment such as exemption from required advance deposits, government financing for investment, etc. Also, goods in the special category could be imported only with great difficulty by other importers if a domestic similar existed. (The special category was abolished in March 1967.) Private importers could import general category goods even if a domestic similar existed, but in that case would not be granted any exemptions, government loans, or other special treatment to which they might be entitled in the absence of the Law of Similars. This last provision had little effect, however, since almost all similars were special category goods. Exceptions to all these general rules were and are made, sometimes towards liberalizing and sometimes towards tightening the provisions.

Public corporations and authorities, and private importers who received special favourable treatment, have to have a licence to import anything. A licence is also necessary for anyone to import goods in the special category. This licence is granted by the foreign trade department (C.A.C.E.X.) of the Bank of Brazil. C.A.C.E.X. tends to be more protectionist than the C.P.A., and has sometimes refused to grant licences even if there was no similar registered with the C.P.A. In cases where goods were not standardized (especially capital goods), the C.P.A.'s register tended to omit many goods for which domestic similars had recently come into existence. C.A.C.E.X. used an informal procedure and was more restrictive on licensing; a private importer who did not receive a licence from C.A.C.E.X. could, however, forego any special privilege and import without a licence if the goods were in the general category. In October 1967, C.A.C.E.X. was given complete authority to enforce the Law of Similars, and can be expected to use its informal and broader concepts of determining if a similar exists.

There are several products for which the Government grants an import monopoly, or sets quantitative restrictions and price controls. The most important instances are salt, soda ash, steel, and rubber. These arrangements are usually made to protect extremely high-cost domestic production (salt, soda ash because salt is an important input, and rubber), but in the case of steel have resulted in domestic prices not too much higher (at times, not at all higher) than in exporting countries.

On the export side, the system of multiple bonuses instituted in 1953 lasted until 1959. During 1959 the rate for more and more products was freed; by the end of the year proceeds from all exports except coffee, cocoa, mineral oil, and castor oil beans could be sold on the free market.

The continuous rise in domestic prices and only occasional readjustments in the export rate had caused wide variations and uncertainty as to the real export exchange rate. The average (of absolute values) monthly variation in the real rate was over 3·8 per cent. Periods of three to six months in which the real rate dropped 10 or 15 per cent were not uncommon. Moreover, during the 1953–9 period the rate for individual products fluctuated even

D

more, and was more uncertain, than the average rate. This effect may not have been too serious with regard to supply of primary commodities, which made up (with coffee) about 80 per cent of the total value of exports. Judging from conversations I have had, it may have been a significant discouragement to a number of industrial firms. While the additional manufactured exports resulting from a more favourable exchange rate might not have been very significant as a percentage of the total value of exports, a less discouraging policy might have significantly reduced the inward-looking attitude of Brazilian industry.

The details of the administrative regime were also far from optimal from an export-promotion view. Throughout the entire post-war period licences were necessary, and the various bonuses, freedom to sell part of foreign exchange receipts from exports of certain products on the free market, and other schemes used to compensate for the over-valued cruzeiro complicated matters considerably. Licences were refused in various instances, the most important being when the Government wanted to keep domestic food prices down and therefore prohibited the export of certain food products. Licences to export manufactured products were rarely refused, although the exporter was required to prove that at least 70 per cent of the value of the product could be attributed to domestic inputs.[1]

There were periodic official protestations that exports should be encouraged, and various modifications to the basically discouraging rate were actually made. Nevertheless, Brazilian policy never really was concerned about promoting exports of anything except coffee and, to some extent, a very few other primary commodities.

In March of 1967 the special category for imports was abolished, and tariffs were generally lowered. Most products which had been in the special category did not receive higher tariffs to compensate for the removal of the exchange premium. The all-inclusive protection—tariff plus exchange rate premium—for these products thus dropped from the 180–220 per cent range to the 60–100 per

[1] See Nathaniel H. Leff, 'Export Stagnation and Autarkic Development in Brazil, 1947–1962', *Quarterly Journal of Economics*, May 1967, for a discussion of export policies in general. Leff goes a bit far in describing the evils of the licensing system when he says, '. . . export licences were denied if . . . the domestic price was rising'. In a footnote he explains that this means the absolute price (p. 290). If this were true, there would have been virtually no exports from Brazil.

cent range.[1] Tariffs on other products were typically reduced by roughly 20 per cent. Administrative procedures for exports have been made much simpler, and it appears that drawback privileges have been made available.

II. BIASES CAUSED BY COMMERCIAL POLICY

Starting in 1947, gaps were opened between the various import and export exchange rates. The size of these gaps, and the way they affected resource allocation in Brazil, can be viewed in several different ways, such as agriculture *v.* industry, export promotion *v.* import substitution, and the inter-industrial structure of protection.

The first step in analysing these biases is to measure the cruzeiro value of one dollar's worth of imports and of exports. The results are presented in Table 3.2. A dollar of imports cost over twice the value of a dollar of exports (the average for 1954–64 was 2·7); this gives a good indication of one dimension of the distortions caused by commercial policy.

Product and effective protection

A more relevant measure than the bias between product prices, however, is the bias between the margins available for value added in the different activities. This concept has recently become popular among economists under the name of 'effective protection'.[2] The basic idea is that production utilizes tradable inputs as well as labour and capital, and that not only product prices but also input prices are affected by commercial policy. The effective tariff measures the net effect; i.e. the increase in the margin available for value added caused by the policies in question. Thus, we would like to know not only the difference caused by commercial

---

[1] Since December 1968 the tariffs on most of these products were raised by 100 percentage points.

[2] See, for example, Bela Balassa, 'Tariff Protection in Industrial Countries: An Evaluation', *Journal of Political Economy*, December 1965; C. L. Barber, 'Canadian Tariff Policy', *Canadian Journal of Economics and Political Science*, November 1955; W. M. Corden, 'The Structure of a Tariff System and the Effective Protection Rate', *Journal of Political Economy*, June 1966; and Harry G. Johnson, 'Trade Preferences and Developing Countries', *Lloyds Bank Review*, July 1966. For a recent criticism of the concept see William P. Travis, 'The Effective Rate of Protection and the Question of Labor Protection in the United States', *Journal of Political Economy*, May–June 1968.

policy in the domestic price of a product, but also the difference in the margin available for domestic value added.

TABLE 3.2
AVERAGE EXCHANGE RATES: 1946–67

| | Non-coffee exports, including bonuses | Imports: | | Ratio of import rate to export rate |
Year		Basic rate	Including protection	
		(cruzeiros per dollar)		
1946	18·40	18·60	18·60	
1947	18·40			
1948	18·40			
1949	18·40			
1950	18·40			
1951	18·40			
1952	18·40			
1953	22·50			
1954	27·00	41·80	62·30	2·3
1955	41·30	63·80	91·90	2·2
1956	44·90	73·80	173·00	3·9
1957	53·00	65·60	173·00	3·3
1958	65·40	149·00	173·00	2·6
1959	114·00	202·00	291·00	2·6
1960	160·00	223·00	321·00	2·0
1961	245·00	268·00	611·00	2·5
1962	370·00	390·00	1,040·00	2·8
1963	553·00	575·00	1,670·00	3·0
1964	1,210·00	1,284·00	3,000·00	2·5
1965	1,874·00	1,899·00	3,930·00	2·1
1966	2,200·00	2,220·00	3,750·00	1·7
1967[a]	2,700·00	2,730·00	3,730·00	1·4

Notes: Average export rate does not include adjustments for proceeds from hard-to-export goods being sold on the free market prior to 1953. Source: E.P.E.A., *Comércio Internacional*, op. cit.

See Appendix 3 for methology.

[a] Data for 1967 are for April–December only, to show clearly the effects of the February–March reforms.

Just as the tariff on the product regulates the domestic price of the *product* relative to the price at which the product can be purchased from abroad, the effective or value-added tariff regulates the domestic value added in the production *process* relative to the value added in that process in the absence of protection. To be precise:

$$t = \frac{X}{P} - 1 \qquad (1)$$

$$z = \frac{X - \sum X_i}{P - \sum P_i} - 1 \qquad (2)$$

where $t = $ *ad valorem* tariff rate on product;

$z = $ effective tariff rate on process;

$X = $ maximum domestic unit value of the product permitted by foreign competition, with protection;

$P = $ unit value of the same product, imported, C.I.F.;

$X_i = $ value of tradable input i needed to produce one unit of product, at maximum price permitted by foreign competition, with protection;

$P_i = $ value of tradable input i needed to produce one unit of product, at C.I.F. import price.

Thus, the effective tariff measures the margin available for value added as a percentage of what that margin would be in a free trade situation.

If the difference between domestic and C.I.F. import prices is in fact equal to the tariff, as in equation (1), or if we define the 'tariff' by the price ratio given in that equation, then formula (2) for effective protection can be reduced to formula (3):

$$z_j = \frac{t_j - \sum a_{ij} t_i}{1 - \sum a_{ij}} \qquad (3)$$

In formula (3), the j's refer to the process and to the product of that process, the i's as before to the tradable inputs to the process, and the a_{ij}'s are Leontief-type input–output coefficients at free trade prices.

We can get a better feel for the idea of effective protection by considering a few simple cases as examples. First, consider a process which uses no tradable inputs (all $a_{ij} = 0$). Effective protection is then equal to the tariff on the product. Second, consider a situation where there are no tariffs on any of the tradable inputs (all $t_i = 0$). Effective protection is then given by the product tariff, divided by the proportion of value added in the value of the product. This is an example of the general principle that, when tariffs are higher for finished goods than for inputs, effective protection is relatively high for an 'assembly-only' process (where tradable inputs are a large proportion of the value of the product, and value added is small), and relatively low for a process with more vertical integration (where tradable inputs are a smaller proportion, and value added is a larger proportion of the value of the product). As a third example, consider the situation where all tariffs are equal (each $t_i = t_j$). Here effective protection is equal to the product tariff, for any process whatsoever. As a final example we may note cases where tariffs raise input costs to a level above the product price ($\sum a_{ij} t_i > t_j$). Effective protection in this case is negative; that is, the margin for value added is reduced by the tariffs on inputs more than it is increased by the tariff on the product.

Before presenting detailed numerical results for Brazil, some words of caution and further explanation are necessary. Numerical estimates give an impression of precision which is often misleading. The analysis presented in this chapter is unfortunately a good example of lack of precision in results, and the reader should be aware of this.

First, the basic data for the analysis is imprecise. The exact tariff rate is known for each commodity, and the effects of surcharges, auction premia, advance deposits, etc., can be included without much error. But other factors which affect the ratio of maximum possible domestic price to import price—the whole idea of protection is to increase this ratio—are harder to quantify precisely. These include various quantitative restrictions and exemptions, which are described above and for which every effort has been made to adjust, and also monopoly power of importers, differentials in transport costs, and other factors for which no adjustments have been made.

Second, presenting the all-inclusive estimates of protection for each of the thousands of products listed in the tariff code would not help the reader very much. These estimates must be aggregated to a point where some sense can be made of them. However, averaging presents both conceptual and empirical difficulties. In addition, estimating effective protection implies further assumptions and approximations. (These are thoroughly discussed in the articles cited above and will not be repeated here.)

The special problems in concept, methodology, and measurement which arose in this study are discussed in Appendix 3. The net effect might be described as follows. The numerical results presented throughout this chapter should be taken as showing only the general structure and approximate level of protection. For example, the estimate that the protection of a sector is, say,

47 per cent, means that 47 per cent is the best estimate, but that a variation of, say, ±10 per cent of the estimate is not unlikely— the true figure might well be 42 per cent, or 52 per cent, or something in between. The results give a picture of the structure and level of protection which is accurate enough for a general evaluation such as the one presented in the final sections of this study. I do not claim more precision than this.

One additional matter should be noted. The estimates presented are estimates of the maximum protection which the actual system, as legally constituted and as actually administered, allows. This protection may not always be fully exploited by domestic producers. This less-than-complete exploitation is often referred to as 'redundant protection'. There may be various reasons for redundancy; for example, domestic competition may force prices below the levels permitted by protection. A further complication in the Brazilian case is caused by the continuous inflation and only occasional exchange rate adjustments which characterized the post-war period. In such a situation, the (nominal) domestic price of imports remains constant from one devaluation to the next, while the price of the domestic product often goes up in many frequent, smaller steps. This is most common in non-durable consumer goods. In this situation, the exploitation of available protection is low immediately after a devaluation, and rises with the inflation until the next devaluation. The two sets of estimates presented below are for different phases of the cycle. June 1966 was midway between devaluations, and the estimates of protection for that date therefore contain some redundancy. They can be taken as roughly the average available protection over the inflation–devaluation cycle. April 1967 was shortly after a tariff reform which brought the real cruzeiro cost of imports to a level which was the lowest in many years (see Table 3.4 below); these estimates therefore contain less redundancy. This is discussed further in Appendix 3; the important conclusions are: first, all estimates of protection should be taken as estimates of the maximum available protection; second, there is little (if any) redundancy except for non-durable consumer goods; third, the estimates for April 1967 contain very little (if any) redundancy for all sectors.

Table 3.3 shows the estimates of product and effective (value added) protection, with the tariffs and other aspects of the system at June 1966 and at April 1967.

TABLE 3.3
THE STRUCTURE OF PROTECTION IN BRAZIL, 1966 AND 1967

| | June 1966 | | April 1967 | |
Sector	Product protection	Effective protection	Product protection	Effective protection
Primary vegetable products	36%	35%	10%	8%
Primary animal products	137	164	17	17
Mining	27	25	14	13
Non-metallic mineral products	79	86	40	39
Metallurgy	54	58	34	36
Machinery	48	41	34	32
Electrical equipment	114	215	57	97
Transport equipment	108	151	57	75
Wood products	45	45	23	25
Furniture	132	239	68	124
Paper and products	93	118	48	59
Rubber products	101	136	78	116
Leather products	108	117	66	85
Chemicals	53	59	34	42
Pharmaceuticals	48	39	37	35
Perfumes, soaps, etc.	192	8,480	94	3,670
Plastics	122	183	48	58
Textiles	181	379	81	162
Clothing	226	337	103	142
Food products	82	87	27	40
Beverages	205	447	83	173
Tobacco	193	313	78	124
Printing and publishing	122	142	59	67
Miscellaneous	104	128	58	72
Average, all sectors	85	181 (118)	37	76 (48)
Average, manufacturing	99	254 (151)	48	117 (73)

Notes: 'Product protection' is tariffs plus exchange premia, port charges, etc., less taxes on domestic production, with adjustments made for restrictions and exemptions. See Appendix 3 for details. Averages in parentheses exclude the perfumes sector.

Over-valuation and protection

The results in Table 3.3 show protection relative to Brazil's 'basic' import exchange rate. That is, the data compare the actual cost of imports, with what that cost would have been if the 'basic' exchange rate prevailed and there were no tariffs or other protective devices. But there is no reason to suppose that, if tariffs were eliminated, the rate which would prevail would be the actual 'basic' import exchange rate. This 'basic' rate is arbitrary, and protection measured relative to that rate does not mean very much. A more useful measure of protection would be relative to the exchange rate which would maintain equilibrium in the balance of payments if tariffs, export taxes and subsidies, etc., were removed.[1] Only by coincidence would this equilibrium free trade exchange rate be the same as the actual basic import exchange rate.

To see this point more clearly, consider the removal of all tariffs. Imports would rise, exports would be unchanged, and the current account balance of payments deficit would increase. Something else would presumably have to happen: devaluation, loss of reserves, or increased capital inflow.

To put the point in a different way, consider an initial equilibrium free trade situation, and a subsequent application of tariffs. Imports will decrease; if equilibrium is to be maintained, the exchange rate will have to be revalued upward. The economic effect of imposing tariffs will therefore be not only to make imports more expensive, *but also to make exports less profitable*. The tariff thus taxes imports less than is apparent, and taxes exports more than is apparent.

It is therefore interesting to analyse protection relative to the exchange rate which would compensate for the removal of all tariffs, subsidies, etc., in the effect on the balance of payments. That is, to compare a situation with tariffs to one without tariffs, it is more interesting to change the exchange rate so as to hold the balance of payments constant, rather than to hold the (arbitrary) exchange rate constant and thus imply changes in the balance of payments.

Such an analysis is inherently hypothetical. It is not possible to define one unique new situation in a non-arbitrary way, much less to estimate precisely the equilibrium exchange rate for it. What I have done is the following. First, coffee policy is assumed unchanged. The new situation, which for convenience will be called 'free trade', is therefore really a 'quasi-free-trade' situation; coffee exports are still taxed. Second, to estimate the equilibrium free trade exchange rate, the response of exports and imports to

[1] See Bela Balassa and Daniel M. Schydlowsky, 'Effective Tariffs, Domestic Cost of Foreign Exchange, and the Equilibrium Exchange Rate', *Journal of Political Economy*, May–June 1968, esp. pp. 356–9.

changes in price must be known. The usual way to do this is through estimates of the price elasticities of supply and demand for imports and exports. This is a complex problem, both conceptually and empirically. The elasticity of demand for imports, for example, may well depend on the magnitude, direction, and duration of the price change. It will certainly depend on how the structure and level of domestic industrial production and income react. If no other policy changes are made, reducing the price of imports would probably have decreased import substitution (i.e. shifted the demand for imports to the right) and also decreased domestic income and demand for industrial inputs (i.e. shifted the demand for imports to the left). Is it more appropriate for our purposes to assume that no compensating policy changes would have been made, or to note Brazil's drive for development and assume that lowering the price of imports would have been done only in conjunction with compensating industrial subsidies? The latter assumption seems more appropriate. (As we shall see later on, many of the new industries established during the period did not enjoy high protection, so this is not quite as drastic as it might seem. Furthermore, this assumption is probably better for 1966 and 1967, where it is used to calculate the data in Table 3.5, than for the earlier years shown in Table 3.4. In any case it seems more relevant than the alternative assumption of no other changes in policy, which implies hard-to-predict changes in income level, structure of production, etc., as well as even harder-to-predict effects of these changes on imports.) The reader is warned that a *ceterus paribus* assumption about policy, rather than about domestic income and production, would probably imply a greater devaluation, a higher free trade rate, and lower protection relative to that rate than the results presented here. Full details of the calculation are discussed in Appendix 3.

Detailed numerical results

In Table 3.4 the estimated free trade exchange rate is shown, as well as protection against imports and implicit export taxes relative to that rate. In the same table are index numbers of the real (i.e. at constant prices) value of the free trade exchange rate, and of the real cruzeiro value of one dollar of exports or imports. These last data are also shown in Figure 3.1. They are not only interesting in themselves; trends in the real value of the free trade exchange rate give some indication of whether the estimates are reasonable. The rise in the real rate in the late 1950s and early 1960s, and its subsequent drop, do seem reasonable; the Brazilian economy was growing very rapidly through 1962 (the year when the rate attained its maximum) and did not grow thereafter. Since imports

TABLE 3.4
PRODUCT PROTECTION, EXPORT TAXES, AND THE FREE TRADE EXCHANGE RATE

Year	Free trade rate	Product protection	Implicit export taxes	Import rate	Free trade rate	Export rate
				Indices of real values		
	(cruzeiros per dollar)	(per cent of free trade rate)		(free trade rate for 1954 = 100)		
1946						117
1947						111
1948						103
1949						98
1950						95
1951						79
1952						70
1953						74
1954	38	64	29	164	100	71
1955	57	61	28	204	126	92
1956	71	144	37	314	129	81
1957	81	114	35	275	129	84
1958	95	82	31	240	132	91
1959	160	82	29	283	156	111
1960	210	53	24	238	155	118
1961	350	75	30	322	185	129
1962	550	89	33	366	193	130
1963	830	101	33	333	166	110
1964	1,700	76	29	330	187	133
1965	2,500	57	25	281	179	134
1966	2,800	34	22	190	142	112
1967[a]	3,100	20	13	150	125	109

Notes: Coffee exports are not included.
'Protection' is calculated as the import rate including tariffs, etc. (Table 3.2), divided by the free trade rate, less unity.
'Export taxes' are calculated as unity, less the export rate (Table 3.2) divided by the free trade rate.
'Indices of real values' were obtained by deflating the nominal rates by the index of wholesale prices excluding coffee (*Conjuntura Econômica* index No. 45).
[a] Data for 1967 are for April–December only, to show clearly the effects of the February–March reforms.

as a whole respond quite markedly to domestic economic activity, and non-coffee exports as a whole are unrelated except to variations in harvests, it is reasonable for an equilibrium exchange rate to rise slowly during periods of growth (up to 1962) and to fall during periods of recession or stagnation (1963–6).

In the period 1954–64, protection averaged 86 per cent, and implicit export taxes 31 per cent, of the free trade rate. After 1964 both protection and export taxes declined, reaching the relatively low levels of 20 and 13 per cent respectively in 1967.[1] The average product protection to the manufacturing sector in 1967 was only 30 per cent. These results show the very high taxes Brazil imposed on international trade. The extremes of high import prices in

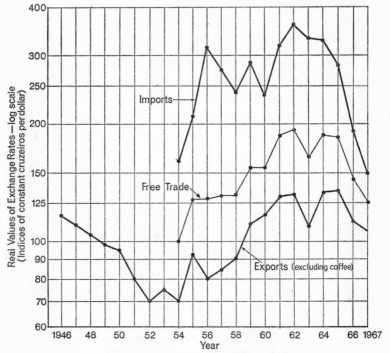

Figure 3.1. Real exchange rates, 1946–67.

years such as 1956 and 1961–4 probably include significant redundancy; protection on many items was probably higher than necessary to prevent imports. But even in years of minimum import cost (1954, '55, '58, and '60), average protection was in the 50–80 per cent range.

Starting around 1964 or 1965, the real exchange rates for im-

[1] The breakdown of the margin between the import and export rates into import tariffs and export taxes reflects our assumptions of elasticities, etc., and says nothing about the intent of government policy in regard to the breakdown of taxation between imports and exports.

ports and exports started moving down and also closer together, so that both protection and export taxes declined. The Brazilian economy in 1967 was unusually open to foreign trade, compared to its own recent past or compared to other L.D.C.s. The drastic drop in the real cost of imports could probably not have occurred in the absence of two other conditions: a generally depressed economy, which reduced import demand and slightly increased export supply, and a plentiful supply of foreign aid. It is likely that in more normal conditions, the real import exchange rate will be raised above the 1967 level.[1]

The real value of the export exchange rate is also interesting in itself. In 1945–6 this was also the import exchange rate. As mentioned earlier, the cruzeiro was substantially over-valued at that time (i.e. the cruzeiro value of dollars was too low). The evidence for this was that Brazil's balance of trade was in serious deficit, and that the nominal export rate had remained constant while Brazilian prices had risen about 80 per cent more than U.S. prices during the period 1937–45. The already-over-valued cruzeiro then became even more over-valued, the price of dollars falling 40 per cent in real terms from 1946 to its minimum value in 1952. However, this additional over-valuation was more than erased by the rise during 1954–62. Since 1952 the export exchange rate has kept up with the Brazilian inflation (at least in annual averages). The problem has been the maintenance of existing over-valuation, not a continuous increase in over-valuation.

The structure of protection relative to the free trade exchange rate, before and after the reform of February–March 1967, has also been analysed. These results are shown in Table 3.5.[2] Before

---

[1] This in fact has been happening since late 1968.

[2] The protection shown in Table 3.5 bears a simple algebraic relation to that in Table 3.3. This is because, in all cases, the combination of protection and the exchange rate relative to which protection is measured must equal the same actual total cost of imports:

$$r(1 + t) = r'(1 + t')$$
$$\frac{r}{r'} = \frac{1 + t'}{1 + t}$$

where r = basic import exchange rate
t = product protection relative to r
r' = free trade exchange rate
t' = product protection relative to r'

As Corden shows (op. cit.) the same equation holds for effective protection:

$$\frac{r}{r'} = \frac{1 + z'}{1 + z}$$

the 1967 tariff reform, average available product protection was 47 per cent for all sectors, and 58 per cent for manufacturing. Effective protection averaged 72 per cent for all sectors, and 98

TABLE 3.5
THE STRUCTURE OF PROTECTION IN BRAZIL, 1966 AND 1967
(relative to the free trade situation)

	June 1966		*April 1967*	
Sector	Product protection	Effective protection	Product protection	Effective protection
Primary vegetable products	8%	7%	−4%	−5%
Primary animal products	88	109	2	2
Mining	1	0	−1	−1
Non-metallic mineral products	42	47	22	22
Metallurgy	22	25	17	19
Machinery	17	12	17	16
Electrical equipment	69	149	37	73
Transport equipment	65	99	37	53
Wood products	15	15	7	10
Furniture	84	168	46	96
Paper and products	53	73	29	39
Rubber products	59	87	55	89
Leather products	65	72	44	62
Chemicals	21	26	17	25
Pharmaceuticals	17	10	19	18
Perfumes, soaps, etc.	131	6,710	69	3,210
Plastics	76	124	29	39
Textiles	123	279	57	130
Clothing	158	246	77	112
Food products	44	48	10	23
Beverages	142	333	59	139
Tobacco	132	227	55	96
Printing and publishing	76	92	38	46
Miscellaneous	62	81	37	51
Average, all sectors	47	122 (72)	20	55 (31)
Average, manufacturing	58	180 (98)	30	91 (52)

Notes: See Table 3.3.

per cent to manufacturing.[1] After the reform, average product protection was 20 per cent, with the average for manufacturing 30 per cent; effective protection for all primary and secondary

[1] This average excludes the perfumes sector, for which the estimate of effective protection appears to be far too high. See Appendix 3. This is the measure used whenever over-all averages of effective protection are mentioned.

sectors averaged 31 per cent; and for manufacturing 52 per cent. A rough breakdown of levels for manufacturing is shown in Table 3.6. In 1966, over half of value added in manufacturing was

TABLE 3.6
NUMBER OF MANUFACTURING SECTORS IN GIVEN RANGES OF
EFFECTIVE PROTECTION
(relative to the free trade situation)

| | Number of sectors | | Per cent of 1964 value added |
Range	1966	1967	1966
Less than 50%	7	10	54
Less than 100%	13	17	71
Less than 200%	16	20	81
200% and above	5	1	19
TOTAL	21	21	100

in sectors where effective protection averaged less than 50 per cent.[1]

Unfortunately, the Brazilian industrial classification does not distinguish clearly between components, semi-finished goods, finished producer goods, and finished consumer goods. Average product protection for sub-sectors has been calculated, and re-aggregated to type of good by use. The results are shown in Table 3.7. Here the cascading is clear: of the uses shown, protection before the 1967 reform was lowest on capital goods. Next came intermediate goods (this class is closer to primary products than 'parts and components'), then construction materials, then parts and components, and finally finished consumer goods. Intermediate goods dropped slightly below capital goods in 1967, but the general structure is similar. As can be seen in Table 3.5, unprocessed raw materials received the lowest protection.

The cascading of product protection causes effective protection to be generally higher than product protection, especially for consumer goods. Some approximate estimates of average effective protection have been made for capital goods, intermediate goods, and finished consumer goods. These results should be taken as indicating only relative orders of magnitude. (The methodology is explained in Appendix 3.) The results, for tariffs of 1966, are

[1] This last should be taken as very approximate, because protection within many sectors varied quite a bit. For example, the average effective protection for transport equipment was 99 per cent, but this includes automobiles which received roughly 180 per cent protection.

as shown in Table 3.8. The wide range of protection within each category should be noted. For capital and intermediate goods this range reflects the low product protection on most goods not domestically available, and the moderately high protection for some of the goods which are produced in Brazil.

TABLE 3.7
PRODUCT PROTECTION BY USE OF PRODUCT
(relative to the free trade situation)

A. Disaggregation

Sector	Use of product	June 1966	April 1967
Non-metallic mineral products:	Construction materials	40%	23%
	Consumer durables	51	8
Machinery:	Parts and components	16	16
	Capital goods	7	10
	Consumer durables	47	27
Electrical equipment:	Parts and components	39	28
	Capital goods	35	40
	Consumer durables	151	67
Transport equipment:	Parts and components	61	47
	Capital goods	38	28
	Consumer durables	139	63
Paper and products:	Intermediate goods	34	22
	Consumer non-durables	107	43
Rubber products:	Intermediate goods	43	38
	Consumer durables	63	56
Chemicals:	Intermediate goods	17	16
	of which: fertilizers	−3	−8
	Consumer non-durables	25	15
Textiles:	Threads and yarns	113	39
	Fabrics	159	75

B. Re-aggregation

Sector	Use of product	June 1966	April 1967
All 21 manufacturing sectors:	Capital goods	24%	22%
	Construction materials	40	23
	Intermediate goods	35	19
	Parts and components	49	38
	Consumer durables	84	45
	Consumer non-durables	70	27

We have seen that the average bias to import substitution in manufacturing, compared to importing, was about 98 per cent as of 1966 (measured by effective protection). It was greatest for consumer goods (roughly 100 to 500 per cent), less for intermediate goods (roughly negative to 100 per cent), and least for capital goods (ranging from negative values up to perhaps 75 per cent). There was a great deal of variation, both among sectors and within given sectors. In earlier years these biases were even greater; in 1967 they were reduced.

The bias to production for domestic consumption, compared to export, was also very large.[1] On the average, non-coffee export products bore an implicit tax of roughly 22 per cent in 1966. During 1954–64 this tax averaged 31 per cent. For primary production, commercial policy was roughly neutral as to inputs. Since in these sectors value added is about 84 per cent of value of product at free trade prices, the implied tax on value added for

TABLE 3.8
EFFECTIVE PROTECTION FOR TYPE OF GOOD BY USE
(relative to the free trade situation)

| Category | Effective protection, 1966 | |
	Typical range	Average
Capital goods	Negative to 75%	15%
Intermediate goods	Negative to 100%	50
Finished consumer goods	100 to 500%	190

Note: 'Typical' means that there are probably a few processes outside the range.

export was roughly 37 per cent during 1954–64, was 26 per cent in 1966, and roughly 15 per cent in 1967. That is, value added for export was 15 per cent less than value added for domestic production in 1967. This is for exports of primary products, excluding coffee.

For exports of manufactures, the bias is even greater. This is shown in Table 3.9. Even assuming full drawbacks in 1967, the margin available for value added for one of the twenty-one manufacturing sectors when producing for export would have been negative. The bias was over 50 per cent for all but three of the twenty-one manufacturing sectors and over 100 per cent for all but nine. This bias was even larger in earlier years, as the spread between import and export exchange rates was greater. One does not have to go further to understand why Brazil has so few regular exports of manufactures.

In very approximate terms, commercial policy was roughly neutral in regard to protection of agriculture. That is, the margin available for value added in Brazilian agriculture was roughly similar to what that margin would have been in a free trade

[1] This bias was calculated as follows:

$$\text{bias} = \frac{\text{(value added if sold domestically)}}{\text{(value added if exported)}} - 1$$

E

situation. For export, however, commercial policy discriminated against agricultural exports (excluding coffee) roughly to the extent shown by the export taxes in Table 3.4. (In terms of product prices. In terms of value added the discrimination was somewhat greater, as estimated above: roughly 37 per cent

TABLE 3.9
BIAS TO MANUFACTURING PRODUCTION FOR THE DOMESTIC MARKET RATHER THAN FOR EXPORT

Sector	1966	1967
Non-metallic mineral products	138%	57%
Metallurgy	135	48
Machinery	106	40
Electrical equipment	a	176
Transport equipment	1,640	118
Wood products	91	29
Furniture	9,430	211
Paper and products	674	84
Rubber products	295	145
Hides and skins	a	133
Chemicals	198	51
Pharmaceuticals	103	51
Perfumes, soaps, etc.	a	a
Plastics	1,060	103
Textiles	a	427
Clothing	a	195
Food products	a	52
Beverages	a	632
Tobacco	a	151
Printing and publishing	528	94
Miscellaneous	251	104

Notes: No drawbacks are assumed in 1966, and full drawbacks in 1967. This underestimates the bias in 1967.
a Value added for export would be negative; i.e. the bias is infinite.

during 1954–64.) Since manufacturing received rather high protection, as shown in Table 3.5, commercial policy certainly tended to increase the profitability of manufacturing relative to agriculture, and therefore presumably to induce resources to move into manufacturing rather than agriculture.

III. TAXES ON ACTUAL IMPORTS

All the analysis of import taxes, etc., so far presented has been relative to 'potential' imports. Tariffs, premia, and other taxes on imports have been weighted by the sums of imports plus domestic production. In this final section estimates of taxes actually paid on goods actually imported will be presented. These estimates are based on the results of a study by Samuel A. Morley, cited above. Morley estimated the actual total cruzeiro cost of one dollar's worth of actual imports, for each of nine types of goods by use, for each year from 1953 to 1965. I have aggregated these to five classes, and taken averages for two periods: 1954–6 to represent the multiple-rate period, and 1958–64 to represent the tariff system during that time. The results are presented in Table 3.10, relative to my estimated free trade exchange rate. These results show that most goods actually imported were cheaper under the actual system than they would have been under free trade.[1]

These surprising results can be checked by comparison with taxes, etc., actually collected. This has been possible only for all imports combined. The results are as follows: taxes, premia, etc., averaged 23 per cent of the value of imports at the basic exchange rates, for both 1954–6 and 1958–64. As a percentage of the free

TABLE 3.10
TAXES ON ACTUAL IMPORTS
(relative to the free trade situation)

Period	Fuels	Wheat	Processed intermed. goods	Capital goods	Finished consumer goods	Total imports
1954–6	−24%	−48%	−6%	−11%	−3%	−16%
1958–64	−6	−38	0	−19	24	−10

Source: Calculated from data in Morley, op. cit. See Appendix 3, Table 4.

trade exchange rates, taxes, etc., were 2 per cent for 1954–6, and −17 per cent for 1958–64.[2] This suggests that the estimates in Table 3.10 are a bit too low for 1954–6, and a bit too high for 1958–64.[3]

We can conclude that most actual imports were cheaper under the actual system than they would have been under a free trade

[1] As explained in Appendix 3, my estimated free trade exchange rate is, if anything, too low (in terms of cruzeiros per dollar). This means that the taxes presented in Table 3.10 are, if anything, too high.

[2] Calculated from data in E.P.E.A., *Comércio Internacional*, op. cit., and E.P.E.A., *Diagnóstico Preliminar, Finanças Públicas*, Ministry of Planning, Rio de Janeiro, December 1965 (mimeo). See Appendix 3 for details.

[3] The differences are on the order of 10 to 20 per cent. For example, for 1954 my averages of Morley's results imply average effective costs of imports of Cr$33/dollar; actual collections imply a cost of Cr$39/dollar. For 1958, the two figures are Cr$86/dollar and Cr$79/dollar.

exchange rate and no taxes. This shows just how well commercial policy worked to facilitate the operations of Brazilian manufacturing. Protection was high for goods produced domestically, and very low for goods which had to be imported.

During the regime of multiple rates (1953–7) there must have been many exemptions for imports of processed intermediate goods and capital goods, in order to reduce the protection shown in Table 3.1 to that in Table 3.10. Under the tariff regime since 1967, exemptions continued to be important for some goods, but the tariff schedule itself discriminated very finely among goods available or unavailable domestically.[1]

IV. SUMMARY

In summary, commercial policy in post-war Brazil has had four outstanding characteristics:

1. Discrimination against producing for export, rather than for the domestic market. This has been strong for primary products and even stronger for manufactures.

2. Generally high protection of domestic manufacturing against imports.

3. Great inequality in the inter-industrial structure of protection, with generally low protection for raw materials, higher for capital goods, higher still for intermediate goods, and highest for finished consumer goods.

4. A concern for established domestic manufacturers, shown by a combination of high protection for products of existing firms and low cost of importing products which were not available domestically.

---

[1] The C.P.A. could change tariff rates, or move a product to the special category, by its own administrative ruling. The tariff rate classification was also designed for easy discrimination; for example, many types of motors were divided between light (domestically produced; 60–80 per cent tariff) and heavy (not domestically produced; 30 per cent or less tariff). One observer has described the system as 'tailor-made'.

4

Other Elements in the Post-war Environment

I. INFLATION AND PUBLIC FINANCE

The post-war period was one of chronic inflation. Prices rose about 10 per cent per year during 1948–52, and around 20 per cent per year during 1953–60. In 1961 the rate of inflation surpassed 30 per cent for the first time in the post-war period, and rose to about 50 per cent in 1962, 70 per cent in 1963, and 90 per cent in 1964. The data are shown in Table 4.1.

It is obvious that much of the inflation before 1961, and certainly most of it thereafter, can be attributed to excess demand.

TABLE 4.1
GROWTH AND INFLATION, 1948–64
(annual percentage increases)

Year	Real growth in output		Increase in prices (G.D.P. implicit deflator)
	G.D.P.	Manufacturing	
1948	9·5	11·9	3·9
1949	5·6	10·6	9·3
1950	5·0	12·3	11·9
1951	5·1	6·1	14·9
1952	5·6	5·0	8·9
1953	3·2	9·9	18·5
1954	7·7	9·0	20·4
1955	6·8	11·0	16·6
1956	1·9	6·6	25·3
1957	6·9	5·4	11·8
1958	6·6	16·9	16·2
1959	7·3	12·6	28·1
1960	6·7	10·6	25·6
1961	7·3	11·1	34·8
1962	5·4	8·2	49·2
1963	1·6	0·0	71·7
1964	3·1	5·1	90·8
1965	3·9	−4·7	57·1
1966	4·4	12·2	38·0

Source: Fundação Getúlio Vargas.

Especially after 1955, government spending was increasing rapidly. (See Table 4.2.) The most significant increase in the late 1950s was in investment by the federal government, mixed companies, and public authorities. The Government was also rapidly expanding credit to selected parts of privately-owned industry, through the National Bank for Economic Development (B.N.D.E.) and the Bank of Brazil.

TABLE 4.2
GOVERNMENT SPENDING, 1947–64
(as per cent of G.D.P.)

	Federal budget			Total public sector
Year	Consumption, subsidies, and transfers	Current account surplus	Gross fixed investment	Gross fixed investment
1947	7·9	5·2	1·0	3·2
1948	8·5	4·9	1·3	4·2
1949	9·4	5·5	1·8	4·8
1950	9·1	3·3	1·9	4·8
1951	8·7	4·9	1·2	4·1
1952	8·7	4·6	1·2	4·3
1953	10·7	2·3	1·2	3·9
1954	9·4	4·2	1·3	4·7
1955	9·9	2·5	1·1	3·8
1956	12·2	0·4	1·0	3·5
1957	11·3	0·2	1·5	5·4
1958	11·2	3·5	1·4	6·6
1959	10·9	2·9	1·5	6·6
1960	11·6	4·0	1·2	7·4
1961	13·3	−0·6	1·3	7·6
1962	14·1	−2·8	1·5	8·5
1963	14·4	−0·9	0·8	7·0
1964	14·6	−2·7	1·0	6·7

Source: Fundação Getúlio Vargas.

Tax revenues were increasing rapidly, but not rapidly enough to counteract completely these inflationary forces. Total tax revenues rose steadily throughout the post-war period, reaching a peak of 23 per cent of G.D.P. in 1960. They fell somewhat in the early 1960s, but caught up to the 23 per cent share by 1965 and have since gone even higher. The share of state and local governments in total tax receipts has been falling slightly, and the federal government share rising. Federal tax receipts rose from 9 per cent of G.D.P. in 1950 to 17 per cent in 1965, and have probably risen even further since 1965. Details are shown in Table 4.3.

TABLE 4.3
SHARE OF TAX RECEIPTS IN G.D.P.

Year	Total indirect taxes, all levels of government	State sales tax	Federal consumption tax	Direct business tax	Total federal	Total state and local	Grand total
1950	10%	3%	3%	1%	9%	6%	16%
1951	12	4	3	1	11	7	18
1952	11	4	3	2	11	7	18
1953	11	4	3	1	10	7	17
1954	13	4	3	1	12	7	19
1955	11	4	3	2	10	7	17
1956	13	4	3	2	12	8	19
1957	13	4	3	2	12	8	19
1958	16	4	3	1	14	8	22
1959	16	5	3	2	15	8	23
1960	17	6	3	2	15	8	23
1961	14	4	3	n.a.	13	7	21
1962	14	5	4	n.a.	13	7	20
1963	14	4	4	n.a.	14	6	20
1964	15	4	5	n.a.	15	6	21
1965	15	4	5	n.a.	17	6	23

Source: E.P.E.A., *Diagnóstico Preliminar, Finanças Públicas*, Ministry of Planning, Rio de Janeiro, December 1965 (mimeo).
Details may not add to totals because of rounding.

Indirect taxes have risen from 10 per cent of G.D.P. in 1950 to 15 per cent in 1965. Two of the most important indirect taxes were the federal consumption tax (impôsto de consumo) and the state sales tax (impôsto de vendas e consignações). The latter was levied on sales or transfers at every stage of production, and thus cascaded on products composed of inputs that had gone through many stages of processing.[1] In the major industrial states of São Paulo, Rio de Janeiro, and Guanabara this tax rate was in the range of 4 to 10 per cent in the early 1960s.[2] Thus the total tax burden on manufactured products has been quite heavy.

The over-all tax burden in Brazil since the mid-1950s has also been quite high for a country at Brazil's income level. Nevertheless, high rates of government spending and credit expansion were too much for taxation to counteract, and chronic inflation was the result.

Both the inflation and the growth, which occurred simultaneously until 1963, can be seen as results of a more-or-less common set of policies—some of the policies that spurred the growth also spurred the inflation. Looking at this in reverse might lead one to say that the inflation facilitated the growth. That is, inflation acted as an alternative to taxation, in transferring income from the private sector to the public sector and from labour to capital. This way of viewing the process is somewhat confusing and misleading. The inflation is best seen not as causing the income transfers, but rather as a result of the same policies and conditions which also caused the transfers.

Inflation *per se* probably did ease the transfer from labour to capital; the rapid rise in nominal wages probably made it easier to keep real wages from rising more rapidly than they did. In the 1949–59 period, physical output per worker in manufacturing increased 90 per cent, real wages per worker increased only 26 per cent, and wages as a percentage of value added decreased 18 per cent. Around 1962, real wages in manufacturing started to rise much faster than productivity. This is shown in Table 4.4.

The post-war period up to 1964 can thus be divided into two parts, with the dividing line around 1961. In the first period, government policies were favourable to industrialization and to inflation: income was transferred from wages to profits, and from

---

[1] This cascading was essentially eliminated in 1966.
[2] E.P.E.A., *Finanças Públicas*, op. cit.

the private to the public sector. Public sector investment rose strongly, and protection and investment subsidies, plus strong aggregate demand, induced a high rate of private investment as well. While the inflation as such also had some negative effects, the net result was rapid real growth.

TABLE 4.4

LABOUR PRODUCTIVITY AND WAGES IN MANUFACTURING

Average percentage annual increase in:

Period	Average productivity	Average real wage
1949–59	6·6	2·4
1955–62	6·1	0·9
1962–4	2·7	13·1

Source: Manufacturing production: Real product indices of the Fundação Getúlio Vargas. Number of workers and nominal wages: Industrial Census for 1949 and 1959; *Registro Industrial* for 1955 and 1962; G.E.T.E.I. for 1964. Wages deflated by cost of living index for São Paulo (*Conjuntura Econômica* index No. 4).

Choice of initial and final years was constrained by lack of comparable data for all years.

The climax of this period came with the Kubitschek Administration of 1956–60. This government adopted rapid growth and industrialization as deliberate, high-priority goals. Their success was notable. After growing at an unusually low rate of only 1·9 per cent in 1956, real G.D.P. grew by 6·9 per cent in 1957, 6·6 per cent in 1958, 7·3 per cent in 1959, and 6·7 per cent in 1960. In the first year after Kubitschek left office, G.D.P. growth was 7·3 per cent; thereafter the growth rate declined. Manufacturing grew at an even more rapid rate through this period. In the five Kubitschek years it grew at an average of 10·3 per cent a year, and continued at over 10 per cent in 1961 and over 8 per cent in 1962 before stagnation set in in 1963. The inflation exhibits similar behaviour: the rate of price increase never exceeded 30 per cent until 1961; in that year it was 35 per cent, and rose to 49 per cent in 1962 and 72 per cent in 1963.

The Kubitschek Administration seems to have done well in balancing the political–economic pressures inherent in rapid development. Federal government consumption, subsidies, and transfers were certainly higher than an austere economist would have recommended—these items jumped from an earlier average of about 9 per cent of G.N.P., to about 11 per cent during Kubitschek's term—but they were still under control and did not rise continuously as they were to do later under Goulart. Investment, on the other hand, rose rapidly, and so did tax revenues; the latter attained quite a high level by the end of the period. It is not easy to raise taxes faster and to higher levels than was done in Brazil in this period, and high government expenditures on current account are a good way of building a political base. If a chronic inflation of 15 to 20 per cent per year was the price to pay for rapid development in a poor country with a low tax base, the price may not have been too high.

Starting in 1961 the situation began to change radically. Economic growth and industrialization lost their top priorities. The vacillation and inconsistency of policies under Presidents Quadros (who resigned after only seven months in office in 1961) and Goulart (1962–4) resulted in neither stable prices nor sustained growth. Public investment was reduced as a counterinflationary measure, but current expenditures were permitted to rise even more rapidly than in the past and the net deficit increased rapidly. As an E.C.L.A. study concluded:

... economic policy in the early sixties contrasted sharply with [the preceding period]. The measures adopted, viewed in sequence, were directed by no clear-cut purpose, but aimed in divergent directions. A swarm of provisions defeated one another's differing ends. None of the proposed systems lasted any length of time; within a matter of months, each gave way to the next. The whole course of events suggested that economic policy was drifting rudderless.[1]

The inflation was now propagated as much through wage increases as through investment demands; the government deficit no longer could be excused as permitting public investment. Those policies which earlier had spurred inflation were continued, and indeed were augmented by allowing more rapid real wage increases; those policies which had spurred growth were largely abandoned. Moreover, the inflation was now galloping at ever-increasing rates, which in itself must have greatly increased uncertainty, and retarded productive investment and industrial growth. Some of the changes between the 1950s and the early 1960s can be seen in Table 4.2, which shows rising government consumption, falling government investment, and rising government deficits.

[1] E.C.L.A., 'Fifteen Years of Economic Policy in Brazil', *Economic Bulletin for Latin America*, November 1964, p. 198.

Inflation—Industrialization interactions

Excess demand was not the only proximate cause of the inflation. Industrialization had various effects which tended to feed the inflation. The rapid structural change caused continued rapid changes in demand for various goods. Thus import substitution and growth caused shifts in relative prices which, as always and especially in a growing economy, moved upward more readily than downward. Second, many industries were monopolistic or oligopolistic in structure and, since they were strongly protected from foreign competition, tended to sell at high prices relative to imports. Thus the continuing import substitution caused more and more price increases as supply shifted from imports to higher-priced domestic production.

The inflation had some bad effects on technological efficiency in industry. In the inflationary environment, profits were highly sensitive to inventory management and financial management. Cost reductions from improving technical efficiency of production would be swamped by windfall profits or losses from inventories, or from arranging a loan at a favourable or unfavourable interest rate. Indeed, the inflation made cost accounting, which provides the feedback necessary for increasing production efficiency, much more difficult to implant. Brazil has long been backward in this area, and still is today. Even in a competitive market structure, businessmen may tend to adopt price-leadership behaviour if they don't know what their costs are. And in an inflationary economy, they seldom know their costs. If one sees his competitor raising prices, he can't follow the classic profit-maximizing behaviour and say, 'I'm making money at the old price; I'll just stay there and take his customers away' because he doesn't know whether in fact he is making profits at the old price.

The inflation also hindered the development of the capital market.[1] The laws of Brazil permitted a short-term market (180 days or less) to function fairly well. But any longer-term funds were virtually unavailable, except to favoured industries from official sources. This was because the law forbade adjusting the nominal interest rate after the loan was made. Uncertainty as to

---

[1] See Mário Henrique Simonsen, 'Inflation and the Money and Capital Markets in Brazil', in Howard S. Ellis (ed.), *The Economy of Brazil*, University of California Press, 1969.

future inflation was such that the maximum nominal rate which the borrower would pay was less than the minimum that the lender required, for loans of more than 6 months. Added to the already weak market for equity capital, this caused many problems for industry. Financing working capital requirements, let alone expansions, was an enormous problem. In the absence of a good financial market, most firms had to meet any needs for increased liquidity through increased retained earnings. The national accounts show that, during 1955–60, retained earnings of corporations amounted to 93 per cent of gross fixed investment in the private sector.[1] This figure is even more striking in light of the large amount of that investment which was undertaken by new firms, which of course did not have any earnings to retain.[2]

The need to finance capital requirements from retained earnings led in turn to increased pressure on prices of sales. Indeed, since many firms had no idea of whether they were operating at a profit or a loss, prices were commonly set by watching the cash flow. As long as liquidity was satisfactory, prices might remain stable; a drop in liquidity was a signal for a price increase.

II. INFRASTRUCTURE

In the theory of development, investments in infrastructure are usually seen as an inducement to growth of the manufacturing sector. Hirschman has a well-known contrary view: the manufacturing (or other 'directly productive') sector grows and causes shortages in supply of transportation or energy. These shortages in turn induce government to increase investment in infrastructure.[3] Brazil is a prime example of the accuracy—if not the optimality—of the Hirschman view. Deficiencies in energy, transportation, and communications have hindered growth and increased costs in manufacturing throughout the post-war period, and continue to do so to this day.

Citizens of the U.S. who go abroad often impress the people in the lands they visit as obsessed with plumbing. A short time in Brazil, however, creates an almost insane desire for a functioning

---

[1] *Revista Brasileira de Economia*, March 1962.

[2] This also suggests that private investment may be underestimated in the national accounts.

[3] Albert O. Hirschman, *The Strategy of Economic Development*, Yale University Press, 1958, especially Chapter 5.

telephone system. A friend of the author, returning to the U.S. after about one year in Rio de Janeiro, made a call from the airport where he landed. As he tells it, the power of having a telephone in his hand that actually gave him a dial tone when he picked it up, and that connected him to the number he dialled, affected him so strongly that he placed call after call. By the time he recovered he had spent a small fortune on perhaps a dozen calls to points all over the country, in about the same time it takes to get a dial tone for a local call on any afternoon in Rio.

The return on improved telephone systems within and among the major cities of Brazil would probably be higher than on any other investment, public or private, of similar or larger size. The cost of the deficiencies of the present system in time lost and communication foregone must be enormous. As always, there are reasons for the deficiencies. Most of Brazil's telephone systems were built and operated by foreign firms. During the post-second world war period, Brazilian governments did not allow rates to keep pace with rising price levels. The telephone companies reacted by not making any investments (on a gross basis; there was probably *net* disinvestment). In the last few years most of the firms have been nationalized, and some progress on improving service is being made, although one does wonder why it takes so long. Perhaps a good study of the actual benefits of improved service would spark more action; all of the 'feasibility studies' I have seen are over-reliant on financial revenues as a measure of benefits. Evidence that the problems persist is the following article:

Two psychiatrists here, pursuing independent lines of research, have come to an identical conclusion: Increasing numbers of subscribers to Rio's quaint telephone service are suffering from anxiety neurosis, or acute frustration.

The findings of Professors David Akstein and Galindo Perez, published in a recent issue of the Daily *Jornal Do Brasil*, came as no surprise. No one needs a degree in psychiatry to know that making a phone call in this otherwise charming city can be a maddening experience. In the best of circumstances, one waits two to five minutes for a dial tone. At times the wait can be as long as 45 minutes. Then, more often than not, the result is a wrong number, or perhaps total silence.

Officials of the Brazilian Telephone Co. contend they are doing their best with the ancient, inadequate equipment purchased by the government two years ago when a Canadian firm was bought out.

Even a light shower, one official told a reporter, is enough to soak underground cables and put entire exchanges out of order for days.

To expand and improve the service, the company has succeeded in having a tax of 30 to 40 per cent tacked onto telephone bills, and new subscribers are required to buy about $600 worth of shares in the company as a kind of installation fee. Some hopeful residents have been on the waiting list for up to 20 years. Some simply buy a phone on the black market, an expensive undertaking that usually involves a payment of $1000 or more.

Meanwhile, tempers grow shorter. 'The man who can't get a line to summon a doctor or close a business deal is in danger of becoming seriously neurotic,' Akstein said. Perez said that time lost in this way can be so exasperating that 'professional men often take out their frustration on clients, friends and families, which further complicates their problems'.[1]

Electric power is another problem sector. Publicly-owned organizations (including federal, state, mixed companies, and public authorities) account for about 55 per cent of installed capacity. Another 10 per cent is owned by industrial companies who generate their own electricity but do not sell any; private firms account for the remaining 35 per cent. More and more of the public firms are coming under the control of the federally-constituted public authority Electrobrás, which acts as a holding company and controls new investments, rates, etc., in the operating companies it controls.[2]

In spite of the large investments in this sector—installed capacity has been growing at an average rate of 9 per cent per year since 1945—most of Brazilian industry still does not enjoy a reliable supply of energy at reasonable cost. The widespread reliance on 'self-supply'—manufacturing firms which build and operate generation facilities for their own use only—confirms the unsatisfactory nature of the service provided by the public utility firms. Severe rationing due to natural disasters (both floods and droughts) which occur almost every year is common and can last for months. The situation is well described in a recently published study by Judith Tendler:

[1] San Francisco *Chronicle*, 30 August 1968.
[2] Data about the electric power sector is taken from E.P.E.A., *Diagnóstico Preliminar, Energia Elétrica*, Ministry of Planning, Rio de Janeiro, 1967, and E.C.L.A., 'Fifteen Years . . .', op. cit.

The power supply to metropolitan Rio and São Paulo was almost always on the brink of crisis during the postwar period. Up to 1946 the two systems had been able to keep pace with the growth of demand for electricity, and even to stimulate it because of the slack capacity in their plants ... Throughout the succeeding twenty years the systems were never able to satisfy fully the demands made upon them. In its Annual Report of 1947, the company announced that it was operating without adequate reserve capacity, that there was a grave risk of being unable to maintain service in case of equipment breakdown, and that rationing had already been introduced in São Paulo. This was to be the case in varying degrees for the next eighteen years.

After 1946 the two subsidiaries never ended a year without a backlog of unattended requests for power connections. In four years—1956, 1957, 1958, and 1965—the company reported that it was able to supply the connected load, as opposed to demand for new connections, with no restrictions. During these years, however, external circumstances had usually limited demand.

By comparing the yearly observations on rainfall conditions with those on the condition of power supply, one discovers that inadequate rainfall was not the sole contributor to the power shortage ... Though shortage always worsened during low rainfall years ... restrictions were prevalent in average rainfall years as well, making clear that installed capacity was never enough. Figure 1.1, for example, shows the continuous existence from 1946 through 1954 of substandard voltage and frequency during the peak hours, which was one method of limiting load to fit within the bounds of installed capacity. Even for the years when significant additions to installed capacity entered service, restrictive measures were not always dispensed with.

* * *

The power shortage that prevailed throughout the postwar period plagued the consumer in the Rio–São Paulo metropolitan area. 'There are deficiencies in transmission and distribution, and in the servicing of new customers,' said the Director of the Water Division (Divisão de Águas) of the National Department of Mineral Production (Departamento Nacional de Produção Mineral). 'There is a waiting list of 6,000 requests for new connections, for example, in the city of Rio ... We get complaints about the problem of new connections and extensions, complaints about the rates, complaints about decreases in the voltage, and complaints about variations in the frequency of power received.'

It would seem that this twenty-year shortage of power should have seriously retarded economic growth, especially in a region that had enjoyed a surplus of power for many years. In 1949 a Brazil–United States Technical Commission had already noted that in São Paulo further industrial expansion was seriously handicapped by the inadequacy of power facilities. In 1954 the Joint Brazil–United States Economic Development Commission described graphically what it was like to be engaged in industrial production in a region with chronic power shortages: 'At times of serious system overload the power company has no option but to disconnect certain circuits ... without warning to the power users concerned ... Tiremakers lose a day's production when such stoppage occurs, and another day is required to clean out the machinery. Stoppage of power to glass furnaces cuts off the air circulation used to cool the walls of furnaces, endangering the strength and life of these walls ... [In polystyrene factories] the material flowing through the production equipment solidifies, causing a shutdown of no less than 10 days and up to 3 weeks, while polystyrene is manually chipped out of the vessels ... [Another] difficulty arises from low voltage and low frequency during periods of overload. Motors burn out, much equipment operates improperly with very widespread losses ... [Textile] looms operate improperly because shuttles slow down at such times, resulting in cloth whose quality is substandard.' Of course, the years when these observations were made—1953, 1954, and 1955—were the worst years in the power history of the south-central region: power cutoffs reached five to seven hours a day in Rio and São Paulo, and unforeseen cutoffs were common. Such severe conditions did not prevail throughout the postwar period, but substandard voltage and frequency were permanent features of the shortage, as well as quotas and other less severe forms of limiting the load.[1]

In spite of these problems, as Miss Tendler notes, industrial growth proceeded rapidly. The explanation is largely in terms of decreased quality of service, and increased self-supply by industrial consumers:

... the governor of São Paulo followed a policy of allowing the company to continue new connections, in order not to discourage the industrial influx into São Paulo. The new connections to the net were made at the sacrifice of the rest of the consumers, including the already existing industrial consumers, by making cuts and quotas even more severe. In face of inadequate installed capacity, in other words, the increase in sales was achieved by a continual decrease in the quality of service rendered to each customer.

What was important about this increasingly defective share of power received by each consumer was that the industrial sector—the

[1] Judith Tendler, *Electric Power in Brazil*, Harvard University Press, 1968, pp. 9–15.

greatest contributor to economic growth—was the consumer most able to adapt to defective supply, through the use of voltage regulators, for example, and more important, the supplementary use of his own generators. In 1956 the São Paulo Electrification Plan reported that supply to industry had been accomplished increasingly by the use of 'own power', especially since 1950. During the 1952–1955 crisis the São Paulo Federation of Industries (Federação de Indústrias do Estado de São Paulo) reported that by 1954 São Paulo industry had installed more than 100,000 kw in diesel generators. They represented about 20 percent of the installed capacity of the São Paulo Light system. Ten years later during the 1963–1964 crisis most major industries in Rio de Janeiro and São Paulo were equipped with standby power. At the end of 1963 the CANAMBRA group estimated the installed capacity of own-power installations in the state of São Paulo at 125,648 kw, or about 9 percent of the capacity of the São Paulo Light system. The group estimated, moreover, that 20,000 kw of this capacity would exist regardless of the adequacy of public power supply, so that a more accurate estimate of private capacity installed because of the shortage of public power would be 105,648 kw, or about 8 percent of the capacity installed in the public system of São Paulo Light.[1]

Just as in the case of telephones, rates were held below cost for years, thus impeding the industry in financing its own expansion. Various devices were used to compensate for the very low levels of the basic rates, including forcing industrial consumers to pay for additions to the power facilities:

There was an even more important area in which distribution allowed the Light company to exact a contribution from the consumer: that of forced consumer financing of the connection to the net. Upon receiving application for a large connection, the Light would inform the potential consumer that it had the power but not the financing to make the necessary installations. The applicant then had the choice of paying for the connection or of not having access to the public power system. A factory in the industrial zone of Guanabara, for example, requested in 1963 an increase in its load from 500 to 600 kva, allowing for a future increase to 1,000 kva. Rio Light informed the company that it would be necessary to expand the capacity of the secondary distribution net to accommodate this increased load— namely, to build a new receiving station. The industrial establishment would have to pay for this station if it wanted to increase its consumption.

* * *

[1] ibid., pp. 19–21.

F

... such financing was an integral feature of the *modus vivendi* in the Rio–São Paulo power system, as the Light itself admitted. 'Due to the lack of financial resources caused by inadequate tariffs,' the company stated in its 1962 Annual Report, 'many utilities have had to resort to consumer financing in recent years, and this has become an indispensable source of capital funds . . .'

Consumer financing in the Light system started in the early nineteen fifties. At the end of 1964 the amount outstanding was equivalent to approximately $22.7 million, comprising non-repayable contributions and repayable financing outstanding . . .[1]

The manufacturing sector thus grew, dragging the electricity sector behind it, rather than vice versa.

Nowhere is Brazil's 'social overhead capital' so deficient as in education. Fifty per cent of the population is illiterate. Sixty per cent of those students who enter first grade do not enter second grade.[2] In Harbison and Myers' correlation of their 'composite index of human resource development' with G.N.P. *per capita*, Brazil has one of the largest negative deviations. That is, Brazil's level of human resource development is more deficient—given its income level—than all countries in the sample of 72 except Saudi Arabia, Rhodesia, Liberia, Haiti, Guatemala, The Dominican Republic, Indonesia, Malaysia, and Canada.[3] Here indeed is an investment with high external economies and linkages which has been overlooked.

To most of the Brazilians who count, the function of education is to prepare young people for the roles appropriate to the socio-economic status of their families. For example, there are very few free-tuition secondary schools. In the big cities of the centre-south, the middle classes have succeeded in enlarging and improving the system to provide more aid to developing future generations than was done in the past. But for most Brazilians, the educational system does more to preserve the *status quo* than to assist in development.

The problems for industry are most serious in the area of skilled production workers, clerical workers, and middle manage-

[1] ibid., pp. 97–9.
[2] See E.P.E.A., *Diagnostico Preliminar, Educação*, Ministry of Planning, Rio de Janeiro, June 1966, for a detailed analysis of the Brazilian system of education.
[3] Calculations from data in Frederick Harbison and Charles A. Myers, *Education, Manpower, and Economic Growth*, McGraw-Hill, 1964, pp. 33 and 42.

ment. That is, it is the deficiencies in the high school and college levels which are the most serious for industrial development.

There are no comprehensive estimates of the cost savings and productivity increases which might be achieved through reasonable improvements in transportation, communication, electric power, and education. Deficiencies in these service sectors raise manufacturing costs in many ways. Everyone agrees that the deficiencies are there, and are serious.[1]

III. PUBLIC ENTERPRISES IN INDUSTRY

In a study of the period 1956–60, Villela found that the flow of investment into industrial enterprises which were operated or chartered by the federal government rose from 2·7 to 7·2 per cent of total gross fixed investment in Brazil. No estimates of total investment in industry are available, but if we take a rough estimate of one-third of over-all investment, the average federal government share of industrial investment was about 15 per cent. Villela also presents estimates of federal government share in income originating in industry: this increased from 3·9 per cent in 1956 to 6·3 per cent in 1960. The most important government investments were in steel, chemicals, and mining.[2]

In steel, the federal government owns or controls about 70 per cent of the country's ingot capacity, including the C.S.N. (Volta Redonda) which is the oldest and largest integrated steel mill in Latin America. In chemicals, 84 per cent of all petroleum refining (about 150,000 barrels per day) is controlled and operated by the federally-constituted public authority Petrobrás; private companies are not permitted to expand or to install new refineries. The Companhia Nacional de Alcalis is the only domestic producer of caustic soda. The federally-owned Companhia Vale do Rio

---

[1] A typical comment is: 'Inadequacies of public services in communications, transportation, and especially electric power have been another source of difficulty . . . They have sometimes caused investors to set up inefficient private substitutes, and in general have substantially increased the costs of doing business. Weaknesses in the educational structure have also made it difficult to secure middle-level managerial personnel and have required the establishment of special company training programs in clerical and industrial skills.' Lincoln Gordon and Engebert Grommers, *United States Manufacturing Investment in Brazil*, Harvard University Press, 1962, p. 151.

[2] Anníbal Villela, 'As Emprêsas do Governo Federal e Sua Importância na Economia Nacional—1956/1960', *Revista Brasileira de Economia*, March 1962.

Doce mines and exports about 80 per cent of Brazil's iron ore exports of over 13 million tons per year (equivalent to over $100 million in value). The Government also made investments in aluminium refining (Companhia Brasileira de Alumínio: 20,000 ton capacity, equivalent to over half total capacity in the industry and about 45 per cent of consumption), trucks and automobiles (Fábrica Nacional de Motores: a small portion of total production), shipbuilding, lead refining, electrical equipment, and pulp and paper.[1]

In addition to these federal enterprises, there are many significant state-chartered firms. The two newest Brazilian steel mills, for example, were directly promoted by the governments of São Paulo and of Minas Gerais. (See Appendix 1.)

Present policy is to continue the recent trend towards more restricted government investment in industry. The B.N.D.E. is no longer a major investor; its main activities are now financing small projects and working capital loans. In infrastructure, steel, and petroleum exploration and refining, public organizations will continue to be important. In other sectors of industry public activities are not expanding, and the public share is diminishing.

The motivation of direct public investment in industry has been two-fold. The first major instance was Volta Redonda, started during the second world war. The Vargas government had decided that Brazil should have an integrated steel mill. Private financing and operation was sought; only when it was not forthcoming did the Government act directly. This motivation of public investment as a last resort to achieve desired results, or at most as an inducement and bottleneck-breaker, was continued by the B.N.D.E., which in the 1950s was the channel for most public investment in industry. The second type of motivation—nationalism—made its first significant appearance with the establishment of Petrobrás in 1953. (By 'nationalism' I mean that foreign private investment was willing to act, but the Brazilian Government preferred to do the job itself.) The nationalistic motivation is also important in C.V.R.D. (iron-ore mining and export). But even in these companies, the motivation was by no means purely nationalistic. It was felt that private interests probably would not carry petroleum exploration and refining to the extent optimal for

[1] For a more detailed analysis see Samuel A. Morley and Gordon Smith, 'Import Substitution as an Industrialization Strategy in Brazil', 1969 (mimeo).

Brazil. In the case of iron-ore mining, the Government felt that Brazil could reap larger benefits by doing it herself. In neither case have events proved that Brazil suffered economically from decisions which were taken on partly nationalistic grounds.

Government investment in other industries has not always fared so well. The shipbuilding experiment has never got off the ground; orders are not steady and there is a lot of excess capacity and need for continued subsidies. The National Motor Factory (F.N.M.) produced a large number of heavy trucks in its early years, but has now suffered greatly from competition from private firms linked to foreign producers. The National Alcalis Company (C.N.A.) is forced to buy salt, its basic raw material, at a very high cost in order to support an inefficient but labour intensive salt industry in the north-east, and an even more inefficient system of transporting the salt.

IV. INVESTMENT SUBSIDIES

Incentives to private investment in favoured sectors have been very important in Brazil's industrialization, especially under the Kubitschek government of 1955–60.

For domestic private investment in traditional sectors (i.e. non-durable consumer goods), incentives were limited to protection against imports. This was already quite significant; at least from 1949 on, there was a conscious effort to extend protection to domestically produced products and to facilitate imports of those raw materials, spare parts and components, and capital goods not domestically available. The resulting high effective protection is of course equivalent to a subsidy in its effect on profits.

Access to long-term, low- or negative-real-interest capital was an important subsidy granted to favoured industries. This was done principally by the B.N.D.E., and also to some extent by the Bank of Brazil. Allocations of B.N.D.E. resources from its founding up to 1964 are shown in Tables 4.5 and 4.7. Over one-third went to manufacturing, within which steel and chemicals (mostly equity participation in public and mixed enterprises) and motor vehicles (mostly loans to mixed and private firms) absorbed most of the funds. The subsidy element—i.e. the difference between the social and the private cost of capital—is probably between 50 and 75 per cent of the total, or roughly $250–$350 million to manufacturing, and \$600–\$900 million to industry as a whole, including infrastructure. No precise breakdowns of total investment by sector of destination are available in Brazil, but using the rough estimate that annual gross investment in manufacturing was on the order of \$1 billion, the subsidy was, very roughly, around 3 per cent of total investment in manufacturing, and perhaps around 5 per cent of total investment in industry as a whole during the 1952–64 period.

TABLE 4.5
ALLOCATION OF B.N.D.E. RESOURCES, 1952–64
(flows in billions of 1953 cruzeiros)

Period	Energy and transport	Agriculture	Manufacturing	Total
1952–6	9·0	0·3	1·1	10·4
1957	3·1	0·2	0·9	4·2
1958	2·7	0·2	2·5	5·3
1959	1·7	0·1	1·4	3·2
1960	0·5	0·0	2·8	3·3
1961	2·8	0·1	1·3	4·2
1962	1·3	0·1	0·4	1·9
1963	0·3	0·1	3·2	3·7
1964	1·2	0·0	0·6	1·8
TOTAL	22·6	1·1	14·2	38·0
Per cent of total	59	3	37	100

Note: An approximate exchange rate for 1953 is Cr\$30/dollar. Thus the total B.N.D.E. investment in manufacturing was about \$470 million, and in manufacturing, energy, and transport a total of \$1·2 billion.
Source: Calculations from B.N.D.E., *XIII Exposição Sobre O Programa de Reaparelhamento Econômico*, 1964. Data in current cruzeiros was deflated by *Conjuntura Econômica* index No. 2; deflator for 1955 used for 1952–6. Details may not add to totals because of rounding.

Allocation of foreign financing was also controlled by the Government. This applied principally to official and semi-official resources, but allocation of private foreign investment was also strongly influenced by whether special treatment was available, on the one hand, and whether there was a threat that imports would be excluded, on the other. Allocation of these funds is shown in Tables 4.6 and 4.7. Here again we see manufacturing absorbing almost half, with steel and motor vehicles accounting for the lion's share.[1]

[1] The funds in Tables 4.5 and 4.6 are *not* mutually exclusive.

TABLE 4.6
ALLOCATION OF EXTERNAL FINANCING, 1955–61
(annual flows in million dollars)

Year	Energy and transport	Agriculture	Manufacturing	Other	Total
1955	74	1	17	19	111
1956	107	9	198	53	367
1957	174	40	255	91	560
1958	320	17	221	32	590
1959	171	10	250	32	463
1960	105	12	202	93	412
1961	66	4	75	22	167
TOTAL	1,017	93	1,218	342	2,670
Per cent of total	38	3	45	13	100

Note: Coverage is all investment authorized by S.U.M.O.C. or licensed by
C.A.C.E.X.; includes both private and public funds.
Source: E.C.L.A., 'Fifteen Years of Economic Policy in Brazil', op. cit.,
Table 21.

TABLE 4.7
ALLOCATION OF RESOURCES WITHIN MANUFACTURING
(per cent of total to manufacturing)

Sector	External resources, 1955–61, Table 4.6	B.N.D.E. resources, 1952–64, Table 4.5
Steel	27%	68%
Motor vehicles	57	6
Non-ferrous metals	1	5
Cement	2	n.a.
Chemicals	1	11
Pulp and paper	4	3
Shipbuilding	2	3
Other metal products	2	3

Sources: Same as Tables 4.5. and 4.6.

Foreign private investment

Inducements to foreign private investment have been very
important, being a judicious combination of carrot and stick. The
principal carrot was the large Brazilian market. As Gordon and
Grommers concluded:

> More important than any of the specific inducements . . . has been
> the general conviction . . . that Brazil presents a large and potentially
> rapidly growing market . . . Apart from size, postwar Brazil has had
> the further attraction of almost continuous economic growth . . .[1]

[1] Gordon and Grommers, op. cit., p. 148.

The principal stick was the threat of loss of the Brazilian market. High tariffs and possible import prohibition under the Law of Similars often meant that firms either had to manufacture in Brazil, or lose the market to other firms which would do so. Gordon and Grommers cite this as the single most important direct cause of investment in Brazil among the U.S. firms they studied.

Protection against imports was thus a double-action instrument: the foreign firm in its home country suffered loss of markets; a subsidiary established in Brazil enjoyed a protected market. Other subsidies and special treatment furnished further inducements: remittances of earnings and capital were virtually unrestricted from 1953 until 1962. This was probably more important as a psychological signal of a welcoming atmosphere than in actual operation, however: the inflation and difficulty of obtaining domestic financing for expanding (or even constant) levels of operation required reinvestment of a high percentage of earnings for most firms, foreign or domestic.

Special treatment for imports of both capital equipment and current inputs was probably the most important type of direct subsidy to foreign investment. Two instruments were used here. From 1955 on, capital goods could be imported by foreign firms without any foreign exchange transactions, under S.U.M.O.C. Instruction 113. If certain requirements were met, and the foreign investor accepted a cruzeiro equity share in the Brazilian enterprise as payment, no tariffs had to be paid and no foreign exchange had to change hands. The rate at which foreign exchange would have had to be sold in order to buy cruzeiros was lower (i.e. cruzeiros were more costly) than the rate at which the foreign exchange had to be bought to import the machinery. Avoidance of the foreign exchange transaction was therefore a significant benefit; the rate for buying foreign exchange for most machinery imports (excluding tariffs) ranged up to 56 per cent higher than the rate at which the foreign exchange was sold to buy cruzeiros. This special treatment was important during 1955–60; during this period costs of favoured imports would have been roughly 45 per cent higher in the absence of S.U.M.O.C. 113. If the alternative is considered to be the free trade situation, costs would have been roughly 39 per cent higher.

The requirements which had to be met to take advantage of this benefit were two: first, the investment had to be in an industry which the Government wanted to develop. Second, the investor and the Government had to agree on various operational plans, the most important being a programme for domestic procurement of inputs. Brazilian policy was to avoid a lot of 'assembly-only' investments; vertical integration of the industry (not necessarily of the firm) was strongly desired. The agreements which set up the timetables for Brazilian procurement of more and more of the raw materials and components were negotiated with the manufacturers, and were usually based on a fairly accurate estima-tion of the initial availability and the feasible rate of expansion of domestically produced inputs. The timetables almost always provided for faster 'nationalization' than the manufacturer wanted. But if the manufacturer made a serious attempt to follow the agreement, whatever imports had been permitted under it were allowed without question or problems, and usually with tariff exemptions or at subsidized rates.

This policy had both good and bad effects for Brazil. It forced foreign investors to use and even to develop Brazilian sources of supply. To some extent this involved extending technical assistance and credit, in addition to orders, to Brazilian firms. On the other hand, the policy involved setting up some processes which were inherently less efficient in Brazil (usually because of the small scale of operation) than in other countries. It also resulted in drastically reducing the demand for imports of manufactured products and thus in reducing much of the pressure on the balance of payments which usually accompanies rapid growth and industrialization. On the level of the firm, the policy virtually eliminated the situation (so common in some other L.D.C.s) where new industries have great difficulty in obtaining permission to import inputs even though the inputs are not available domestically, and where extra capacity is built simply to get enough import licences to operate a little more of the presently existing, largely idle plant.[1] Once established, the Brazilian firm might have had to use some inferior or higher-cost domestic inputs, but it did not stand idle because it could get neither the domestically produced input nor the licence to import it.

[1] For evidence of this see J. Bhagwati and P. Desai, *India: Planning for Indus-trialization*, Oxford University Press, 1970; S. Dell, *Trade Blocs and Common Markets*, Knopf, 1963; S. Lewis, *Pakistan: Industrialization and Trade Policies*, Oxford University Press, 1970; A. Waterston, *Development Planning: Lessons of Experience*, Johns Hopkins University Press, 1968.

Another device which helped to attract both foreign and domestic investment was the forming of 'Executive Groups' for various industries. These were high-level bodies, constituted of the representatives of Ministers of relevant ministries, the Presidents of the B.N.D.E. and the Tariff Council, etc. They worked hand-in-glove with the managers of firms in their sectors. These groups combined the responsibilities to plan and to implement arrangements for investment, operations, and all relevant government policies and regulations in the industries of their concern. These groups, where they functioned, were very effective in implementing decisions and eliminating red tape. They are discussed further in Section V, below.

The automotive industry furnishes outstanding examples of the application of the policies just discussed. Executive Groups were also important in shipbuilding, capital goods, chemicals, and iron-ore mining. Other industries where foreign interests are important are automotive industries, chemicals, electrical equipment, rubber products, special steels, aluminium, home appliances, cigarettes, perfumes and soaps, and pharmaceuticals.

The amount of direct foreign private investment is shown in Table 4.8. Most of this investment, especially since around 1950,

TABLE 4.8
DIRECT FOREIGN PRIVATE INVESTMENT, 1947–64
(annual flow in millions of U.S. dollars)

Year	Amount
1947	$36
1948	25
1949	5
1950	3
1951	−4
1952	9
1953	22
1954	11
1955	43
1956	90
1957	144
1958	110
1959	124
1960	98
1961	108
1962	69
1963	30
1964	28

Source: Bulletins of S.U.M.O.C. and the Central Bank.

went into manufacturing. The levels of foreign private investment in the 1956–62 period were quite significant, averaging slightly over $100 million per year, or roughly 10 per cent of total investment in manufacturing.

Some idea of where foreign private investment went can be had from a study made by Editôra Banas, a market research and business consulting firm in São Paulo. Banas surveyed Brazilian firms, and reported on the total stock of foreign capital, and on the total stock of equipment that had been imported under S.U.M.O.C. 113, as of the end of 1960. The former data are in cruzeiros, and since the methods of adjusting asset value to the inflation were quite poor and quite arbitrary, they should be taken as providing only a very general indication.

The Banas data, summarized in Tables 4.9 and 4.10, show that most foreign private capital went to manufacturing, and within that sector the lion's share went to the automotive industry.

TABLE 4.9
DESTINATION OF MACHINERY IMPORTS UNDER S.U.M.O.C.
INSTRUCTION 113
(total through 1960)

Sector	Value (million dollars)	Per cent of total
Automotive	201	53
Chemicals	44	12
Machinery and equipment	29	7
Non-ferrous metals	19	5
Rubber and products	17	4
Textiles	14	4
Steel	11	3
Others	46	12
TOTAL	381	100

Source: Editôra Banas, *O Capital Estrangeiro no Brasil*, São Paulo, June 1961 (third edition). The total reported by Banas appears to be only about three-quarters of all imports under S.U.M.O.C. 113.

Chemicals was second, followed by sectors such as machinery, metallurgy, food products, rubber products, textiles, and pharmaceuticals.[1]

The data in Table 4.8 show that foreign private investment was very much higher when S.U.M.O.C. 113 and the other devices described above were operating, than either before or

[1] See also Morley and Smith, op. cit.

after. This suggests that these subsidies and special arrangements may have been quite important. The total value of investment licensed under S.U.M.O.C. 113 for the period 1955–60 was $507 million, which is about 83 per cent of total foreign private invest-

TABLE 4.10
FOREIGN PRIVATE CAPITAL IN BRAZIL
(total value of assets as of 1960)

Sector	Amount (billion cruzeiros)	Per cent of total
Manufacturing	259·2	90
Commerce and services	18·6	7
Mining, including petroleum	6·9	2
Others	2·5	1
TOTAL	287·2	100

Within manufacturing:

	Amount (billion cruzeiros)	Per cent of total
Automotive	61·0	24
Chemicals	26·2	10
Food products	23·4	9
Machinery	21·4	8
Textiles	14·2	6
Steel	13·8	5
Pharmaceuticals	11·2	4
Rubber products	10·9	4
Non-metallic mineral products	10·6	4
Non-ferrous metals	5·4	2
Others	61·1	24
TOTAL	259·2	100

Note: An approximate exchange rate for 1960 is Cr$210/dollar. The total value of foreign capital invested in Brazilian manufacturing as of 1960 was thus over $1 billion.
Source: Banas, op. cit.

ment in the period. (If a one-year lag between licensing and investment is assumed, the percentage drops to 74 per cent.) This is on the order of 7 to 10 per cent of total investment in industry during the period.

V. THE ADMINISTRATIVE ENVIRONMENT; PLANNING

Government administrative procedures are mentioned in various parts of this study, especially in preceding parts of this chapter and in Chapter 3. However, this area deserves specific and comprehensive evaluation, even at the cost of repeating some of the earlier discussion.

The government administrative environment relevant to a private manufacturing firm in Brazil has been, on balance, rather favourable, or at least not exceptionally unfavourable. Most Brazilian governments of the post-war period have been well disposed towards private enterprise, and even the most socialistic government—that of Goulart in 1962–4—did not adopt policies which seriously hampered the operations of private manufacturing firms.[1] Brazil did not exhibit the 'we will tolerate you, but we don't like you and will constantly harass you' behaviour which is common in many L.D.C.s blessed with the combination of 'socialist' governments and much private capital in manufacturing. Industrialization was a conscious, high-priority goal, at least during the mid-1950s. In some sectors public enterprises were given the dominant or only place, but where private enterprise was permitted to operate in manufacturing—and this was in almost all of manufacturing—the administrative environment was designed to help it rather than to control it, on balance.

The favourable environment was a matter of the *detail* of control, and the *flexibility* of control. The administration of commercial policy is a good example of both.

Many L.D.C.s require licences for all imports. (Many also require licences for investment.) This is not the place for a general evaluation of alternative methods of planning and implementation, but it seems fair to say that the results of most instances of such detailed planning in L.D.C.s have ranged from poor to awful. The desired benefits usually are not achieved, because decisions are not taken on the bases of the desired criteria or with the relevant accurate information. The costs expand, in terms of red tape, corruption, delays, idle capacity, etc.[2] Control by taxation, rather than by direct quantitative controls, seems to work better in practice.

Brazil has never required licences or other government approval for investment. Licences for all imports were required during 1947–53; in spite of the Brazilian genius for getting along in any

---

[1] Only *direct* administrative policies are meant to be included here. The galloping inflation, which was largely a result of policies under Goulart, certainly did not help most firms, nor did the rapid increases in real wages which Goulart permitted, nor the increasingly high tax burden since the mid-1950s.

[2] See especially J. Bhagwati and P. Desai, op. cit.

situation, the results—typical of those mentioned above—were poor enough that the system was abandoned.[1] Nevertheless, import licences were and are required for goods for which domestic similars exist, and for importers who receive various exemptions or special treatment. The effect of this on producers is small, however, because many of these licensing requirements either fall on consumer goods imports, or can be avoided if the importer is willing to pay the regular tariff, etc. There are, however, producer goods for which domestic similars exist and for which import licences are therefore required. This does result in some effort expended either to get the licence or to get around a possible prohibition of the import,[2] or in buying a domestic substitute which may not be a perfect substitute or as good a value.

These restrictions are far from optimal, from the viewpoint of the consuming firm. But they are also far from the practice of many L.D.C.s of putting quantitative restrictions on imports regardless of the non-existence of domestic substitutes, causing periodic and sometimes chronic idle capacity because of lack of inputs. In Brazil it may be costly or impossible to use an import instead of an available domestic product, but it is virtually never impossible to import a producer good which is not available domestically—quite the contrary, importers of producer goods not available domestically generally face low tariffs and no administrative barriers. (See Section III of Chapter 3.)

The flexibility achieved in administering the import control system was outstanding. The multiple rate system from 1953 to 1957 worked well, but did not give as much control over the composition of imports as was desired. The tariff reform of 1957 created the Tariff Council (C.P.A.) which had broad powers to change tariff rates, move products from one to the other of the two remaining categories, and decide which products should be recognized as domestic similars.[3] Note the conclusions of an E.C.L.A. study of 1962:

[1] See Donald L. Huddle, 'Balanço de Pagamentos e Contrôle de Câmbio no Brasil: Eficácia, Bem-Estar e Desenvolvimento Econômico', *Revista Brasileira de Economia*, June 1964.

[2] In cases where the import of a much-preferred item would be prohibited because of the existence of a domestic similar, it is not uncommon for the would-be importer to arrange for the domestic supplier to state that he is unable to supply the product in this instance (thus permitting the import), in return for purchase of something else, or some other sort of bribe.

[3] The Foreign Trade Department of the Bank of Brazil (C.A.C.E.X.) had to

... the Council has given the application of the customs tariffs the efficiency and pliability which are indispensable attributes for the operation of any instrument in a country that is undergoing a rapid process of economic change ... The combination of the tariff and the Council constitutes the most precise and well-adjusted instrument of economic policy existing in Brazil.[1]

I join in E.C.L.A.'s admiration of the C.P.A.'s administrative flexibility, even if I cannot go so far in approving the tariff structure itself. This flexibility is such that (as noted in Chapter 3) one cannot give a detailed, accurate description of how the system of protection operated since 1957. It is too complicated. The system was administered so as to protect industries which had been or were to be established, with a minimum cost on imports of producer goods that could not be produced and which were needed as inputs. Cases of new industries which had not yet grown large enough to satisfy all demand furnish a good example: the C.P.A. permitted imports at low or zero tariffs if the importer bought a proportionate amount of domestic production. The proportion was set just high enough to assure full use of what domestic capacity did exist.

The bad aspects of the administration of commercial policy are seen principally on the export side. Fluctuating rates and administrative red tape added their effects to other policies and conditions which discouraged exports.

The best instances of efficient, flexible administration are those of some of the Executive Groups, in which representatives of the various Ministers and the heads of the C.P.A., Bank of Brazil Foreign Trade Department, B.N.D.E., etc., worked intimately with the management of the private (and public, if any) firms in their part of the economy. In the more successful of these groups, a comprehensive plan was developed with management of the businesses concerned, covering output, investment, a timetable for increasing domestic procurement of inputs, and the governmental regulations needed to implement the plans. For example, the timetable of domestic procurement of inputs was used to project needed imports of capital equipment, components, and raw materials. These imports were then given favourable treat-

---

licence imports of special category goods. In 1967 the power to recognize the existence of domestic similars also passed to C.A.C.E.X.
[1] E.C.L.A., 'Fifteen Years of Economic Policy in Brazil', op. cit.

ment, the details of which were worked out in the Executive Group, by the representatives of the responsible government agencies. In many cases—notably chemicals and automobiles—the group negotiated hard with various potential investors so as to strike an agreement with the least tariff concessions and the most rapid reduction of imported inputs. But once the agreement was reached, the firms got the imports they needed.

A crucial factor in the success of the Executive Groups (where they succeeded—some did not) was that the planning was done by the people who had to implement it. If tariff concessions were needed, the C.P.A. and C.A.C.E.X. had participated in planning them. If other tax concessions were to be granted, the representative of the Minister of Finance had played a major role in designing them. If a significant amount of transport facilities had to be constructed, representatives of the relevant ministries had helped to decide on them. The business firms did not get everything they wanted, but at least they were able to bargain directly with the men who had the power, and the mission, to implement whatever final agreement was reached.

At least until 1964, there were no attempts to make comprehensive national plans for economic development in Brazil. The most ambitious attempts covered only a few important sectors, and all but one of these plans were complete failures. The S.A.L.T.E. plan (Saude, Alimentação, Transporte, and Energia = health, food supply, transport, and energy), a five-year programme for public investment in the four-named sectors, was abandoned after one year (1950). A joint team of E.C.L.A. and B.N.D.E. personnel made some macro-economic projections in 1955, but this was in no sense a plan. A Three-Year Plan was made for 1963–5 under the direction of Celso Furtado. This was a combination of macro-economic projections plus a price stabilization programme; President Goulart abandoned the latter after only a few months.

The one moderately successful plan was President Kubitschek's 'Target Plan' (Programa de Metas), which set detailed targets for output and investment in each of thirty sub-sectors of energy, transport, food production and marketing, manufacturing, and education. Not all of the targets were met, especially in food marketing facilities, but the period of the plan (1955–61) was one of extremely rapid over-all growth of output, industrialization, and modernization generally.[1] In spite of widespread corruption and waste, the Kubitschek regime is remembered with great nostalgia by many Brazilians—especially in the lower and working classes—and many observers believe that Kubitschek would have been the most likely winner if a free election for the Presidency of Brazil had been held as scheduled in the mid-1960s.

The original Executive Groups and the Tariff Council were created to help to formulate and to implement the Target Plan. There was some co-ordination by the B.N.D.E. and the monetary authorities, since most of the financial resources for the plan flowed through them.[2] But the broadest scope of any real co-ordination was within each of the Executive Groups and a few public authorities. The former co-ordinated activity over sectors such as the automotive industry, shipbuilding, tractors and earth-moving machinery, heavy equipment, and railway equipment; the latter controlled significant parts of petroleum refining and exploration, electric energy, and marketing of food products. There was certainly a sense of priorities implicit in the formulation of the plan, but explicit or detailed comprehensive planning was completely absent.

The project and sector planning done by and for the Executive Groups and public authorities was, on the whole, competent and very useful. This is not to say that implementation was always very close to the economic optimum. In the automotive industry, as will be shown in Chapter 7, excessive fragmentation and over-zealous requirements for domestic procurement raised costs significantly. In chemicals, a few tremendously inefficient plants were built, most of them for particular political reasons. But the over-all results were certainly a great amount of real growth, and the desired drastic changes in the structure of production and trade were achieved. As to the lack of over-all, comprehensive planning, it is far from clear that Brazil suffered very much from this omission.

[1] For a detailed description and evaluation of the Target Plan, see E.C.L.A., 'Fifteen Years of Economic Policy in Brazil', op. cit. In this article, the author's high degree of objectivity fails to conceal his predilection for comprehensive central planning, even as he extols the success of the essentially unco-ordinated development under Kubitschek.

[2] Roberto Campos, president of the B.N.D.E. for much of this period, has often expressed himself on the internal inconsistency of the phrase 'comprehensive planning in Brazil'.

G

VI. SUMMARY

Brazilian governments of the post-war period have not been bashful about public investment, both in infrastructure and in manufacturing. Total public investment as a percentage of G.N.P. was quite respectable by the late 1950s, probably even if the (unknown) cost of Brasilia is deducted. Progress has certainly been made in some important sectors such as electric power and highways. But little or no progress has been made in other areas, and even electric power and transport in general are still far from satisfactory. On balance, infrastructure in Brazil is clearly and significantly deficient. This deficiency is equivalent to what I call a 'negative subsidy'. Adequate service is often not available at any price, and the value received for taxes and fees for telephone service, electric power service, etc., in Brazil is far below that in most advanced countries. The idea of government intervention in infrastructure is to provide services at lower real costs than would be possible if each industrial firm had to provide these services for itself, or if it were left to private firms to provide them. In fact, government interference with private firms in infrastructure, and deficient operation of public firms, have resulted in higher real costs of infrastructure services to manufacturing than in advanced countries, and in some cases even in higher real costs than would have been likely in Brazil if government had not intervened.

What are the areas where government actions increased real costs to manufacturing? This is 'negative subsidy' in the strictest sense. Two areas are outstanding: rate regulation of private firms in communications and electric power in the 1950s and early 1960s, and the effects of inflation on capital markets and on technological efficiency in manufacturing. Rate regulations kept nominal utility rates from keeping up with the inflation, the utility firms responded by cutting investment, and service deteriorated steadily. Inflation together with the legal prohibition on adjustable nominal interest rates completely eliminated the market for private loan capital of more than 180 days maturity. Inflation also reduced the ability to increase technological efficiency by increasing the difficulty of cost accounting, and decreased the motivation to increase technological efficiency by making inventory management and financial management more important determinants of profits.

In other areas of infrastructure, government action was not negative, but was insufficient—infrastructure services in Brazil are not as good as in the countries Brazilian manufacturing must compete with. This is true in physical infrastructure—notably electric power, railroads, and coastal shipping—and also in education and in market organization—the last notably in capital market regulation, and agricultural marketing services such as grading, credit, bonded warehouses, etc.

Theory indicates that subsidies to manufacturing might well have been justified, because of wage distortions, external economies, and because of the 'infant economy' effect. But in infrastructure—physical, social, and organizational—Brazilian manufacturing was and is *less* well served than manufacturing in advanced countries. Brazilian costs are raised, rather than lowered, in relation to costs of competitors.

In compensation for these 'negative subsidies', favoured Brazilian industries have received positive financial subsidies as well as special treatment administratively. These were mostly creations of the Kubitschek administration (1956–60), and many are still functioning today. The financial subsidies were mostly special treatment for imports of machinery and equipment for favoured user industries, and long-term, low-interest loans to the same industries. For essentially the same favoured industries, the administrative environment was eased by Executive Groups, the interministerial bodies which made plans in co-operation with the industry concerned, and then saw to the government actions necessary to implement these plans with a minimum of further administrative problems for the industries. Except for the automotive, these favoured industries were all makers of producer goods. As to the administrative environment, this may not have been as favourable as in many advanced countries, but at least seems to have been much more favourable than in many L.D.C.s.

PART III

Results

5

Structural Change in the Post-war Period

IN the two previous chapters the policies which the Brazilian Government used to promote industrialization were described. In this chapter we will see the over-all picture of the results of those policies, in terms of the structure of imports, domestic manufacturing, and exports. In the two chapters which follow we will examine some of the results in more detail.

I. INTER-INDUSTRIAL CHANGES AND IMPORT SUBSTITUTION

Manufacturing output grew at a rapid and rising rate from 1939 to 1962. The early post-war structure was heavily concentrated on food products and textiles. These activities are still important but have been joined by diversified chemicals, metallurgy, and machinery and equipment sectors. Paper products and rubber products, although much smaller, have also been growing rapidly. In the most general terms the evolution has been more or less typical, with emphasis shifting from consumer goods to producer goods, and from traditional to modern industries. This history is summarized in Tables 5.1 and 5.2.

The process of change in the industrial structure must be studied in conjunction with the import-substitution process which gave it its main impulse and also its structure. At the beginning of the post-war period, there were already very few imports of non-durable consumer goods. During 1947–55 the outstanding progress in import substitution was made in consumer durables; by the late 1950s most of these goods were produced domestically.

As imports of consumer goods were reduced, the import substitution process entered the stage of producer goods. (The term 'producer goods' is meant to include both capital goods and

TABLE 5.1
EVOLUTION OF THE STRUCTURE OF BRAZILIAN MANUFACTURING, 1939-64

Sector	Value added, in millions of U.S. dollars				Percentage distribution				Average annual growth rates			
	1939	1949	1959	1964	1939	1949	1959	1964	39-49	49-59	59-64	39-64
Food, beverages, and tobacco	345	612	1,118	1,859	30	27	21	22	5·9%	6·2%	10·6%	7·0%
Textiles and clothing	307	537	815	1,164	27	23	16	14	5·7	4·3	7·4	5·5
Wood, paper, and products	79	200	456	519	6	8	8	6	9·8	8·6	2·6	7·8
Leather and rubber products	26	75	181	239	3	3	3	3	11·2	9·2	5·8	9·3
Chemicals, pharmaceuticals, etc.	124	230	723	1,386	11	10	14	17	5·6	12·2	13·8	10·2
Non-metallic mineral products	61	165	356	355	5	7	7	4	10·5	8·0	nil	7·3
Metals and metal products	150	349	1,437	2,547	13	16	27	31	8·8	15·2	12·0	12·0
Others	54	129	247	288	5	6	4	3	9·1	6·8	3·0	6·9
TOTAL manufacturing	1,146	2,297	5,333	8,357	100	100	100	100	7·2	8·5	9·4	8·3

Source: Industrial Censuses for 1939, 1949, and 1959; I.B.G.E., *Indústrias de Transformação Dados Gerais—1963/64*, Rio de Janeiro, April 1966 for 1964. Adjustments for comparability made by the author. These data are based on value added deflated by a general price index (the G.D.P. implicit deflator) except for 1939, and hence show somewhat different values than the physical product indices cited elsewhere.

intermediate goods.) Both domestic production and imports of capital goods increased rapidly during the initial years of this stage (roughly 1955–9). Domestic production of intermediate goods also expanded at a rapid pace; so rapid that imports of intermediate goods remained at a more-or-less constant absolute level. By around 1959, the investments made during the period had entered into full-scale operation. There was a marked decline in total manufactured imports as a percentage of total imports, while imports of larger quantities of certain raw materials were consumed by the new industries.

Until the early 1960s, the process of progressive vertical integration and self-sustaining growth can be seen. Investments caused the simultaneous creation of both demand and supply for a wide variety of industrial products. As Baer and Kerstenetsky concluded, 'The picture which emerges . . . from the simultaneous growth of industries which to a large extent are each other's customers is that of a remarkably balanced growth . . . Many complementary industries grew up simultaneously and acted as self-re-enforcing factors.'[1] The value of total imports, which was 16 per cent of G.D.P. in 1947–9, fell to 10 per cent in 1948–50 and to 8 per cent in 1960–2. The share of processed products in total imports fell from 87 per cent in 1953 to 58 per cent in 1965; a different source shows the share of processed products falling from 90 per cent in 1948–50 to 70 per cent in 1959–61.[2] The most important single elements of this shift from processed products to raw materials were in petroleum products, metals and metal products, and wheat. Industrial growth was rapid and diversified enough to keep imports of manufactured goods roughly constant in absolute value; this is remarkable in the face of the rapid income growth which was occurring. Table 2.1 shows the shift in the structure of trade.

Table 5.2 and Figure 5.1 show how imports of manufactures fell as a percentage of total supply. As noted above, imports of non-durable consumer goods were already insignificant in 1949; imports of durable consumer goods were substituted rapidly

---

[1] Werner Baer, *Industrialization and Economic Development in Brazil*, op. cit., p. 142.

[2] Author's calculation from I.B.G.E., *Números Indices*, op. cit., and E.C.L.A., 'The Growth and Decline of Import Substitution in Brazil', op. cit. The former starts in 1953, and the latter ends in 1961.

during the early 1950s, and of capital goods and intermediate goods throughout the period.[1]

Import substitution has also been analysed according to the Brazilian census classification. This has manufacturing divided among 21 sectors. Unfortunately, many sectors contain very different types of goods. This is the only way that most of the data are available, however, and it has been used throughout this study.

TABLE 5.2
STRUCTURE OF IMPORTS AND DOMESTIC PRODUCTION OF
MANUFACTURED PRODUCTS, BY USE

Year	Consumer goods		Producer goods		All manufactured goods
	Durables	Non-durables	Intermediate	Capital	
		Imports (billion cruzeiros of 1955)			
1949	8·9	5·4	18·2	15·8	48·3
1955	2·1	4·5	22·6	13·7	42·9
1959	2·9	2·8	21·2	29·2	56·1
1964	1·5	3·9	18·6	8·7	32·7
		Domestic production (billion cruzeiros of 1955)			
1949	4·9	140·0	52·1	9·0	206·0
1955	19·0	200·9	104·0	18·0	341·9
1959	43·1	258·0	159·6	59·5	520·2
1964	93·8	319·5	261·2	79·7	754·2
		Imports as percentages of total supply			
1949	64·5	3·7	25·9	63·7	19·0
1955	10·0	2·2	17·9	43·2	11·1
1959	6·3	1·1	11·7	32·9	9·7
1964	1·6	1·2	6·6	9·8	4·2

Source: Imports from I.B.G.E., *Números Indices*, op. cit. Gross value of industrial production from Industrial Census, Registro Industrial and indices of physical production from *Conjuntura Econômica*. Imports of 1949 projected backward using data in E.C.L.A., 'The Growth and Decline of Import Substitution in Brazil', op. cit. Data adjusted to relative prices of 1955, to remove the effects of changes in relative prices.

Import ratios for 1939, 1949, and 1962 are shown in Table 5.3. These are estimates for two different measures. One is the gross value of imports and the gross value of domestic production. The second is the value added content of imports and of domestic

---

[1] Imports of capital goods in 1964 were abnormally low because of the very low volume of investment; imports drop much more rapidly than domestic production in a recession. This in itself shows how well developed the Brazilian capital goods industry has become. The normal share of imports in total supply of capital goods, as of the mid-1960s, is roughly 30 per cent.

production. The estimates of the second measure, which is much more meaningful for many purposes, are preliminary results kindly made available by Samuel A. Morley and Gordon Smith.[1] Morley and Smith applied the inverse of the 1959 Brazilian input–output table to the import bill, to get the total production in each

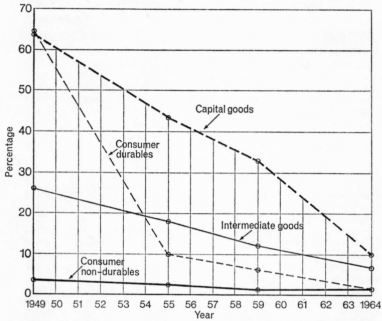

Figure 5.1 Imports as percentage of total supply of manufactured products.

sector which would have been required to produce the imports in Brazil. Applying the ratio of value added to gross production for each sector (also from the 1959 table) then gave the estimates of the value added content of imports.[2]

[1] 'On the Measurement of Import Substitution', *American Economic Review*, to appear.
[2] In matrix algebra terms:

$$X = (I - A)^{-1}M$$
$$V = RX$$

where $(I - A)$ = identity matrix minus the input–output coefficient matrix,
$\quad M$ = vector of gross value of imports,
$\quad V$ = value added content of imports,
$\quad R$ = matrix with off-diagonal elements of zero and diagonal elements of the ratios of value added to gross value of production for each sector.

Table 5.3 shows again the broad scope and extent of import substitution in manufactured products. Imports were drastically reduced in every sector, and are down to very small percentages of domestic production in all but capital goods and chemicals.

TABLE 5.3
RATIO OF MANUFACTURED IMPORTS TO DOMESTIC PRODUCTION

	Gross value			Value added	
Sector	1939	1949	1962	1949	1962
Non-metallic mineral products	0·157	0·095	0·039	0·270	0·077
Metallurgy	0·705	0·238	0·102	1·160	0·502
Machinery	0·842	1·641	0·754	1·860	0·630
Electrical equipment	0·197	0·875	0·170	5·400	0·248
Transport equipment	7·191	1·248	0·185	4·470	0·119
Wood products	0·043	0·016	0·006	0·122	0·065
Furniture	0·010	0·003	0·000	0·025	0·011
Paper and products	0·600	0·226	0·126	0·471	0·248
Rubber products	0·680	0·011	0·004	0·127	0·027
Leather products	0·082	0·039	0·004	0·104	0·037
Chemicals	1·022	0·709	0·227	8·730	0·346
Pharmaceuticals	1·871	0·167	0·051	0·277	0·102
Perfumes, soaps, etc.	0·029	0·013	0·021	0·007	0·003
Plastics	0·000	0·054	0·002	0·965	0·024
Textiles	0·079	0·050	0·003	0·084	0·019
Clothing	0·036	0·018	0·004	0·002	0·001
Food products	0·022	0·027	0·017	0·060	0·031
Beverages	0·092	0·023	0·020	0·118	0·034
Tobacco	0·000	0·000	0·000	0·000	0·000
Miscellaneous	0·740	0·376	0·273	0·399	0·171

Note: The printing and publishing sector is omitted.
Source: Gross value of manufactured imports, Fundação Getúlio Vargas, unpublished worksheets. Gross value of industrial production, Industrial Censuses for 1939 and 1949, and Industrial Register for 1962. Value added ratios, preliminary results of Morley and Smith, op. cit.

We have seen that industry led post-war Brazilian growth in a structural as well as in an arithmetic sense. Industrial growth was largely based on import substitution (including induced new demand for producer goods).[1] The import-substituting industrialization did not stop at consumer non-durables plus assembly of some consumer durables, as so often happens.[2] It went on to

[1] For a quantitative analysis of the importance of import substitution in industrial growth in Brazil, see Morley and Smith, op. cit.
[2] See Carlos Diaz, 'On the Import Intensity of Import Substitution', *Kyklos*, XVIII, No. 3, 1965; and Albert O. Hirschman, 'The Political Economy of Import-Substituting Industrialization in Latin America', *Quarterly Journal of Economics*, February 1968.

include all consumer durables, almost all intermediate goods (semi-finished goods and components), and over two-thirds of the apparent consumption of capital goods.

Industrialization on a broad front, with widespread protection, investment subsidies, and tariff exemption for some of the inputs which had to be imported, was easier to sell politically and psychologically than narrower efforts might have been. Since the mid-1950s, there was a strong public spirit of industrialization,[1] and there was less of an impression of unfairness because virtually all industrialization efforts were receiving public support. Adverse reaction from the large agricultural sector was reduced by partially subsidized imports of tractors, fertilizers, and other agricultural inputs, some negative-real-interest loans, and also by separate policies for coffee and some of the other main export crops.

The import substitution phase of the Brazilian industrialization was almost complete by the early 1960s. Imports of manufactures had been reduced to insignificant proportions of apparent consumption except for some chemicals and the technologically more complex capital goods. Even in these sectors imports were only about 10 and 30 per cent, respectively, of apparent consumption. However, exports of manufactured products, the sign of the desirable next phase of industrialization, have not appeared in significant value, range of products, or continuity. This is shown in Table 5.4, where the shares of exports in domestic production of the individual manufacturing sectors are shown.

II. BIASES AND THEIR RESULTS

In the section above we saw the over-all picture of the structural changes in domestic manufacturing, imports, and exports. The relation of the policies described in Chapters 3 and 4 to these changes can now be analysed. The first part of this section will deal with manufacturing as a whole, relative to imports, exports, and also relative to domestic agriculture. In the second part the focus will move to the relationship between the inter-industrial structure of protection and of import substitution: which sectors got how much protection, and what happened? This forms the basis for some tentative conclusions on questions such as how

---

[1] *Desenvolvimentismo*, of which industrialization was an important element. See Thomas E. Skidmore, *Politics in Brazil*, op. cit., pp. 87–100.

well the structure of protection was designed, what effects did it have, and to what extent was it necessary; how did the other policies (discussed in Chapter 4) interact with commercial policy; and why did Brazil get so far in import substitution of producer goods?

TABLE 5.4
RATIO OF MANUFACTURED EXPORTS TO GROSS VALUE OF PRODUCTION, 1949 AND 1962

Sector	1949	1962
Non-metallic mineral products	0·002	0·002
Metallurgy	0·017	0·001
Machinery	0·016	0·009
Electrical equipment	0·002	0·001
Transport equipment	0·000	0·008
Wood products	0·021	0·193
Furniture	0·000	0·000
Paper and products	0·000	0·004
Rubber products	0·001	0·002
Leather products	0·396	0·069
Chemicals	0·268	0·076
Pharmaceuticals	0·022	0·004
Perfumes, soaps, etc.	0·000	0·000
Plastics	0·000	0·000
Textiles	0·136	0·097
Clothing	0·001	0·001
Food products	0·389	0·185
Beverages	0·000	0·000
Tobacco	0·000	0·001
Miscellaneous	0·019	0·003

Note: Printing and publishing is omitted.
Source: Manufactured Exports, Fundação Getúlio Vargas, unpublished worksheets. Gross Value of Production from Industrial Census for 1949 and Registro Industrial for 1962.

Output by major sectors and markets

For manufacturing as a whole, the combination of protection, investment subsidies, etc., did result in rapid growth. Moreover, this growth was greater in the post-war period (when protection was deliberate and more varied among industrial sectors, and accompanied by some financial subsidies and administrative inducements) than in the depression-war period of 1930–45 (when protection was involuntary and more uniform in its structure, and the pre-existing industrial base was smaller). The industrialization was principally based on import substitution, including new demand for producer goods induced by the substitution. The ratio of imports to domestic production was sharply reduced in most sectors. Imports of consumer goods were reduced to insignificant levels, and imports of intermediate and capital goods to roughly 10 and 30 per cent of total supply, respectively.

The rapid growth of manufacturing output was exclusively for the protected domestic market. Exports of manufactures, very small to begin with, were stagnant or declining from the late 1940s to the early 1960s.[1] This is really extraordinary in view of the tremendous scope of growth of domestic manufacturing, but is explained by the tremendous bias in almost every sector in favour of producing for the domestic market as against producing for export. (See Table 3.9.) Considering commercial policy alone—forgetting about deficient infrastructure—the margin available for value added when exporting was negative for 8 of the 21 manufacturing sectors in 1966. That means that tariffs raised costs of tradable inputs alone, above the level of revenue fixed by the export exchange rate. Those 8 sectors accounted for roughly 40 per cent of value added in all manufacturing. For the other sectors, the margin available for value added for domestic sales was over twice that available for export, for all but one sector (wood products, where the ratio was 1·9). In earlier years, as we saw in Chapter 3, the bias was even greater. Now, the aggregation hides a lot here. There are export products in sectors where value added for export, on the average, would be negative. But the results do show that the bias against exports of manufactures was generally enormous, even though there were exceptions scattered throughout the industrial classification.

The value of exports as a per cent of domestic production for 20 industrial sectors is shown in Table 5.4. The classification used is very broad in its definition of a manufactured product. Many products which receive minimal processing are included as manufactures, such as coffee beans, milled rice, salt, and sugar. The result is to give the impression that Brazilian industry is more export-oriented than it actually is; even so, exports are insignificant for most sectors. Exports as a percentage of output rose in only 5 of the 21 sectors: wood products, transport equipment, paper and products, rubber products, and tobacco. In all of these but wood products, exports *rose* to less than 1 per cent of

[1] Depending on the definition of manufactures and the exact dates chosen.

output. Exports of wood products were virtually all pine lumber. The tremendous bias against manufactured exports, described in Chapter 3 and earlier in this chapter, has had its effect.

The bias between industry and agriculture is a little harder to evaluate. The effective tariff calculations for agriculture do not take full account of subsidies to agriculture in the form of tariff exemptions and other subsidies to fertilizer, tractors, and other inputs. On balance, I would judge that commercial policy was roughly neutral towards agriculture, as to import substitution. That is, both actual product prices and actual margin available for value added, when producing for domestic sales, were not too different from what they would have been in the free trade situation. Growth in output is not inconsistent with this conclusion: growth in agricultural output for domestic consumption was about 4·9 per cent per year,[1] while growth in population was 3 per cent and in *per capita* income 2·4 per cent. This is analysed in more detail in the first section of Chapter 7.

The bias against agricultural exports is much clearer.[2] The implicit tax on exports (relative to the free trade situation) averaged 31 per cent in the period 1954–64. Again assuming that commercial policy was roughly neutral in its effects on inputs, value added for the domestic market would be over 50 per cent more than for export. In addition to this price bias, quantitative restrictions were placed on exports of food products from time to time. (Non-coffee food products were roughly one-third of total non-coffee exports.)

One of the major causes of the poor performance of Brazilian exports since the second world war was thus the continued over-valuation of the cruzeiro. As we saw in Chapter 3, this over-valuation was already significant at the end of the war. The additional over-valuation accumulated during the late 1940s was more than made up during the 1950s and early 1960s (Table 3.4). The problem was that even at its low points, the export cruzeiro was over-valued. To promote exports, a once-and-for-all real devaluation was needed as well as reductions in fluctuations and administrative restrictions. The result of such a change in policy would have been something like a once-and-for-all increase in the value of exports; it would not have been a continuous increase in

[1] *Conjuntura Econômica*, index No. 38 (1945–7 to 1965–7).
[2] Again coffee is excluded from the analysis.

the value of exports. This point should not be overstressed; policies which made exporting easier and more profitable would have had some effect on long-run growth as well. But the main impact would have been on the level, and not on the long-run growth, of the value of exports. The maximum devaluation, to the free trade situation, would have been about 38 per cent on the average during the 1954–64 period. Using the assumptions about elasticities from Appendix 3, the value of non-coffee exports would have increased by the same percentage, and total exports would have increased by roughly 20 per cent, or $250 million per year.

If export expansion had been the *only* goal, a policy of continual devaluation in real terms, plus taxes on coffee and perhaps a few other products, might well have been successful. The trouble with such a policy is that it probably would not have produced the desired growth in income, industrialization, and modernization.

Further details of Brazil's export performance during the post-war period are shown in Table 5.5. The volume of both coffee and non-coffee exports were essentially stagnant. Exports of manufactures, never significant, were also stagnant or declining. Since the purpose of exporting is to earn the foreign exchange with which to buy imports, it is interesting to analyse the evolution of the purchasing power of exports in buying imports. This index is called the 'capacity to import'. It is equal to the volume of exports, times the price of exports, divided by the price of imports. Components of the change in Brazil's capacity to import during the post-war period are shown in the first column of Table 5.6. Increases in coffee prices were the most significant positive element, while decreases in prices of other exports plus increases in prices of imports were an offsetting negative element. The first column of Table 5.6 shows what actually happened; the second shows a rough estimate of what would have happened if the export cruzeiro had been devalued all the way to the free trade situation.

Throughout the post-war period, exports have been seen as a 'vent of surplus'. This is certainly not true for coffee, and perhaps not completely true for one or two other products such as cacau and iron ore. But for all other products, primary as well as manufactured, both the Brazilian Government and most Brazilian

H

TABLE 5.5
EXPORTS, TERMS OF TRADE, AND CAPACITY TO IMPORT, 1946–64

	Export value, million dollars					Export quantum			Terms of trade	Capacity to import
Year	Coffee	Other food products	Raw materials	Manufactures	Total	Coffee	Other	Total		
	(1)	(2)	(3)	(4)	(5)	(6)	(7)	(8)	(9)	(10)
1946	348	156	410	73	985	100	187	133	51	68
1947	422	192	447	91	1,152	95	177	127	64	81
1948	492	215	428	45	1,181	112	164	131	69	90
1949	631	114	316	35	1,096	125	119	117	63	73
1950	866	150	323	17	1,355	95	117	102	100	103
1951	1,058	167	523	20	1,769	105	120	109	102	111
1952	1,045	114	250	10	1,418	102	65	90	100	90
1953	1,089	148	292	11	1,540	100	100	100	100	100
1954	948	204	395	16	1,562	70	132	86	120	103
1955	844	212	343	24	1,423	88	132	100	94	94
1956	1,030	146	280	27	1,482	108	111	108	86	93
1957	846	198	322	26	1,392	92	124	100	87	87
1958	687	258	274	23	1,243	83	135	96	80	77
1959	733	234	210	105	1,282	112	140	117	72	84
1960	713	223	297	36	1,269	108	150	118	69	82
1961	710	225	418	50	1,403	109	183	128	69	88
1962	642	150	387	35	1,214	105	158	118	66	78
1963	749	219	397	41	1,407	125	155	130	69	90
1964	759	162	434	70	1,430	96	168	116	76	88
Avg. 1946–8						102	176			80
Avg. 1960–2						107	164			83

Source: Columns 1–5: E.P.E.A., *Diagnóstico Preliminar, Setor de Comércio Internacional*, Ministry of Planning, Rio de Janeiro,
     March 1967 (mimeo). Some sums do not equal totals in the source.
    6–8: *Conjuntura Econômica*, indices Nos. 93, 70, and 69.
    9: Column 10 divided by column 8.
    10: E.P.E.A., op. cit.

businessmen have been very pessimistic about the chance of increasing exports, and rather uninterested in attempts to do so. 'The Brazilian market is big, demand for primary products doesn't grow, and other countries would never permit their imports of our manufactures to grow to a significant amount.' Such has been the attitude, and indeed there is much truth in it. From Table 5.6 we can imagine some of the reasons why the

TABLE 5.6
BREAKDOWN OF CHANGE IN CAPACITY TO IMPORT
(1946–8 to 1960–2)

Due to change in:	Actual	With maximum devaluation
Coffee quantum	2%	2%
Coffee price	21	21
Non-coffee quantum	−4	18
All other sources	−15	−15
TOTAL change in capacity to import	4%	26%

Notes: Each of the first three sources of change is defined as the percentage increase in the respective variable, times the share of either coffee or non-coffee exports in the total value of exports in the base period.

The 'all other sources' is defined as the difference between the total change and the other three sources. It includes the effects of the world price of non-coffee exports, the price of imports, second-order effects due to treating finite changes, and a statistical discrepancy because of inconsistency among data sources. In fact it appears to reflect mainly changes in import prices.
Source: Table 5.5.

Brazilian Government did not try to increase non-coffee exports. The influence of coffee prices, and of factors outside the control of Brazil (such as import prices), were the most striking elements in determining changes in the capacity to import. It must have been easy to worry about coffee, throw up one's hands about declining world prices of other exports and rising prices of imports, and ignore the rest. But we also see that if non-coffee exports could have been increased, it would have made a great difference. Disinterest in these may have been understandable, but was also costly.[1]

[1] This is *not* to say that the cruzeiro should have been devalued all the way to free trade equilibrium. This is only an estimate of the cost, in terms of export revenue, of not doing so. Alternative policies are evaluated in Chapter 8.

Inter-industrial biases

We saw above that import substitution has been at the heart of Brazil's industrialization, and that protection and subsidies were key instruments used to promote this process. In this section the relation between the structure of protection and subsidies and the structure of import substitution in the post-war period will be analysed.

There is no general, simple relation between protection and import substitution. The reasons for this are as follows:

1. Import substitution was already virtually complete in many sectors at the start of the period. Moreover, many of these sectors received very high protection.

2. The classification which had to be used often lumps together products and processes which are very different, and which received very different levels of protection. This is especially true of the electrical and transport equipment sectors, which include both capital and consumer durable goods, and of the rubber, leather, and chemicals sectors, which include both intermediate producer goods and finished consumer goods.

3. The measures of the structure of protection are for 1966 and 1967 only. The structure in 1966 was typical of the 1957–66 period, and in a rough way of the 1947–57 period as well. But from 1947 to 1953 imports were controlled by quantitative restrictions, and from 1953 to 1957 by multiple rates (of which there were essentially only six). So the estimates for 1966 are far from perfectly representative of the entire period.

4. The measures of the structure of protection do not take into account the differences in costs of capital equipment, and other subsidies and special treatment (discussed in Chapter 4), as among using sectors. I believe these to have been important influences on structural changes within manufacturing, but they are of course not included in the estimates of protection.

5. The estimates of effective protection are relative to gross value added. A better measure for estimating effects on resource allocation would have been relative to either net return to capital, or net value added. Data to estimate these last measures were not available.

In spite of all these qualifications, it turns out that there is a relationship between the structure of protection and the structure of import substitution. Let us first review the basic data. As a measure of import substitution the ratio of imports to domestic production for 1949, divided by that ratio for 1962, will be used.[1] These ratios will be called the 'import ratios'. A high import ratio indicates much import substitution; a lower import ratio indicates less. Of the two kinds of data on which to base these ratios, the set of estimates which has imports broken down into value added will be used.[2] Domestic value added and effective protection for 1966 will be used with these estimates of the value added content of imports.

It is next necessary to look at exports. Of the five sectors which export more than a negligible part of their production, only wood products and food products can really be considered to be 'export sectors'. Exports of the other three sectors have fallen in absolute value, as well as in percentage of output. The leather products and textiles sectors probably could be export sectors—some of their firms are export firms—but it is more accurate not to consider them so. Wood products and food products, then, will be classified as 'export' or 'high comparative advantage' sectors. They each showed a low share of imports in total supply at the start of the post-war period, and enjoyed relatively low protection.

In analysing import substitution in the remaining sectors, it is necessary to distinguish those sectors where any measure of import substitution is meaningless because the initial share of imports in total supply is so low. Small changes in this share are noise rather than information. These sectors will be called the 'daddy' sectors—they were already well-established at the start of the post-war period. Even though this distinction makes perfect sense, there is no objective, *a priori* way to fix the dividing line. I have therefore done it on the basis which best reveals a relationship between protection and import substitution for the remaining sectors. Therefore statistical results for this analysis are not presented; I merely divide the non-export sectors into three groups, as follows:

---

[1] 1949 is the first post-war year for which data on the structure of domestic production are available. 1962 is the last year of the post-war industrial growth, and also has better information than any year from 1959 to the present.

[2] Analysis with the other set gives very similar results.

1. 'Daddies': all sectors with imports less than 13 per cent of domestic production in 1949.

2. Highly protected infants: protection above a certain level (98 per cent), and import substitution above a certain level. (Import ratio, 1949 relative to 1962, greater than 11.)

3. Less-protected infants: protection below 98 per cent and import ratio less than 11.

There are no sectors among the infants with high protection and low import substitution, or vice versa. This means that if sectors with very little scope for import substitution in 1949 are excluded, a relationship does exist among those sectors remaining: high protection is associated with high import substitution, and vice versa. The results are shown in Table 5.7.

We can see that the classification in Table 5.7 makes sense by comparing the average parameters for each of the four groups of sectors. The results, in Table 5.8, clearly show the distinctions among the groups: the low export ratio for all but the export sectors, the low initial import ratio and very high protection for the 'daddies', and the greater reduction of the import ratio for the highly protected infants than for the less-protected infants. The import ratio for the highly protected infants in 1949 was higher than for the less-protected, and by 1962 had become lower than for the less-protected.

Let us look more closely, first at the 'daddies'. These sectors, already well established at the end of the second world war, generally received higher protection than the infants![1]

The 'daddy' industries not only received the highest protection, they also failed to export. In some cases these industries had no inherent disadvantages—there are firms in leather products, textiles, and tobacco which export regularly. So not only the justification but also the need for high protection for these sectors is doubtful. The high costs observed in most firms of many of these sectors are probably *results* of high protection. This question will be dealt with in more detail in Chapter 6.

---

[1] Some qualifications should be noted: the consumer durables parts of electrical and transport equipment were infants, and received very high protection. Rubber products, on the other hand, includes automotive tyres and tubes, a real infant; imports were low in 1949 because the Brazilian motor vehicles industry had not yet been started, but imports of cars were extremely expensive and therefore limited.

TABLE 5.7
RELATION BETWEEN PROTECTION AND IMPORT SUBSTITUTION IN
BRAZILIAN MANUFACTURING

Sector	Ratio of exports to domestic production, 1962	Ratio of imports to domestic production, 1949	'Import ratio', 1949 relative to 1962	Effective protection 1966
Export Sectors: low initial import ratio and low protection:				
Wood products	0·193	0·122		15%
Food products	0·185	0·060		48
Daddies: low initial import ratio and high protection:				
Furniture	0·000	0·025		168
Rubber products	0·002	0·127		87
Leather products	0·069	0·104		72
Perfumes, soaps, etc.	0·000	0·007		6,710
Textiles	0·097	0·084		279
Clothing	0·001	0·002		246
Beverages	0·000	0·118		333
Tobacco	0·001	0·000		227
Highly Protected Infants: high protection and much import substitution:				
Electrical equipment	0·001	5·400	21·7	149
Transport equipment	0·008	4·470	37·0	99
Plastics	0·000	0·965	41·7	124
Less-protected Infants: lower protection and less import substitution:				
Non-metallic mineral products	0·002	0·270	3·52	47
Metallurgy	0·001	1·160	2·31	25
Machinery	0·009	1·860	2·95	12
Paper and products	0·004	0·471	1·90	73
Chemicals	0·076	8·730	10·31	26
Pharmaceuticals	0·004	0·277	2·73	10
Miscellaneous	0·003	0·399	2·33	81

Turning to the infants, we see that they include all of the sectors which received investment subsidies in the form of low interest loans, special treatment of imported capital equipment, etc. They are mostly producer goods sectors. They also tend to be the sectors where foreign private investment is most important.[1] Note that even the less-protected infants, which received quite low average protection, have had a great deal of import substitution. Imports were reduced from one and one-half times domestic production, to only one-third of domestic production, even though protection (as measured in 1966) averaged only 30 per cent. This shows the importance of the investment subsidies and other special treatment discussed in Chapter 4. All of these instruments were applied almost exclusively to the infant sectors.[2]

TABLE 5.8
PROTECTION AND IMPORT SUBSTITUTION: FOUR GROUPS OF SECTORS

Group	Ratio of exports to domestic production, 1962	Ratio of imports to domestic production 1949	1962	Import ratio 1949/62	Effective protection 1966
Export sectors	0·186	0·070	0·036		44%
Daddies	0·055	0·074	0·017		(244)
Highly protected infants	0·005	4·536	0·145	31·3	120
Less-protected infants	0·024	1·504	0·346	4·4	30

Note: Average protection for daddies excludes perfumes.

Much of the post-war import substitution thus took place in sectors enjoying moderate to low protection. Import substitutes among consumer durables did enjoy high protection, but in intermediate goods (most of the 'less-protected infants') and capital goods (machinery, plus parts of electrical and transport equipment) protection was relatively low. Of those processes which were highly protected, most were already supplying virtually all of Brazil's needs at the start of the post-war period.

We are now able to understand how protection, subsidies, and similar aspects of the environment influenced the structure of post-war industrialization in Brazil. Brazil was already virtually self-sufficient in non-durable consumer goods at the start of the post-war period. These sectors received high protection, but no subsidies. Durable consumer goods had been mostly imported before the second world war. They were, of course, largely

[1] Rubber products is also among these sectors; as explained above, it should perhaps be considered an infant; the import ratios put it near the borderline.
[2] The only exception is that some foreign private investment into some of the daddy sectors did take advantage of S.U.M.O.C. 113 to import equipment.

unavailable throughout the war, and imports were severely limited by the quantitative restrictions of 1947–53, as well as by the multiple rates and tariffs which followed. These sectors, such as the automotive industry, received significant subsidies and special treatment as well as high protection during the period. The result was that by 1949 imports of durable consumer goods were already down to about 60 per cent of total supply, and were further drastically reduced to only 6 per cent by 1959 and 2 per cent by 1964.

So far the policies and their results are not very different from those of a number of other L.D.C.s. But the Brazilian experience is quite unusual in its success in continuing import substitution 'backward' through intermediate goods and capital goods. How did this happen, and was it a good thing?

First, note that import substitution of producer goods has been incomplete. Significant percentages of capital goods, chemicals, intermediate metal products, and other producer goods are still imported. Moreover, the limits of the import substitution seem to make some sense. Among capital goods, imports are technologically more advanced than domestic production; the imports have a much higher content of engineering design in their cost.[1] Capital goods as a whole have received little protection or direct subsidies, and the growth of domestic production has been pretty much limited to internationally competitive products. Of course, the enormous growth in demand for capital goods (see Table 5.2) caused by the industrialization was a crucial factor. Among intermediate goods, the bulk of imports are products of process industries where economies of scale are significant up to levels far above the levels of Brazilian demand. This is not to say that there are no producer goods industries in Brazil which are not internationally competitive. But those which have *not* been established have tended to be those which are the *most* non-competitive. This is probably related to the prevalence of private capital, and to the absence of over-all planning, especially of the material balance variety.

Now let us look more closely at intermediate goods. The

---

[1] See I.P.E.A., *Plano Decenal*, Tomo V, Vol. 2, *Industria Mecânica e Elétrica*, Ministry of Planning, Rio de Janeiro, 1967, especially p. 27. As a quantitative index of technological sophistication, imports of machine tools have an average price of over $3,000/ton, while domestic production averages $1,500/ton.

tremendous growth of intermediate goods production which took place was the deliberate result of a number of actions taken with that specific purpose, in addition to the rapid growth and high level of demand for these products. Value added in manufacturing in Brazil had reached over $5 billion by 1959, which is roughly as much as is produced by any manufacturing sector in the under-developed world. Because economies of scale are so important for many intermediate goods, import substitution probably could not have proceeded so far if the market had been smaller, at least without much higher protection.

What were the actions taken specifically to induce growth in intermediate goods sectors? Intermediate goods on the average were subject to product protection which varied between 35 and 50 per cent during the 1953–67 period. Effective protection was somewhat higher, averaging roughly 50 per cent. These estimates are for all intermediate goods taken together; those produced domestically typically received more protection, including in many cases import restrictions under the Law of Similars or the proportional controls mentioned in Chapter 3. Table 3.10, and the more detailed Table A.25 in Appendix 3, show that inter-mediate goods which were actually imported were not taxed very much at any time during the post-war period.

All industries receiving special treatment such as direct public investment, B.N.D.E. loans, special treatment of imported equipment under S.U.M.O.C. 113, and the other benefits dis-cussed in Chapter 4 were under pressure to expand domestic procurement of inputs as rapidly as possible. These firms, many of them with foreign connections, often were forced to assist their Brazilian suppliers with credit and technical assistance. They were able to get special treatment for imports of inputs not domestically available by following the agreements they had made for purchasing the inputs which were and would come to be produced in Brazil.

The Government took further specific steps to establish many intermediate goods industries through Executive Groups and similar arrangements. These were in the chemicals, rubber, pulp and paper, non-ferrous metals, and cement sectors. In steel, alcalis, petroleum products, rubber, and aluminium, direct public investment was an important instrument. The importance of direct and indirect government investment in these industries can be seen in Tables 4.5, 4.6, and 4.7; most of the B.N.D.E. investment, and much of the foreign private investment during the 1950s and early 1960s went into intermediate goods industries.[1]

Capital goods did not benefit from most of these promotional devices, but evidently the high level of demand plus a natural advantage was sufficient to support rapid growth and import substitution in those sectors.

To sum up: as a result of both the large scale of demand and the specific promotional policies adopted, imports of producer goods were far below levels which would be expected in a country as underdeveloped, and as rapidly developing, as Brazil was from 1945 to 1962. Domestic production of producer goods rose very rapidly, and imports rose far less rapidly than total consumption, as shown in Table 5.2. Brazil's success in carrying import substitution back through producer goods was due to a combination of rapid growth and high level of demand, natural advantages in many sectors, and strong government promotion in many sectors.

The over-all picture of the policies used to promote import substitution in the post-war period can be summarized as follows:

Sectors	Protection	Subsidies and other promotion	Import substitution
Daddies:			
consumer non-durables	Very high	Little or none	Had already happened
Infants:			
consumer durables	Very high	Strong	Virtually complete
intermediate goods	Low to moderate	Strong	Great
capital goods	Low	Little	Great

Carrying the import substitution back into producer goods was not accomplished without some loss of efficiency; especially among intermediate goods many of the new products could have been imported for less. The outstanding horror stories of high cost—alcalis, synthetic rubber, one or two non-ferrous metals—are the results of direct government action in those sectors.[2] But the

[1] This is also shown in Morley and Smith, 'Import Substitution as an Industrialization Strategy in Brazil', 1969 (mimeo).

[2] Most of these instances of extreme inefficiency are the results of social and political pressures to provide or maintain employment in certain areas; they are *not* the result of a blind impulse to import substitution. Examples

rest of these sectors—the great majority of firms making producer goods—operate with prices within 20 or 30 per cent of the cost of imports at the free trade exchange rate (in 1966).

In the following chapter, the development of some of these industries will be dealt with in more detail.

---

are as follows. High-cost coal for steel making: to keep coal mines open in Santa Catarina. High cost of soda ash and caustic soda: to support inefficient salt production and transport in the north-east. High-cost synthetic rubber: to provide a market for sugar-cane in the north-east (the rubber is made from alcohol, which in turn is produced from the sugar). All these are cases of an inefficient supplying industry which employs a significant amount of labour in a particular region.

6

Results in Particular Industries

In this chapter I want to look at a few industries in more detail. To evaluate Brazil's industrialization and trade policies, we need not only the over-all results described in Chapter 5, but also more specific information. To what extent did the establishment of an industry depend on government support, or to what extent was it a 'natural' result of the Brazilian environment? What are costs of production in Brazil and how do costs and prices compare with those in other countries? Prices of most manufactured products are higher in Brazil than in most developed countries; to what extent is this due to high costs of production, or to high taxes, or to monopoly profits? To what extent could high costs of production be reduced by better organization of the industry or by better management of the firm?

These questions are not easy to answer, and fully satisfactory answers to most of them are still far away. But even the limited information available is useful for the more general purposes of this study.

I. THE STEEL INDUSTRY[1]

Development of the industry

Iron working activities in Brazil can be traced back to the middle of the sixteenth century. Forges operated at various times in the present state of São Paulo in the sixteenth and seventeenth centuries and in Minas Gerais at the time of the gold rush in the

---

[1] Most of this section is taken from Appendix 1, by Werner Baer. Indeed, parts of this section are taken verbatim from the Appendix. Baer thus deserves the credit for providing most of the information and analysis, but does not necessarily agree with conclusions expressed in this section. Baer's full study will be published by the Vanderbilt University Press as *The Development of the Brazilian Steel Industry*.

eighteenth century, producing utensils for the mines. In the early nineteenth century, with the ending of the formal colonial status of Brazil, government stimulus was given to establish iron smelting operations, as well as tool and machinery fabrication.

Scientific interest in iron ore and iron and steel production was maintained throughout the nineteenth century. The School of Mines at Ouro Prêto, the Escola Politécnica of São Paulo, and the army's Escola de Engenharia do Exército have produced some of Brazil's finest geologists and engineers. Thus, although the first substantial spurt of steel production in Brazil did not occur until the fourth decade of the twentieth century, a future destiny as a large steel producer had long been foreseen.

The growth of iron and steel production which took place in the first three decades of the twentieth century was mainly based on the initiative of private entrepreneurs. In 1921 the Belgian–Luxembourg A.R.B.E.D. group, at the invitation of the governor of Minas Gerais, founded the firm Companhia Siderúrgica Belgo-Mineira. In the 1920s other small firms were founded, especially in the São Paulo area. In the mid-1930s Belgo-Mineira built its mill at Monlevade, and by the end of that decade the steel industry had made substantial progress. Pig iron production reached 185,000 tons in 1940, and steel ingot production 141,200 tons. Brazil had stopped being an importer of pig iron and steel ingots. However, it still imported 70 per cent of the rolled products it consumed.

Throughout the 1930s there was a powerful movement within the Government to create a large-scale fully integrated steel mill based on coke. When the U.S. Steel Corporation decided not to build a plant, even though the report of its experts had made a favourable recommendation, the Government decided to build an integrated steel mill itself. After a period of negotiation in which the Brazilians used the interest of the Germans in building a plant in Brazil as an implied threat, the U.S. Export–Import Bank agreed to finance the building of the steel works at Volta Redonda. With the full functioning of Volta Redonda in 1948, Brazil became the first Latin American country to have a fully integrated coke-based steel mill.

During the fifties plans for the construction of two new large integrated mills were conceived. The basic ideas for the creation of these firms stemmed from private and state government interests. Usiminas was constructed by a Japanese steel consortium, which originally participated with a 40 per cent ownership. The Brazilian ownership was originally divided among the state of Minas Gerais, the B.N.D.E., some other state-owned companies, and a smaller group of private interests. As the project's costs increased during construction beyond what was originally planned, the B.N.D.E. had to increase its contribution and gradually became the majority owner, Japanese interest shrinking to about 20 per cent. The Cosipa company was originally created by private interests. However, by the late fifties the government of the state of São Paulo and the B.N.D.E. had to enter the picture to get the project under way. Again the B.N.D.E. was obliged to acquire controlling interest in the company. Both Usiminas and Cosipa are fully integrated coke-based plants, specializing in flat products. Usiminas began operations in October 1962; Cosipa, which began operation of its rolling mills in December 1963 (rolling ingots from Volta Redonda), started to function as a fully integrated mill in early 1966.

The growth of steel output is shown in Appendix 1, Table A.4. A summary is reproduced here in Table 6.1. Brazil is now virtually

TABLE 6.1
IMPORTS AND PRODUCTION OF IRON AND STEEL

	Pig iron		Steel ingot		Rolled steel products	
Year	Production (thousand tons)	Imports as per cent of supply	Production (thousand tons)	Imports as per cent of supply	Production (thousand tons)	Imports as per cent of supply
1925	30	28	8	47	0	100
1940	186	0	141	5	135	69
1960	1,750	0	1,850	0	1,712	20
1965	2,260	0	2,980	0	2,100	9

Source: Table A.4, Appendix 1.

self-sufficient in steel products, with a production in 1966 of 3·8 million ingot tons. In terms of value added, production of basic iron and steel accounted for just under 5 per cent of all manufacturing activity in 1959, or roughly U.S.$160 million. Value added in casting, forging, and rolling accounted for another 2·7 per cent, or U.S.$90 million.[1] Today the total value added is over U.S.$300 million.

[1] Industrial Census of 1960. Conversion to dollars at free trade rate of Cr$160/dollar.

Structure of the industry

Production capacity in 1965 was 5 million ingot tons. This was divided as shown in Table 6.2. Cosipa and Usiminas are the two newest mills, and will soon be expanded to 1 million tons and more. Volta Redonda will probably soon be expanded to 2·5 million tons. A few of the smaller mills will also be expanded, but most of the rest of additional capacity will come from further expansions of Usiminas and Cosipa, and from new mills.

TABLE 6.2
STEEL-MAKING CAPACITY IN INGOT TONS, 1965

Firm	Capacity (thousand ingot tons per year)
Volta Redonda (C.S.N.)	1,400
Cosipa	625
Usiminas	634
Belgo-Mineira	450
Mannesmann	328
Acesita	120
All other	1,521
TOTAL	5,078

Source: Table A.3, Appendix 1.

Economies of scale are quite important in each of the three major phases of steel-making (blast furnace, steel shop, and rolling mill). In the blast furnace and the steel shop, unit costs decline more or less continuously as the individual units get bigger. In the rolling mill strict indivisibilities are important; for example, the minimum capacity of a rolling mill which can roll plates over 2·5 metres wide is about 1 million tons. An additional source of economies of scale in each part of the mill is the existence of more than one, or many similar units, to enable the mill to continue operating during shut-downs for maintenance or repair of a particular unit.

Most of Brazil's steel firms are well below optimum scale. Only Volta Redonda can be said to be near a reasonable size for a modern mill. (Many of the smaller mills, using charcoal rather than coke, are less subject to economies of scale and were not so inefficient when they were built.)

Government policies

About two-thirds of Brazil's steel capacity is in government-controlled firms. The Government's percentage of total capital investment in the industry is between 50 and 60 per cent. Before any of these firms existed, Brazil already had 27 private firms producing iron and/or steel, with a production in 1945 of 260 thousand tons of pig iron and 206 thousand tons of steel ingot. The Government built Volta Redonda in the 1940s only after foreign private interests were approached and had refused to participate. In Cosipa and Usiminas, in the 1950s, the Government started as a minority participant and assumed a controlling interest only as the private participants became unwilling or unable to finance the full costs of the projects. Government will probably continue to be important in future expansions and new mills.

Official tariffs were not relevant to protection or pricing of steel in Brazil during most of the post-war period. Until 1961, C.S.N. and Acesita were the only entities allowed to import any basic steel products. These companies, controlled by the Government, set domestic prices independently of tariff considerations. C.S.N. was also the largest and strongest domestic producer, and was the price leader for most steel products. Since 1961, imports have been allowed only for products in short supply.

Until 1963, C.S.N. generally set prices high enough for it and most other companies to operate at a profit. Since 1963, the Government has kept a tight rein on steel price increases, keeping them generally behind the rate of inflation.

Government policies affect costs in the steel industry in four major areas: capital equipment, iron ore, coal, and infrastructure.

Most of the capital equipment which has been imported, from the construction of Volta Redonda in the 1940s to the present, has received special treatment. In the case of Volta Redonda, taxes on imports of capital goods were not significant. Most of the imported equipment for Usiminas and Cosipa took advantage of S.U.M.O.C. Instruction 113. (See Chapter 4. Banas estimates the total value of machinery imported under S.U.M.O.C. 113 by the steel industry as $11 million; this seems to be an underestimate.) It is doubtful that any duties were paid on imported equipment for steel mills, since such duties went into effect in 1957.

I

On the other hand, new steel firms (or existing firms which were expanding) were under considerable pressure to use domestic equipment to the extent it was available. Only since the mid-1950s has a significant amount of such equipment been available. However, a tour of the newest mill, Cosipa, reveals a large number of domestic travelling cranes, trucks and all sorts of material-handling equipment, foundry equipment, electrical equipment such as generators, motors, and transformers, and even some rolling mill parts and accessories.

Brazilian steel mills receive iron ore at the mill at a cost of about $3.00 per ton. The price of iron ore exported from Brazil, F.O.B., is about $8.50 per ton. It has not been possible to make a precise estimate of the social opportunity cost of the iron ore. Because of Brazil's enormous reserves, this cost is less than the export price (except in the very short run). On the other hand this cost may well be more than the price to Brazilian steel mills. In any case, the maximum estimate of the subsidy to the mills, implied by taking the export price as the opportunity cost of ore, would represent a reduction in the total cost of rolled steel products of about $5.00 per ton, which is only 3 per cent of the total cost.

A number of Brazilian mills were located far from existing towns and transport facilities. The steel firms themselves have directly borne the cost of constructing many of these facilities. Volta Redonda is the most striking example: Its location between Rio and São Paulo, in the state of Rio de Janeiro, was chosen as a political compromise. The company builds and maintains all workers' housing, health services, extensive recreation facilities, schools, training programmes, local roads, water supply, etc. While some of these costs are the result of political considerations, others are simply unavoidable costs of progress in a country where infrastructure of all kinds is deficient. Most of these costs did not have to be incurred in order to have a steel industry—the mills could have been located near existing large cities without significantly increasing transport costs. Therefore these costs do not reflect adversely on the economic rationality of establishing a steel industry in Brazil.

The transport system serving the steel industry is deficient in many ways. Most producers rely heavily on highway transport, which is probably more costly than efficient rail transport would be in many cases. Where railroads have been used, many steel firms have been obliged to purchase their own rolling stock. Use of domestic maritime transport is limited to bringing domestic coal from the mines in Santa Catarina. Its excessive costs and unreliable service make it undesirable.

To sum up, the Brazilian steel industry had its origins very early. In the post-war period, government policy has been one of strong promotion through direct investment, import monopoly, etc., but mixed with deficient infrastructure and other cost-increasing elements.

Production efficiency

The analysis of production costs in Appendix 1 can be summarized as follows.

Raw material cost: Brazil possesses most of the raw materials and other natural resources necessary for the manufacture of steel: iron ore, limestone, manganese, water, and a huge economic hydro-electric potential. The country has one of the world's largest iron ore reserves; known reserves in 1966 amounted to more than 27 billion tons. In quality these ores are among the best in the world.

Coal is the only important raw material whose availability is deficient. The only coal deposits in Brazil are of poor quality (due to high ash content) and cannot be exclusively relied on for producing coke. The domestic coal which can be used has to go through expensive washing operations. Technical studies have estimated that, given the techniques of production currently used in Brazil, Brazilian coke rates could be brought down to levels below those obtained in the United States and many European countries if imported coal were used exclusively.

Capital: this is the single most important input cost. Reliable data on capital costs are very difficult to obtain, especially in Brazil where inflation makes current values at different times non-comparable. Thus, while initial investment costs are sometimes available, the costs of expansions are not easily made comparable. However, some qualitative conclusions can be made from the information available.

Capital costs tend to be high in Brazil. For example, the capital-production ratio for Volta Redonda in 1963 implied by the E.C.L.A. study cited in Appendix 1 is over $500 per ton. The use of domestic coal contributes about $90 to this cost; removing this burden would reduce the capital–production ratio to about \$425 per ton. Direct estimates of capital costs for Cosipa and Usiminas, the two newest mills, are around \$400 per ton, at 1 million tons per year capacity.

In addition to expensive plant and equipment, many smaller inefficiencies and organizing deficiencies appear. These have the effect of reducing the output which a given mill actually produces and thus increasing the unit capital charge. In the early stages of the operation of Cosipa, for example, iron ore, which came by railroad, had to be transferred from standard-gauge cars to narrow-gauge cars to descend the steep hill next to the mill. In addition to increasing the cost of the ore, this caused the supply of iron ore to be an effective constraint on the capacity of the mill. Many such examples of minor problems which reduce the effective capacity of various mills at various times could be cited. Such situations are much less common in developed countries with longer histories of industrial operation, greater value placed on efficient organization and operations, and a larger supply of competent middle-level administrators, as well as better physical infrastructure. To develop these institutions, attitudes, skills, and facilities in a country such as Brazil requires time and experience.

Administration and sales: these costs tend to be abnormally high in Brazil. The small scale of firms and minimal pressure to lower costs or to raise profits are probably among the chief causes of this.

Indirect taxes: as for all manufacturing in Brazil, these have been extremely high since the mid-1950s.

In the final section of Appendix 1 there is a social profitability analysis of the operation of Volta Redonda for the single year 1963. The results of that analysis can be presented in two different ways. The gross rate of return, using the free trade exchange rate estimated in Chapter 3, is about 15 per cent. Alternatively, the mill can be viewed as an import-substituting activity which was saving foreign exchange at a cost of 670 cruzeiros per dollar. This can be compared with the average import rate including tariffs of 1,670, the estimated free trade rate of 830, and the average export rate (excluding coffee) of 553. This indicates that the operation of Volta Redonda was efficient in a comparative cost sense.

This conclusion should be qualified in many ways. On the

positive side, we should remember that Volta Redonda was the first large integrated coke-based steel mill built in Brazil. By 1963 it was already 17 years old, and its technology was already partly obsolete (especially in the steel shop). Some inefficiency might be justifiable on grounds of its age and pioneering position. It is striking that this is not necessary.

On the other hand, various negative factors were not included in the analysis. Operation in early years may have been considerably less efficient than in 1963. No charges were made for special infrastructure costs such as workers' housing, local roads, etc., as described above. Both Baer and I believe such costs should be charged to a 'general costs of development' account rather than to the steel industry; others may disagree.

It appears that the two newest mills, Cosipa and Usiminas, will be more efficient than Volta Redonda when they reach 1 million tons per year capacity. (This is planned to happen by 1975 or earlier.) Their actual capital costs were each about \$325 million for about 650,000 tons of ingot capacity (and 1·5 million tons in the rolling mills) and plans for expansion to one million tons call for additional investments of less than \$70 million each. Thus their capital charges should be about 20 per cent lower than the E.C.L.A. estimates for Volta Redonda.

Conclusion

Brazil has most of the natural resources needed for producing steel, including very high-grade iron ore. At least since the 1950s, the level of demand for steel has been enough to support two mills of reasonable size. These factors lead one to expect that Brazil might have a comparative advantage in steel. On the other hand, Brazil is an underdeveloped country, with poor infrastructure and perhaps a short supply of good engineers, managers, etc. Since capital costs are so important in steel-making, the ability to increase output from a given plant is crucial to over-all unit costs. The net result, based on the evidence summarized above, is that at least some of the major firms of Brazil's steel industry are competitive in a comparative cost sense, without any recourse to external benefits or infant industry arguments.

II. THE AUTOMOTIVE INDUSTRY

Today's less developed countries all seem to want to establish two 'prestige' industries: steel and automobiles. The complex and difficult technology, the importance of economies of scale up to very large levels of output, and the heavy capital investments required all raise questions as to the economic wisdom of establishing these industries. In the previous section we saw that Brazil's steel industry, or at least the most modern part of it, appears to be more or less competitive on an international basis. The automotive industry will be analysed in this section.

The automotive industry in general includes the assembly of cars, trucks, buses, etc., and the production of components (carburettors, electrical equipment, tyres, engines, transmissions, chassis, body parts, etc.).[1] A car contains thousands of parts; the engine alone several hundred. Production of these many parts and components is typically decentralized; an assembly plant in a developed country will buy parts from several hundred regular supplying firms.

Automotive industries in L.D.C.s typically start with an 'assembly only' operation; virtually all parts and components are imported. As industrialization proceeds, more and more parts are manufactured domestically. Of twenty-six L.D.C.s producing automobiles in 1965, nine had only assembly plants, and only six produced more than half of the car (by weight) domestically.[2]

Small scale, restrictions on imports, and unreliability of domestic supply make the automotive industries in many L.D.C.s horrible examples of inefficiency.[3] Considering scale alone—which is probably not the chief source of high costs—only four L.D.C.s produced 100,000 units or more in 1965. Significant economies of scale go beyond 100,000 units per year *for one assembly plant*. In the remaining twenty-two countries there were 145 firms which together produced a total of about 276,000 units! Even in the four

[1] Tractors are not considered.
[2] Jack Baranson, *Automotive Industries in Developing Countries*, Report EC-162, International Bank for Reconstruction and Development, Washington, D.C., 31 May 1968, p. 79. See also Baranson's 'Integrated Automobiles in Latin America?,' *Finance and Development*, 1968. In addition to the works cited, I am much indebted to Mr. Baranson for comments on an earlier draft.
[3] See, for example, Leland J. Johnson, 'Problems of Import Substitution: The Chilean Automobile Industry', *Economic Development and Cultural Change*, January 1967.

countries where more than 100,000 units were produced, the total production of 718,000 was divided among fifty-six firms.[1]

Most firms in L.D.C.s are subsidiaries of firms in developed countries, or have arrangements for technical assistance on design, engineering, etc. This applies to virtually all firms which produce the finished automobile, truck, or bus, and also to many parts producers.

Development of the Brazilian industry

Today Brazil produces roughly 125,000 passenger cars, over 60,000 station wagons, pick-up trucks, jeeps, etc., and over 30,000 trucks and buses per year. Over 95 per cent of these vehicles, by weight, is produced domestically. Brazil ranks around tenth among *all* countries in total units produced. Among L.D.C.s, she shares first place with Spain and Argentina, both of which produce about 200,000 units annually, with a 'nationalization index' (per cent of weight produced domestically) of over 90 per cent.[2] Eleven years ago—in 1957—Brazil produced no passenger cars, and only 30,000 other vehicles which contained over 50 per cent imported parts. Roughly 90 per cent of today's industry did not exist in 1957.[3] In terms of value added, the industry in 1959 accounted for about 6 per cent of all manufacturing, or about $200 million. About 75 per cent of this was in firms assembling cars, trucks, and buses, and about 25 per cent in firms primarily producing parts and accessories.[4] If these figures are projected to 1966 in the same proportion as the change in total units produced, value added in 1966 would be over $450 million for the industry as a whole.

The industry existing in 1957 was a small part of that existing today, but it was none the less a significant base on which to build. In the mid-1950s, Brazil had a fleet of trucks and buses numbering roughly 300,000, and of automobiles and light pick-up trucks of over 400,000. In addition to the assembly and manufac-

[1] Baranson, op. cit., p. 79.
[2] Ibid., pp. 78, 79. Data in this source are for 1965, when the Brazilian economy was abnormally depressed.
[3] These data, and other data in this section for which the source is not cited, are from unpublished studies of the Grupo Executivo da Indústria Auto-mobilística (G.E.I.A.), the Associação Nacional dos Fabricantes de Veículos Automotores (A.N.F.A.V.E.A.), I.P.E.A., and various newspaper articles.
[4] Industrial Census of 1960. Conversion to dollars at the free trade rate of Cr$160/dollar.

ture of 30–50 per cent by weight of 30,000 trucks and buses per year, there was a large spare-parts industry. This industry had grown in response to the difficulty of obtaining spare parts during the second world war, and had been protected and encouraged by restrictions on imports, especially under the Law of Similars, in the post-war period. There were about 700 plants regularly making spare automotive parts.[1] Most of these were strictly Brazilian in ownership and management, and many made other metal products as well.

The assembly plants existing in 1957 were the Fábrica Nacional de Motores (F.N.M.), Ford, General Motors, and Mercedes Benz (all making principally medium and heavy trucks) and Willys (making jeeps). Ford, General Motors, and Mercedes were of course subsidiaries of foreign companies, and Willys was an offspring of Kaiser. The F.N.M. was a publicly-owned Brazilian enterprise, with design and other technical assistance from Alfa Romeo.

Willys started producing passenger cars in 1959 (the Dauphine, under licence from the French company) and in 1960 started production of the Aero Willys, taken from the American Kaiser. The F.N.M. started producing a very small number of luxury cars (Alfa Romeo) in 1960. Ford started passenger car production in 1967, and General Motors evidently intends to start producing the Opel within a year or two. Simca (a French company recently merged with Chrysler) started producing passenger cars in 1959, and Vemag (largely Brazilian-owned but with minority participation and technical assistance from the West German firm Auto Union G.M.B.H.) in 1958. Volkswagen, which today produces over half the passenger cars and about 40 per cent of all vehicles combined (over 100,000 units per year), started producing their passenger sedan in 1959. Production of the 'Kombi' had started in late 1957.

Most of the large manufacturers of parts and components, which are also linked to foreign companies in one way or another, also were founded in the late 1950s. Purely local parts suppliers also grew rapidly, and this branch of the industry now numbers over 1,500 firms.

The industry developed extremely rapidly, both in number of

---

[1] E.C.L.A., 'Fifteen Years of Economic Policy in Brazil', *Economic Bulletin for Latin America*, December 1964, p. 169.

units produced and in the nationalization index, which was greater than 90 per cent by 1962. Total production in 1962 was greater than in any succeeding year until 1966; we can get a good idea of the structure of the industry at the end of its initial 'working-in' period by looking at 1962. The structure of production for that year is shown in Table 6.3.

The creation of new assembly plants was regulated to some extent by the Government, through the inter-ministerial Grupo Executivo da Indústria Automobilística (G.E.I.A.), which was created in June 1956. The regulation was exercised through G.E.I.A.'s discretion in granting subsidies; these were so great that it is hard to imagine any new assembly operations being started without them. Nevertheless, it appears that G.E.I.A. did not turn down any interested firm, and we see from Table 6.3 that the industry was excessively fragmented from the point of view of production efficiency.

Eight different passenger cars were produced. (The recent entry of Ford makes nine.) Starting from the least expensive, there was the Volkswagen sedan, the Dauphine, D.K.W., Simca, Aero Willys, and the F.N.M. 2000. There were also two expensive sports models, the Karmann Ghia and the Interlagos. (The latter is a small sports car with the Renault engine and a hand-made fibreglass body.) The number of different trucks also appears to be unnecessarily large, although economies of scale are not so important with truck assembly.

While the number of firms was certainly too great to take maximum advantage of scale economies, the Brazilian industry was not so excessively fragmented as that in some other countries. For example, in 1965 in Argentina there were thirteen firms, the largest of which produced 57,000 units;[1] in 1964 in the free port of Arica in Chile there were twenty firms producing 25 models, the largest of which produced 1,500 units![2]

In recent years the structure of the industry in Brazil has been consolidating. Vemag merged with Volkswagen, and production of the Vemag models was discontinued in 1967. Shortly after Ford started producing a luxury passenger car in 1967, it merged with Willys. This may result in the future discontinuation of the Aero Willys. Sales of the Gordini and the Simca have fallen off

[1] A.D.E.F.A., cited in Baranson, *Automotive Industries* . . ., op. cit., p. 83.
[2] American Embassy, Santiago; cited in Johnson, op. cit., p. 205.

TABLE 6.3
AUTOMOTIVE PRODUCTION IN 1962

Type	Firm	Model	Units
Passenger cars	F.N.M.	2000 ('J.K.')	378
	Simca	Chambord (and variants)	6,689
	Vemag	D.K.W.	7,123
	Volkswagen	sedan	38,430
		Karmann-Ghia	759
	Willys	Dauphine-Gordini	11,782
		Aero Willys	9,508
		Interlagos	218
	TOTAL		74,887
Station wagons	General Motors	Chevrolet 9-passenger	968
	Simca	station wagon	215
	Vemag	station wagon	7,806
	Volkswagen	Kombi	14,563
	Willys	Rural (2 models)	11,903
	TOTAL		35,455
Jeeps, etc.	Toyota		627
	Vemag	2 models	615
	Willys	4 models	21,005
	TOTAL		22,247
Pick-ups	Ford		6,506
	General Motors	5 models	5,508
	Willys	2 models	6,921
	TOTAL		18,935
Trucks, medium	Ford	5 models	15,207
	General Motors	2 models	12,353
	International	2 models	711
	Mercedes Benz	2 models	7,836
Trucks, heavy	F.N.M.	3 models	892
	International		561
	Mercedes Benz	2 models	461
	Scania Vabis	2 models	722
	TOTAL		38,743
Buses, chassis	Five firms		297
Buses, complete	Mercedes Benz		630
	TOTAL		927
TOTAL vehicles			191,194

Source: Associação Nacional dos Fabricantes de Veículos Automotores
(A.N.F.A.V.E.A.), *Indústria Automobilística Brasileira*, 1966.

greatly in the last few years, and their continuation is doubtful. The Government has been considering selling the F.N.M. for some years, as its sales also (mainly heavy trucks) have fallen badly. The likely evolution of the passenger car and station wagon industry is shown in Table 6.4.

TABLE 6.4
EVOLUTION OF PASSENGER CARS AND STATION WAGONS

	1962	1967	Guess at 1970
Passenger cars, regular	V.W. sedan	V.W. sedan	V.W. sedan
	D.K.W.	—	—
	Dauphine-Gordini	Gordini	—
	Simca	Simca	Simca or replacement
	Aero Willys	Aero Willys	?
	F.N.M. 2000	F.N.M. 2000	—
		Ford Galaxy	Ford Galaxy
			Ford, smaller model
			G.M. Opel
Passenger cars, sports	Karmann Ghia	Karmann Ghia	Karmann Ghia
	Interlagos	Interlagos	Interlagos
Station wagons, etc.	Chevrolet (9-passenger)	Chevrolet	Chevrolet
	Simca	Simca	?
	Vemag	—	—
	V.W. Kombi	V.W. Kombi	V.W. Kombi
	Willys Rural	Willys Rural	Willys Rural
			some small U.S.-type station wagon

Imported technology has been crucial in the development of the Brazilian automotive industry. Every assembly operation, and most of the large-scale parts manufacturing, have been based on foreign designs. Foreign participation in the ownership of many firms—even assemblers—is small, but foreign 'know-how' has been uniformly important.

Government policy

Governmental stimuli to the Brazilian automotive industry started under the second Vargas administration: in 1952 imports of parts for which domestic similars existed was prohibited. A few other steps were taken under Vargas, but only with the inauguration of President Juscelino Kubitschek in 1956 was any significant progress made. Kubitschek had advocated the establishment of the industry during his campaign, and on 16 June 1956 he created G.E.I.A. to plan and implement the programme.

GEIA was formed by representatives of the Banco do Brasil's foreign exchange and foreign trade departments, of CPA, of BNDE, of SUMOC and of the principal ministries concerned. Under the plans drawn up for the motor-vehicle industry, enterprises which fulfilled certain requisites (the attainment of given proportions of domestic content, in terms of the weight of the vehicle, by specified dates) enjoyed a variety of concessions: reservation of foreign exchange, at a stable and subsidized rate, for imports of spare parts; a preferential exchange rate for repayment of external credits and loans; duty-free importation of capital goods and spare parts; provisional exemption from excise taxes on motor vehicles (other than private cars); official financing by the Banco do Brasil, for periods of one to three years, of exchange surcharges deriving from imports of spare parts; and, on occasion, long-term financing accorded by BNDE for investment purposes. After studying and approving the different projects submitted by manufacturers of vehicles and spare parts, GEIA authorized the extension of the above-mentioned benefits. Similarly, the Group saw that the directives issued were implemented, proposing the measures it deemed necessary. In view of the nature of the Executive Groups, their proposals were hardly likely to be passed over, since in them the various official bodies were represented in conjunction. Thus, besides serving the sectors concerned as centers for the coordination of incentives, they were the means of removing bureaucratic stumbling-blocks to the attainment of the sectoral objectives pursued.[1]

G.E.I.A. worked with interested investors to plan the development of the industry. The government actions necessary to implement these plans were then taken speedily and as planned, because the government agencies involved had helped formulate and already agreed to the plans.

The B.N.D.E. channelled Cr$866 million (1953 prices), or roughly U.S.$20 million into the automobile industry, mostly during 1956–9.[2] According to the Banas survey quoted in Chapter 4, over $200 million worth of equipment was imported duty-free under S.U.M.O.C. Instruction 113. The industry received more equipment under S.U.M.O.C. 113 and more total foreign financing than any other Brazilian industry. The B.N.D.E. also contributed more capital to the automotive industry than to any except

---

[1] E.C.L.A., 'Fifteen Years . . .', op. cit., pp. 193–4.
[2] Calculated from B.N.D.E. annual reports. Data cover 1952–64.

steel and chemicals. President Kubitschek's two biggest projects were Brasilia and the automotive industry, and Kubitschek was not a man for half-way measures.

The double action of protection is seen clearly in the automotive industry. Foreign companies which exported automobiles to Brazil faced a clear choice of either co-operating in the establishment of the Brazilian industry or losing that market. Protection was very high; during the mid-1950s and early 1960s product protection was at least 200 per cent and effective protection was even higher. Once the industry was established, imports were cut to a few hundred units per year. With a subsidiary in Brazil the manufacturer enjoyed virtually complete protection; otherwise he was excluded.

From the beginning G.E.I.A. forced the pace of domestic procurement of inputs. The general plans for progressive 'nationalization', adopted during 1956 and early 1957, were as shown in Table 6.5. By the end of 1961 all vehicles were to attain at least 98

TABLE 6.5
TARGETS FOR DOMESTIC PROCUREMENT

	Per cent of weight to be produced domestically (*July 1*)			
	1957	*1958*	*1959*	*1960*
Passenger cars	50	65	85	95
Station wagons, pick-ups, etc.	50	65	75	90
Jeeps	60	75	85	95
Trucks	40	65	75	90

Source: Decrees 39,568, 39,569, 39,675, and 41,018.

per cent domestic procurement. These plans were slightly modified in some cases, but were generally followed and met. By the early 1960s all vehicles claimed over 95 per cent domestic content, and even allowing for some devious accounting it is fair to say that the targets have essentially been fulfilled.

This caused a tremendous boom in auto parts manufacturing, as well as in capital goods, steel, and other indirect supplying sectors. G.E.I.A. did not regulate the parts suppliers, but did see to it that they got the same privileges as the assemblers. The number of supplier firms doubled (from about 700 in 1956 to over 1,500 in the early 1960s), some of the most important new firms being subsidiaries of foreign firms.

Costs and prices[1]

Passenger cars receive very high protection in Brazil, and sell for very high prices. The average retail price of a standard Volkswagen sedan during 1966–7 was roughly $2,500–$2,800 (conversion at the free trade exchange rates). Bigger cars were proportionately more expensive; the Ford Galaxy has cost over $7,000 since its introduction in 1967. Retail prices of cars in Brazil generally average roughly twice retail prices in developed countries.

A good deal of this difference seems to be in wholesale and retail margins, probably largely due to the high cost of working capital for these sectors. For one large Brazilian manufacturer, ex-factory prices have been roughly 25 per cent higher than C.I.F. prices, which is equivalent to slightly under 50 per cent higher than ex-factory prices in the home country.[2]

A large part of the differential in ex-factory prices can be attributed to the high indirect taxes in Brazil. A major source of state revenues in Brazil is a sales tax, which until 1966 was levied on manufactured products at every sale. The cost of a finished automobile thus might include taxes on steel, for example, once as steel, once again as components, and yet again as an automobile. Popular mythology among Brazilian economists has it that over 40 per cent of the *retail* cost of an automobile is taxes. Data for one large Brazilian firm show that indirect taxes paid directly by the firm averaged 19 per cent of sales.[3] If this same percentage is applied to the firm's purchases of materials, parts, and components, the estimated share of all indirect taxes in the ex-factory price rises to 27 per cent. This last figure is equivalent to between 30 and 40 per cent of the C.I.F. value of sales, or about 45 per cent of the ex-factory price in the home country. I do not have an estimate of the share of indirect taxes in the ex-factory price in the home country, but it is probably not more than 10 per cent. Thus, perhaps 35 of the 50 per cent difference in ex-factory prices is due to higher indirect taxes in Brazil.

[1] This section is largely based on data collected and analysed by Carlos Sánchez-Marco of the O.E.C.D. Development Centre. I am much obliged to Mr. Sánchez-Marco for making his preliminary results available, as well as for comments on a preliminary draft.

[2] Average for 1963–6; conversion at free trade exchange rates.

[3] Average for 1963–6.

For other, smaller Brazilian firms, diseconomies of small scale are probably responsible for a large part of the excessive costs of production. This is true not only of assembly operations but also of the manufacture of some specialized parts and the stamping of sheet metal for bodies. (The relative unimportance of stamped body parts in the production of trucks is the main reason why economies of scale are so much less significant for trucks than for passenger cars.) The requirements for almost complete domestic procurement raise production costs significantly. This goes hand in hand with scale: The smaller the scale of the assembly operation, the greater the cost of increased domestic procurement. Data for India show that the increase in total cost caused by increasing the domestic content from 60 to 90 per cent is about 37 per cent at 3,000 units per year, but only about 17 per cent at 12,000 units per year.[1] Data from an American firm with subsidiaries in Argentina, Brazil, and Mexico show that specialized parts and sheet metal stamping cost roughly twice as much in Brazil as in the U.S., and that importing these inputs (40 per cent of the weight of the automobile) would reduce total production cost in Brazil by roughly 20 per cent.[2] The firm in question is relatively small in Brazil; the reduction would probably be less important for a larger Brazilian firm. In fact, data for a large Brazilian firm indicate that the average cost of components made in Brazil is actually 15 per cent *less* than the export price of the same components in the home country, if the comparison is made using the free trade exchange rate.

The data mentioned earlier in this section suggest that at least one large Brazilian firm is close to being competitive in a comparative cost sense. Analysis in fact shows that the internal rate of return of this enterprise, from the viewpoint of the Brazilian economy, is at least 25 per cent.[3]

The over-all conclusion is that one large Brazilian firm has real production costs which are not more than 15 per cent higher than

[1] Baranson, op. cit., p. 28.
[2] Baranson, op. cit., p. 33.
[3] In this analysis, all theoretically tradable inputs (including capital equipment), and the output, were valued at world market prices. Taxes and other transfers were not considered as costs. Valuing labour at actual wages gave a return of 25 per cent; using lower values for the opportunity cost of labour gave much higher rates. The methodology followed Little and Mirrlees, *Social Cost Benefit Analysis*, Vol. II of *Manual of Industrial Project Analysis in Developing Countries*, O.E.C.D. Development Centre, Paris, 1969.

in the parent plant in the home country; that this 15 per cent could be cut perhaps in half by relaxing domestic procurement requirements to 80 or 85 per cent by weight (i.e. importing body and power train parts, where economies of scale are most important); and that the Brazilian market is big enough to support two such firms. If Brazilian policy had limited itself to promoting production of only high-volume models (say, one low-priced and one intermediate-priced car such as the Volkswagen or Citroën 2CV, and the Opel or Ford Falcon), with only 80 or 85 per cent domestic procurement, then real costs of these cars to Brazil need not have exceeded the C.I.F. cost of imports. Such a policy would have implied increased imports of parts, and either imports or non-availability of larger, more expensive cars.

I have less data on trucks and buses. Since scale economies are less important here, a similar conclusion would probably be correct: rationalization of the assembly sector and some relaxation of domestic procurement requirements would permit costs to be reduced to C.I.F. import costs, or even less.

III. CAPITAL GOODS[1]

Steel, automobiles, and capital goods are all sectors which one might expect could operate efficiently only in advanced industrial countries. We have seen that the steel industry was to some extent a 'natural' for Brazil, that it also had plenty of government support, and that today it is more or less competitive. The automotive industry was certainly not a natural. It was established only recently, and only as the result of conscious government policy and tremendous support consisting of both subsidies and protection. Costs in most firms tend to be high, although at least one large firm seems to be efficient. The capital goods sector is yet a different case: it has developed with virtually no direct assistance from the Government; appears to be quite competitive, even in export markets, in some lines; but still does not supply some 20–30 per cent of domestic demand. As Leff notes:

[1] See N. H. Leff, *The Brazilian Capital Goods Industry 1929–1964*, Harvard University Press, 1968. The E.P.E.A., *Diagnóstico Preliminar* (1966) and *Plano Decenal* (1967) for the 'Indústria Mecânica e Elétrica', Ministry of Planning, Rio de Janeiro, are also good sources on developments since 1960 and on present policy problems relevant to the sector.

... the Brazilian capital goods industry is not a recent development, the 'final stage' of an industrialization that began with finished products and proceeded by backward linkages to producers' goods. Equipment production developed relatively early in Brazil's industrial history, and by 1947–1949 domestic industry supplied approximately 61 percent of all producers' equipment in Brazil. This domestic supply coefficient was more than three times larger than in Argentina during the same years. Moreover, the Brazilian industry was no artificial creation fostered by government protection. On the contrary, until the early 1960's it had to meet the competition of equipment imports which were accorded preferential exchange-rate treatment and duty-free importation.[1]

Production of both capital goods and consumer durables in 1939 already accounted for 5·5 per cent of value added, and 3·2 per cent of production workers employed, in Brazilian manufacturing.[2] The sector did not grow rapidly during the second world war, probably because of the difficulty of obtaining steel and other inputs which had to be imported. The repair and maintenance functions, of course, were highly stimulated. The existence of a sizeable industrial sector throughout the period of the 1930s and the war, when Brazil could neither import nor produce much machinery or equipment, created an ample number of skilled repair and maintenance personnel which is a notable characteristic of urban Brazil to this day.

After the war the industry grew rapidly. Steel and other inputs, both imported and domestic, were available. The pent-up demand from the previous fifteen years, plus the new industrial growth, provided a strong market. Value added rose from about $93 million in 1949 to about $383 million in 1959.[3] The evolution of

---

[1] Leff, op. cit., p. 8.   [2] Industrial Census of 1940.
[3] Industrial Censuses of 1950 and 1960. Conversion to dollars at free trade rate of Cr$160 per dollar for 1959. For 1949 and 1954 the free trade rate was projected backward according to the wholesale price index excluding coffee. This gave a rate of Cr$28 per dollar for 1949. Leff estimates value added as $306 million in 1949 (op. cit., p. 20). This is based on an estimate in cruzeiros of Cr$5·7 billion and an exchange rate of Cr$18·60/dollar. Leff does not explain how he got his cruzeiro estimate. Reasoning backwards from the data, one possible explanation is that he includes casting, forging, rolling, construction material, and stamping of parts, simple tools, cutlery, etc. Another possible explanation is that he mistook gross value of production for value added. (See my Table 6.6.) Even his estimate of Cr$5·7 billion, however, implies a dollar value of only around U.S.$200 million at any reasonable exchange rate. The rate of Cr$18·60/dollar used by Leff for 1949 was, as explained in Chapter 3 above, very much over-valued.

K

the structure of the industry is shown in Table 6.6, which shows the rapid growth and varied composition of the sector.

TABLE 6.6
OUTPUT OF MAJOR BRANCHES OF THE CAPITAL GOODS INDUSTRY, 1949 AND 1959

	1949		1959	
Subsector	Value added	Gross value of production	Value added	Gross value of production
		(million dollars)		
Capital goods:				
Machine tools	12	22	47	83
Miscellaneous machinery and industrial equipment	22	39	62	112
Electrical equipment	15	33	64	140
Communication equipment	5	10	6	16
Railroad equipment	4	8	13	24
Trucks, buses, jeeps, etc.	28	54	160	314
Other transport and earth-moving equipment	7	14	31	53
SUB-TOTAL	93	180	383	742
Parts and components, construction materials, etc.:				
Castings and forgings	28	55	34	69
Miscellaneous rolled and stamped products (largely construction material, simple tools, cutlery, etc.)	82	159	224	708
SUB-TOTAL	110	214	258	777

Source: Industrial Census of 1950 and 1960. Data converted to dollars at free trade rates of Cr$28/dollar for 1949 and Cr$160/dollar for 1959, as explained in footnote on previous page.

Private foreign investment has been quite important in the post-war growth of the capital goods sector.[1] This is especially true of heavy equipment, where the field is dominated by subsidiaries of General Electric, Siemens, and Brown-Boveri in heavy electricals, and by a subsidiary of the French firm Schneider in heavy mechanical equipment. All of these received government support on importation of equipment, and Schneider also received a B.N.D.E. loan. According to a study by the Ministry of Planning, however,

[1] See Leff, op. cit., pp. 24 and 25.

... the investments in [machine tools and other industrial machinery] were from private sources and were attracted more by the programs to develop infrastructure than by favors conceded by the Government.[1]

That is, the strong market for machinery was more important than direct subsidies to machinery producers in stimulating investments in production of machinery.

Most machine tools, other industrial equipment, earth-moving and transport equipment (except automotive) were assigned low tariffs and placed in the General Category of imports. This meant that effective protection was low—often negative—and that importation was relatively easy, with exemption from the already low tariffs for government and public firms and other favoured importers. Electrical equipment, on the other hand, tended to receive higher protection. Most products in this sector were placed in the Special Category, which limited imports by most public firms. This is shown in the tariff calculations in Chapter 3. In 1966 average product protection was only 17 per cent for the machinery sector, but was 69 per cent for electrical equipment, which was mostly capital goods. For the transport equipment sector the average of 65 per cent reflects the average of the protection for motor vehicles of about 180 per cent, and the close to zero protection for the earth-moving equipment, railroad equipment, farm equipment, and other capital goods in this sector.

The Law of Similars has never worked very well to protect capital goods, because of the lack of standardization, large number of models, rapid change of models, etc. Only the simplest kinds of goods, mostly light electrical equipment, were recognized similars.[2]

In spite of low protection in most branches, we see from Table 6.6 above, and from Table 5.3 in Chapter 5, that the capital goods industry grew rapidly and that the ratio of imports to total supply was steadily reduced. An example of this import substitution is shown in Baer's study of the steel industry:

It is interesting to note the decrease in the import content of investment in the steel industry in Brazil. Whereas the foreign cost of investments amounted to about 60 to 68 percent of total expenditures in the

[1] E.P.E.A., *Diagnóstico Preliminar*, op. cit., p. 36. My translation.
[2] As noted in Chapter 3, in October 1967 enforcement of the Law of Similars moved to C.A.C.E.X., which can be expected to administer it in a more protectionist manner.

1950's, it dropped to a range of 25 to 39 percent in the steel investment plans for the late 1960's and early 1970's. This reflects the impact of the import-substitution industrialization which made it possible for Brazil to rely to a greater extent on its own sources of supply. For example, the foreign cost of the blast furnace of Cosipa (built in the 1950's) amounted to over 80 per cent, while the plans for new blast furnaces at Volta Redonda to be built in the late sixties have a foreign cost component of only 35 percent; the drop of foreign cost for the construction of the LD steel plant was from about 70 percent to about 33 percent; a substantial drop can also be seen in the foundry. The drop was less dramatic in the rolling mills, where most of the machinery still has to be imported; however, there is now a greater capacity in Brazil for producing medium size rolling mill cylinders, various types of cranes, etc.[1]

It would seem that during the post-war period and earlier Brazil has provided a setting where capital goods production was quite efficient. Most capital goods which are produced in Brazil are quite competitive with imports. The major exceptions to this are most electrical equipment, and perhaps trucks.[2] The large and fairly steady demand for capital goods, due to the continuous growth in industry as a whole, was certainly important to whatever growth and efficiency the capital goods industry has attained. The future prosperity of the sector probably depends on two crucial factors: continued (or rather resumed) strong demand, and adequate financing for sales. This latter point deserves further discussion.

International competition in capital goods depends to a considerable extent on financing. Much of the foreign aid programmes of many developed countries are little else but export promotion, through export credits or other financing on more favourable terms. Capital goods are usually among the important exports to be promoted. This creates difficulties for a country like Brazil, not only in its potential export markets but also in its own domestic market.

[1] From Appendix 1.
[2] Electrical equipment is somewhat burdened by the very high domestic price of copper, but this accounts for only a small part of total cost. Trucks suffer from the extremely high domestic procurement requirements, and to some extent from excessive fragmentation of the industry. But economies of scale are not so important in truck production, and Brazil could probably be an efficient producer if the domestic procurement requirements were relaxed a bit.

It probably makes sense for Brazil to continue to be a net borrower from abroad. But one of the conditions for doing this—one of the ways in which the resources must enter—is continued imports of capital goods. This applies to private investment as well as to official aid. Brazil has already reached the point where further import substitution in capital goods means significantly greater difficulties in absorbing foreign capital—given the restrictions presently imposed by capital-exporting countries.

IV. TEXTILES[1]

History and government policy

Brazil's first textile mill was established in 1814. The period of free trade and special advantages for Britain (discussed in Chapter 2) kept the industry from growing very rapidly. In 1844 a tariff of 30 per cent was established and the industry began to grow. Growth in the mid-nineteenth century was largely in the northeast; around the turn of the century more textile plants were established in the centre-south, based on cotton plantings there in former coffee country, and on the growing shift of population from Pernambuco and Bahia southward to Rio and São Paulo. The industry passed through several cycles of growth and decline, climaxed by the second world war when Brazil not only supplied all of her own domestic demand but also exported about 20 per cent of production. Brazil has been self-sufficient in textiles throughout the post-war period. In 1959 the industry accounted for 12 per cent of value added in manufacturing, or about $410 million. Clothing accounted for another 3 per cent, or $120 million. Over 20 per cent of the total labour force in manufacturing was employed in textiles alone.[2]

In spite of several periods of exporting, capped by the large value of exports during the second world war, analysts seem to agree that Brazilian textile manufacturers were never really

[1] My major published sources of information on the textile industry are United Nations, *The Textile Industry in Latin America: II: Brazil*, E/CN.12/623, October 1963; E.P.E.A., *Diagnóstico Preliminar da Indústria Têxtil*, Ministry of Planning, Rio de Janeiro, January 1967 (mimeo); and United Nations, *La Exportación en el Mercado Mundial: Una Perspectiva para el Desarollo de la Indústria Têxtil Latina-Americana*, ST/ECLA/Conf. 23/L.43, March 1966 (mimeo).

[2] Industrial Census of 1960. Conversion to dollars at free trade rate of Cr$160/dollar.

export-minded.[1] Growth was usually behind government protection, and was principally based on expanding domestic demand. Most companies were run by succeeding generations of the same family—this is common even today, especially in the coarse cotton cloth sector—and most of the industry was not and is not known for technological progress, modern management and organization techniques, etc. As Stein puts it, 'The conservatism of textile-mill proprietors, their unwillingness to alter organization and administration stem from the experience of past decades when government aid supported them in times of crisis. Cushioned by this security, why should the industry innovate?'[2] Export sales were sought only at times of domestic crises, and not always even then. In the 1930s, for example, when possible export markets were even weaker than the Brazilian market, imports of textile machinery were forbidden, ostensibly to keep total capacity from expanding.

The prohibition of imports of textile machinery in the thirties, and the difficulty of obtaining equipment during the second world war, accentuated the Brazilian industry's concentration in coarse cotton fabrics. At the end of the war, Brazil had overcapacity in mills which could produce nothing but these low-quality goods, and undercapacity in higher-quality lines.

In 1946 Brazil had an established position in many export markets, and production costs in the exported lines which were not out of line with costs of its competitors. Moreover, factories of many formidable potential competitors had been destroyed. Some of the financial resources built up during the war could have been devoted to modernizing both the textile industry and the system of supply of cotton and wool, to reduce costs and to compete both abroad and at home. Instead, textile exports were prohibited in order to try to bring down domestic prices, and in 1947 a virtual prohibition on imports was established. There being little incentive, the existing industry did little to modernize itself. By the time that exports were again permitted, the industries of Japan and Europe had been rebuilt with modern equipment, while Brazil was still using equipment largely from the 1920s, and even more antiquated organization and management.

[1] See Stanley J. Stein, 'Brazilian Cotton Textile Industry, 1850–1950', in Simon Kuznets, Wilbert E. Moore, and Joseph J. Spengler (eds.), *Economic Growth: Brazil, India, Japan*, Duke University Press, 1959. Also E.P.E.A., op. cit.

[2] Stein, op. cit., p. 447.

Since the mid-1950s the industry has modernized to some extent. This has happened in two different ways. Some older firms have modernized their equipment. Estimates of the extent of this vary widely, but on balance I would judge that, at least until the last three or four years, only a small dent had been made in the needed replacement of obsolete equipment. The more important carrier of modernization has been new foreign private investment. Subsidiaries of foreign firms have brought in more modern equipment, as well as better management and organization techniques. These firms produce higher quality fabrics—mostly blends of natural and synthetic fibres—and together with a few purely domestic firms make up the more modern and efficient part of the industry. They are separated by a tremendous gap from the backward traditional firms. The wide range of productivity and costs in the Brazilian textile industry will be shown in the following section.

Government policy towards the textile industry has been very protective but not at all developmental. The industry has enjoyed moderate to high protection against imports since the mid-nineteenth century. Imports were virtually prohibited under the licensing regime of 1947–53, and also (by very low exchange allocations for consumer goods as a whole) during the multiple rate regime of 1953–7. Since the imposition of tariffs in 1957 textiles have had the highest tariffs available, and in 1966 and 1967 the sector enjoyed higher effective protection than any other except perfumes and beverages.[1] Effective protection for textiles was about 280 per cent in 1966 and 130 per cent in 1967.

As already mentioned, imports of textile machinery were virtually impossible during the 1930s and early 1940s. This led to a considerable domestic capacity for producing textile machinery. During the post-war period, imports generally were not forbidden, but the various special treatments such as B.N.D.E. loans, or tariff exemptions and low exchange rates applied to capital goods imports for favoured industries, were not available to domestic textile manufacturers. The Government has generally been reluctant to promote re-equipment out of fear of reduced employ-

---

[1] There are probably a number of processes within other sectors which enjoyed higher effective protection—the automotive industry is probably the most notable example. These do not show clearly because of the aggregation of the Brazilian census classification.

ment. This problem is aggravated because the firms with the most obsolete equipment tend to be in the north-east, where unemployment is already a serious problem. Under S.U.M.O.C. 113, foreign firms could and did import equipment at much lower rates (see Chapter 4), and some modern new capacity was installed in this way. But on the whole little was done to help the already-established firms keep up to date, modern, and efficient.

Costs and prices

The wide range of costs and productivity in the Brazilian textile industry has already been mentioned. Even though protection was and is high, and exports have declined both in absolute terms and as a proportion of output, as of 1962 the industry still exported 10 per cent of total output. The inefficiency in most of the industry, however, is well described by the E.C.L.A. study of 1963:

Operational conditions in the spinning and weaving industries, which represent approximately 80 per cent of the textile industry as a whole, have progressively deteriorated until they have reached a state deserving a careful analysis.

In brief, the following is the situation described in the ensuing chapters of the present study (which relate only to the states of the [more advanced] Centro-Sul region of Brazil) . . .

The textile industry utilizes a relatively high proportion of its capacity—90 per cent of the machinery and 80 per cent of the working-hours available in the case of spinning, and 95 and 60 per cent, respectively, in that of weaving. It operates on the basis of a reasonable number of shifts (approximately two, if an average is taken for the several kinds of fibre). Nevertheless, its operational yield, in terms both of unit output of machinery and of labour productivity, was found to be extremely low in comparison with that of other countries, even in Latin America . . .

Owing to the poor performance levels of its machinery and man-power, increased costs cancel out the advantages of which the industry could avail itself not only to deliver inexpensive goods to the domestic consumer but also to compete in external markets, and which consist in the relatively low prices and abundant supply of the raw materials needed (especially cotton), low wages, and the ample opportunities for specialization afforded by the large size of the domestic market.

The causes of the industry's operational inefficiency are many and complex. Outstanding among them, however—in an order which does not necessarily reflect their relative importance—are the high degree of obsolescence of its machinery, the deficient internal organization (administrative and technical) of its enterprises, the inadequate vocational training of its labour force and the defective state in which its raw materials (especially cotton and wool) reach the mills. The interdependence of these factors immediately suggests that the situation should be tackled by means of a co-ordinated programme of remedial measures, aimed at a radical reorganization and modernization of the industry.

Given the steady maintenance of such co-ordinated action over a specific period, it should become possible to double the industry's present productivity, thus raising it to a level much the same as that of the textile industries in western Europe and Japan.

To facilitate evaluation of the present state of affairs, standards of comparison were adopted which represented levels of performance considered to be fairly easily attainable in conditions with respect to size of markets, degree of automatic control of machinery and training of manpower that would, broadly speaking, be appropriate in Latin America. These Latin American standards are, moreover, substantially inferior to those reached, on an average, in the corresponding industries in western Europe, not to mention the United States, where the special conditions prevailing would make the comparison less significant.

According to the findings obtained, the output of the existing machinery in cotton spinning mills—14 grammes per spindle/hour—represents only 58 per cent of what was taken as the standard for Latin America. Similarly, in cotton weaving mills the unit output of the machinery—2·93 metres per loom/hour—is only a fraction of the standard figure, not exceeding 54 per cent of the yield that could be obtained with up-to-date and efficiently utilized machinery in Latin American conditions. In the processing of wool, the indices are equally unfavourable, showing only 38 per cent of the theoretical output per spindle/hour for the spinning industry, and 56 per cent of the standard output per loom/hour for the weaving industry.

For productivity, even lower levels are registered. In cotton processing, output per man/hour was 1,995 grammes in the spinning industry (or 46 per cent of the standard volume) and 8·18 metres in the weaving industry (or 30 per cent of the standard length). To show that the standards of comparison adopted are realistic, it will suffice to mention that the standard level of productivity for spinning mills is 4,300 grammes per man/hour whereas the corresponding figures rise to over 5,500 grammes in western Europe and to 12,400 grammes in the United States, for the same yarn count.

A comparison between levels of productivity in Brazil's spinning and weaving industries and in those of other Latin American countries, such as Chile and Peru, is also unfavourable to the former.

These low levels of machine output and manpower productivity are imputable partly to the high degree of obsolescence of the machinery in use and partly to the marked shortcomings in the internal organization of the industry, including the failure to train the workers properly to operate even the existing out-of-date equipment.

The machine inventory in the spinning and weaving industries is characterized by a high degree of obsolescence. The obsolescence of machinery (measured both in terms of age and by certain technical characteristics), in the various phases of the production process and according to the fibres handled, was analysed in detail for the purposes of the present study, with results which bear eloquent witness to the unsatisfactory operational conditions prevailing in the industry. In the cotton sector, the classification of machinery (establishment by establishment) reveals that approximately 80 per cent of the spindles and nearly 70 per cent of the looms are obsolescent. In wool processing, the state of the equipment is not quite so bad, 48 per cent of the spindles and 62 per cent of the looms being obsolete . . .

. . . an estimate prepared for the cotton industry, which is the largest sector in the Brazilian textile industry as a whole, shows that approximately one-third of the total operational deficiency is due to the obsolescence of the machinery, while under-utilization of the existing machinery (irrespective of its age and technical characteristics) as a result of defective internal organization accounts for the remaining two-thirds. The generic term 'internal organization' includes such physical elements as balance of production, distribution of work loads and lay-out of factories, and such human elements as efficiency of administration and manpower training.[1]

In short, costs are sky-high in Brazil, not because of any unavoidable disadvantages, but because of obsolete machinery and what Brazilians call *falta de organização*. The E.C.L.A. study quoted above tried to analyse in more detail the causes of the low productivity they found. The cotton spinning and weaving branch is the most important, accounting for 60 per cent of value added in the textile industry as a whole. The raw cotton is domestically produced, and was found to be adequate and economically competitive. Standards of grading, cleaning, and transportation, however, were found to be inadequate:

Thus Brazil is in a fairly good position as regards its supply of raw cotton, subject to reservations as to cleaning and classification, which cause considerable wastage and entail the expense of reclassification.[2]

[1] E.C.L.A., *Textile Industry*, op. cit., pp. 2, 3.
[2] E.C.L.A., *Textile Industry*, op. cit., p. 86.

Another E.C.L.A. study noted that the long-fibre Brazilian cotton is equal to the best in the world.[1] As already noted, Brazil regularly exports significant quantities of cotton.

Labour costs in Brazil's textile industry are low per man hour, but high per unit of output. Wages are low, even for Latin America, but so is output. This is largely due to labour-intensive equipment, which itself has a low production rate, but another important cause is poor labour training and poor organization of production.

The net effect of raw material and labour costs is shown in Table 6.7. Brazil has an advantage in raw material costs, part of

TABLE 6.7
COMPARISON OF COSTS OF COTTON AND LABOUR FOR THE PRODUCTION OF A YARD OF COTTON FABRIC IN SELECTED COUNTRIES (dollars)

	United States (1960)	Japan (1960)	Chile (1961)	Brazil (1961)
Average price of cotton per kg.	0·72	0·66	0·826	0·51
Average price of cotton per kg. including wastage	0·816	0·757	1·026	0·62
Man-hours per unit of output (index)	100	200	556	707
Cost components of a yard of fabric:				
Cotton	0·0861	0·0805	0·1087	0·0657
Labour	0·0392	0·0172	0·0480	0·0516
Total of the two inputs	0·1253	0·0977	0·1567	1·1173
Indices	100	78	125	94

Source: E.C.L.A., *Textile Industry*, op. cit., pp. 89, 90.

which it loses on the high wastage rates caused by poor cleaning, grading, and packing of the raw cotton. Its low wages cannot offset the even lower labour productivity, and the total raw material and labour costs are roughly 20 per cent higher than in Japan (although 6 per cent lower than in the U.S.).

Machinery is somewhat more expensive in Brazil than in other countries. Tariffs on textile machinery were generally 30 or 60 per cent in 1966, and are now generally 25 to 40 per cent. Over half of apparent consumption is manufactured domestically. The textile industry did not get widespread tariff exemption for imported machinery. Nevertheless, neither the prices nor the availability of machinery seem to be a major problem in the cost of producing textiles.

[1] E.C.L.A., 'La Exportación . . .', op. cit., p. 2.

Capital costs and availability are a problem. As explained in Chapter 4, commercial loans for more than 180 days were just not available in Brazil. The textile industry received very little long-term financing from the B.N.D.E. or similar agencies, up to 1965. Since foreign private investment has been small, most of the industry has not benefited from S.U.M.O.C. Instruction 113 or similar special treatment for imported equipment. All financing for domestically purchased equipment, and much for inventories, had to come from sources internal to the firm.

In a comparison between average French costs and 'one of the best Brazilian mills' in 1964, E.C.L.A. found that variable costs (*not* including raw material) in the Brazilian firm were lower than in France, amortization was about the same, but that 'other fixed costs' in Brazil were much higher. These it attributed to high costs of inventories. High financial costs of carrying inventories are most important on raw materials, for most of which a full year's supply appears on the market within one or two months. The results are shown in Table 6.8.

TABLE 6.8
PRODUCTION COST OF COTTON THREAD
(excluding raw material)

Item	France	Brazil
	(index: total for France = 100)	
Variable labour	44·5	32·0
Variable energy	9·5	10·0
TOTAL variable costs	54·0	42·0
Fixed salaries	11·5	17·3
Amortization	26·0	27·3
Other fixed costs	8·5	18·4
TOTAL fixed costs	46·0	63·0
TOTAL costs	100·0	105·0

Source: E.C.L.A., 'La Exportación . . .', op. cit., p. 6.

For synthetic fabrics, the situation is almost completely reversed. The fibres are more expensive in Brazil—30–50 per cent in 1961 at the exchange rate used by E.C.L.A. and 6–16 per cent if the free trade rate estimated in Chapter 3 is used.[1] The weaving of synthetic and mixed natural-synthetic fabrics, however, tends to be done in the more modern mills, which are also those with

[1] See E.C.L.A., *Textile Industry*, op. cit., Table III, p. 86.

some foreign capital (most notably French) and are therefore modern not only in machinery but also in organization and management.

The duality or diversity of productivity in the Brazilian industry is striking. The wide range of productivity is clear proof that the high costs could be reduced. The E.C.L.A. *Textile Industry* study notes this in many places. For example:

... although average cotton spinning productivity is well below the standard adopted, there are marked differences between the various size groups and areas studied ... The productivity of individual mills ranges from less than 500 grammes per man/hour to over 6,000 grammes, whereas the over-all average is about 2,000 grammes. There are marked differences within individual states, particularly in Minas Gerais. In nearly half the mills surveyed productivity is between 1,000 and 2,000 grammes per man/hour. In almost two-thirds of the mills (63·9 per cent) productivity is below 2,000 grammes per man/hour; since the average for Brazil is 1,996 grammes, this means that the average is surpassed in only 36 per cent of the mills. Of that 36 per cent, 21 per cent are in São Paulo, 7 per cent in Minas Gerais, 6 per cent in Rio-Guanabara and 2 per cent in Santa Catarina and Rio Grande do Sul. The highest percentage of mills with a productivity that equals or exceeds the standard of 4,300 grammes per man/hour is in São Paulo (5·2 per cent), and the lowest in Santa Catarina and Rio Grande do Sul (nil). Of the total number of mills, 4·3 per cent equal or exceed the standard: 2·6 per cent in São Paulo, 1·4 per cent in Minas Gerais, and 0·3 per cent in Rio-Guanabara. The mills with the highest productivity (over 6,000 grammes per man/hour) are in Minas Gerais; the highest individual figure is 6,155 grammes, which is 44 per cent above the standard ...

The great differences between the levels in individual mills, and the fact that some exceed the standard adopted (of which the average for Brazil represents less than 50 per cent), testify to the feasibility of a reorganization programme designed to promote the widespread application of processes and methods of work that are already in full use in some mills.[1]

The study finds the same diversity for weaving. It concludes that:

... what might be called physical factors or production characteristics do not explain the sharp variations in productivity levels in Brazilian mills. Consequently, after studying the limited data available, it must

[1] E.C.L.A., *Textile Industry*, op. cit., p. 58.

be concluded that the explanation of that part of the variation in productivity not attributable to the physical factors involved must be looked for in the human factors in the production process. The most important is mill management, including the whole concept of the entrepreneur's or manager's responsibility as regards use of satisfactory raw material, careful machinery maintenance, manpower training and so forth. The question arises whether manpower training is the direct responsibility of the entrepreneur or whether he should make use of the services of existing training institutions. The plain fact is that labour productivity in some mills is many times that in others, and the explanation of such very different results in the same country would appear to be the concern of the entrepreneur. Differences in productivity, given the same conditions of obsolescence, mill size and even type of product, call for more searching analysis, which is beyond the scope of the present study. Nevertheless, a more thorough knowledge of the reasons for this situation and of the role played therein by the entrepreneur will contribute to the more efficient operation of Brazil's textile industry.

The apparent co-existence, within so wide a market as Brazil's, of factories whose productive results are so different raises the question of how these differences are reflected in final production costs, and what variations exist in this respect. From the standpoint of the possible reorganization or remodelling of the industry in view of the opening up of the Brazilian market for textile goods from the region, production costs (in which labour, and consequently productivity represents the most important input after raw materials) will become a key factor. At the same time the existence in one country of mills working under optimum conditions side-by-side with others where conditions are sadly deficient proves that the levels regarded as optimum can be attained even under existing conditions. For the inefficient mills, attaining these standards might require some time, and perhaps provision of appropriate incentives, but there do not appear to be any insuperable difficulties since the more progressive mills have been able to reach their present standard with the resources now available. The foregoing implies also, *inter alia*, that Brazil possesses sufficient know-how to attain productivity levels comparable with those of Europe, and that this kind of knowledge—whether administrative or technical— could well be channelled into an effort to reorganize the industry on a rational basis to meet future requirements.[1]

What can we conclude from this? *Le défi américain* may be a problem in France, but *o desafio francês* apparently does not

[1] E.C.L.A., *Textile Industry*, op. cit., p. 83.

exist for the Brazilian textile industry. The existence of such wide and widespread differences implies that for many Brazilian textile manufacturers, the best monopoly profit is a quiet life. They would rather relax than reduce costs. For still others, life may be strenuous inside the mill, and efficiency can be high. But this high efficiency is not translated into price competition and expansion; the inefficient firms continue on their own even quieter life of continued inefficiency and presumably lower profits.

It is hard to identify all the causes of this oligopolistic pricing behaviour in an industry whose structure seems conducive to competition. High protection is surely a necessary condition. Inflation probably further reduces the incentive to competitive pricing; when nominal prices are always changing, it's hard for the buyer to shop around.

Conclusion

In 1946 the Brazilian textile industry was one of the largest in the world, supplying all domestic needs and exporting to various countries. Profits made during the war, and foreign exchange saved by the nation as a whole, could have been used to re-equip the industry, and try to exploit Brazil's natural advantage, which clearly exists in cotton at least. Instead, exports were temporarily forbidden in 1946, and imports were virtually prohibited starting in 1947. The industry became less and less competitive, as other countries rebuilt with modern equipment while Brazil continued with antiquated machinery and administration.

There seems to be no reason why the Brazilian industry could not be, at a minimum, competitive at home. Brazil has a clear advantage in cotton, and no great disadvantage in linen, wool, or synthetics. The industry presents no special problems such as complex or especially advanced technology, or economies of scale significant in relation to the Brazilian market. Exports of cotton and wool, the cost studies in the two E.C.L.A. studies cited above, and actual regular exports from a few Brazilian mills show this to be so.

In the last few years the federal government has started to make significant funds available for financing of re-equipment. There is also talk of a concerted programme of technical assistance in production management and administration. In 1967 protection was cut roughly in half, but even so remains over 100 per cent. It would be interesting to see just how much carrot, and how much stick, is needed to raise the efficiency of the Brazilian textile industry to its potential level.

V. FOOD PRODUCTS

This is an industry which one might expect would have few problems in Brazil. In fact it does get along pretty well, with relatively low protection. (Transport costs, of course, are important here.) But there is one type of problem it has, which can teach us something about the nature of underdevelopment and 'negative subsidies'. The common symptoms of trouble in this large and diverse industry are excess capacity, shortage of working capital, and complaints about raw material supplies.

The Fundação Getúlio Vargas, in a survey of 136 firms, found the evidence of idle capacity shown in Tables 6.9 and 6.10. (Data refer to 1962–4.) Fifty-nine per cent of all replies cited either insufficient working capital or irregularity of supply as the principal reason for low use of capacity. In all parts of the industry except

TABLE 6.9
EXCESS CAPACITY IN THE FOOD PRODUCTS INDUSTRY

Per cent idle capacity	Per cent of firms
50 or more	18
40 or more	46
30 or more	61
20 or more	75
10 or more	85

Source: *A Indústria de Alimentos no Brasil*, Fundação Getúlio Vargas, 1966 (mimeo), p. 123.

TABLE 6.10
REASONS GIVEN FOR LOW USE OF CAPACITY

Reason		Per cent of replies
Trouble in obtaining raw materials of which:		54
irregular supply	38	
quality problems	10	
transport problems	6	
Insufficient demand		25
Working capital		21

Source: *A Indústria de Alimentos no Brasil*, op. cit., p. 125.

the dairy products sector (less than 10 per cent of total value of production in the industry, and only 4 per cent of all firms) the irregularity was seasonal. Now, the supply of raw materials to the food products industry is inherently seasonal! The part of the problem subject to change is a shortage of facilities for storing agricultural produce, and of working capital to finance the storage, at whatever stage of processing.

Storage costs may be somewhat less for processed food products than for raw materials, because of volume reduction and reduced spoilage problems. On the other hand, absorbing the basic seasonal variation of supply by storing after processing rather than before requires larger production capacity in the processing industry. There may therefore be a trade-off between additional storage costs to store the unprocessed raw materials, and additional production capacity costs to process the raw materials as they become available. The food products industry in Brazil is far from the optimum position in this respect; storage facilities for farm produce are scarce, and the large excess capacity in the food products industry is in part a result.

A careful study by Gordon Smith, not yet published, suggests that lack of physical storage facilities *per se* is not the main problem. He notes that total storage capacity seems roughly sufficient, although some may be of poor quality, and in some parts of Brazil it may be inadequate in quantity. He finds that improvement is most needed in transportation, credit, warehouse regulation, grades and standards, and market information. In short, physical storage facilities are less available and less useful because of lack of complementary facilities (credit, grading, and regulation) and are more strained than they should be because of lack of substitute facilities (transportation and market information). This furnishes a good definition by example of *falta de organização*.

The over-all picture of the industry is as follows:

Raw materials: Brazil exports many, and is self-sufficient in all but wheat. However, the system of storing, grading, and transporting agricultural products has many deficiencies, and commercial credit for the farmer, the merchant, or the processor was generally either unavailable or very expensive until the mid-1960s.

L

Labour: Productivity relative to wages is high compared with other industries in Brazil.

Capital equipment and technology: No problems of complex or advanced technology, scale economies, etc. Foreign capital is important in a few branches of the industry, such as flour milling and slaughterhouses.

Credit and financial costs: This industry has high working capital needs because of the seasonal nature of raw material supply. In addition to their own inventories, processors have until recently had to bear a large part of the credit needs of their suppliers. It was estimated in 1954 that over half of the credit extended to agriculture came from distribution and processing firms.[1] The inadequacy of supply of facilities for storage of farm products has required processing capacity to expand to handle a larger percentage of the raw materials as they become available, and this has aggravated the problem of working capital and financial charges in general for the processing industry.

VI. CONCLUSIONS

The information presented in this chapter, while incomplete and imperfect, lends support to several important conclusions about industrialization in Brazil. Some of these conclusions are not really surprising—many readers would probably expect them to be true even before seeing any evidence—but it is useful to have some more detailed and more factual bases for them.

First, both government policies, and factors outside of anyone's control, were important in determining growth and efficiency in Brazilian industries. Policies were able to compensate for an unfavourable situation in some cases, and in at least one other case bad policies 'compensated' for a favourable situation.

The automotive industry is an outstanding example of an 'unnatural' industry for any L.D.C., even such a large one as Brazil. Economies of scale up to very high levels of output, and complex technology, make it an unlikely candidate for efficient production. To establish this industry in Brazil, not only very high protection but also every type of subsidy and special arrangement in the Government's bag of policies were used. But the industry was

---

[1] Klein and Saks, *O Problema de Alimentação no Brasil*, Rio de Janeiro, 1954, p. 75.

established, and one firm at least seems to be a socially efficient operation.

The textile industry is at another extreme. It is a 'natural' for Brazil, but has become extremely inefficient behind a very high protective barrier.

The case of capital goods is yet a third extreme. This sector is often thought to be a bad bet for L.D.C.s. Moreover, policies directly affecting the industry were negative: very little protection or subsidies. But an apparent natural comparative advantage combined with the rapid growth of demand which in turn was partly a result of policy provided the basis for rapid and significant growth, and apparently high efficiency.

The costs of deficient infrastructure were seen clearly. Textiles and food products, depending on raw materials from agriculture, show how costs are increased by the lack of storage, marketing, grading, and transport facilities.

This first conclusion, then, can be stated in another way: good policies can create good industries even in somewhat unfavourable conditions; bad policies can induce or permit inefficiency even in favourable conditions, and efficient industries can develop without directly supporting policies, even in a very modern and technologically complex sector such as capital goods.

The second conclusion is that very high protection seems to have been at worst counter-productive, and at best unnecessary for efficient growth. It was certainly counter-productive in the case of textiles. (And there is no reason to believe that it did any good in any non-durable consumer goods sectors.) In the automotive industry, protection could have been much lower if the excessive fragmentation, high taxes, and the overzealous goal of *complete* import substitution had been avoided. If Brazil had settled for, say, one low-priced and one intermediate-priced passenger car, fewer utility vehicles, the same trucks and buses, and only 80 or 85 per cent domestic procurement of inputs, the real social costs of production might have been reduced to near-competitive levels. We saw in the last section of Chapter 5 that most of the import substitution in producer goods took place without very high protection, and that most sectors which enjoyed very high protection were already well-established at the beginning of the post-war period. The only major sectors where there was much import substitution behind high protection were consumer

durable goods, and we have seen in this chapter that, for automobiles at least, other policies could have made the high protection
unnecessary.

From one point of view, the results of industrialization in Brazil
are odd indeed. What are we to make of an L.D.C. which has
efficient producers of steel, automobiles, and capital goods, but
many extremely inefficient textile manufacturers? The stereotypes
just don't apply. Rather, we see that it is indeed possible for
Brazil to have a large and growing industrial sector which is
competitive or very close to it in comparative cost terms. Not only
non-durable consumer goods, but many capital goods, automobiles and trucks, steel, and many other intermediate goods can
clearly be produced efficiently in Brazil. Policies have been
important in determining what happened, and future progress
will depend greatly on future policies.

7

Balance and Imbalance in the Industrialization

THE words 'balance' and 'imbalance' have been used in many different senses in the literature of economic development. There are three different types of balance—three dimensions in which I wish to analyse balance—which will be discussed in this chapter.

The first is the relationship between industry and agriculture; what industrialization policies affected agriculture, and what resulted. The second (closely related to the first) is the structure of labour productivity in the Brazilian economy, and industry's role as an absorber of labour. The third dimension of balance to be discussed is the geographic structure of output and productivity in manufacturing, with some suggestions as to causes underlying this structure. This last topic leads to some insight into one of the most important factors which determine efficiency in industry: industrialization itself is seen to produce the kind of environment in which industry can function efficiently.

I. BALANCE BETWEEN INDUSTRY AND AGRICULTURE

The questions which seem important here are:

1. How have the policies used to promote industrialization affected incentives in agriculture?
2. How has agricultural output responded? How has the structure of the economy, as between the industrial and agricultural sectors, evolved?
3. Are these results good or bad?

I have not studied Brazil's agriculture at all closely, so the analysis will be neither very new nor very profound. I do believe, however, that my answers to these three questions, while perhaps partial and superficial, are correct as far as they go.

Policies affecting agriculture

Brazil's tremendous industrialization, and the many policies which supported it during the post-war period, do not seem to have had a major unfavourable effect on Brazilian agriculture. This does not mean that all policies which affected agriculture were satisfactory. That question is far beyond the scope of this study. It means only that policies *which promoted industrialization* did not have significant negative effects on agriculture. The one great exception is the discouraging of agricultural exports by exchange rate policy. To put the conclusion the other way around, most of the important improvements in policies to affect agricultural output and productivity could have been taken without seriously hindering the industrialization (again with the exception of exports of agricultural products).

The element of industrialization policy which had the most effect on agriculture was the over-valued export exchange rate. This discriminated against exports of all products, industrial, agricultural, or whatever. The maximum devaluation—to the free trade situation—would have averaged about 40 per cent during the period for which I have estimates (1954–67). This would probably have increased non-coffee exports by roughly the same percentage; total exports would have increased by roughly 20 per cent, or $250 million per year.

Such a move would of course have raised domestic prices of agricultural products, and resulted in a large increase in producers' surplus to the agricultural sector—roughly 20 per cent of the value of its entire output—and a corresponding loss of consumers' surplus to Brazilian consumers. Whether the net effect of this would have been good or bad—either on welfare or other grounds—is a complex question. But apparently the answer was clear most of the time to most Brazilian governments; at least until 1964 the net effect of *all* government policies on agricultural prices was to keep them down. This was especially true of food prices. The over-valued exchange rate probably owed its existence at least as much to a desire to keep food prices down, as to a desire to industrialize. In addition to the over-valued exchange rate, other policies tended to discriminate against agriculture in the same way. These policies included price ceilings and export prohibitions, which were typically applied to specific food products during periods of unusually short supply.

The structure of protection against imports gave much higher protection to manufacturing than to agriculture, and this of course reduced the relative profitability of agriculture. Table 3.5 gives a rough picture of this discrimination. In 1966, protection for agriculture was roughly zero.[1] For manufacturing, product protection averaged roughly 60 per cent and effective protection roughly 100 per cent. Important agricultural inputs such as fertilizers and tractors were heavily subsidized. Fertilizers, for example, were available at prices which implied negative protection —the cruzeiro price was less than the C.I.F. dollar price times the free trade exchange rate. This negative protection averaged —43 per cent during 1955–64, and was reduced in the following years to about —10 per cent in 1967.[2]

The internal 'terms of trade' between industry and agriculture should show the net effect of these policies (as well as the effects of all other aspects of the situation) on relative prices of agricultural and industrial products.[3] Unfortunately, there are some serious problems with the data, and one does not know exactly what to believe. Table 7.1 shows, in the first column, an estimate of agriculture–industry terms of trade based on wholesale price indices of the Fundação Getúlio Vargas. The first column is based on prices of all agricultural products except coffee; the second column is based only on food prices (again excluding coffee).

The first column of Table 7.1 seems to show that the internal

[1] Not including the largely redundant protection to primary animal products, and considering the overestimate of protection of agricultural inputs. See Appendix 3.

[2] My calculations from data on C.I.F. dollar prices and cruzeiro prices collected and made available by Peter Knight. Rougher data from the Ministry of Finance are consistent with Knight's estimates, which are based on nutrient values.

[3] The terms of trade, in simplest form, is an index number series which expresses the evolution of the prices of agricultural products relative to the prices of manufactured products. One forms a time series of average prices of agricultural goods, and another time series of average prices of manufactured goods. The terms of trade series is then formed by dividing the first by the second; the result shows the *changes* in relative prices of the two kinds of products.

It would be interesting to have data on prices of inputs as well as outputs. I have attempted to derive such data from the various price series of the Fundação Getúlio Vargas and from other sources, but have been unable to do a satisfactory job.

terms of trade turned against industry in the period 1944-8, and remained more or less the same thereafter. This is just the opposite of what one would expect. The structure of scarcities during and immediately after the war (1944-5) was such that industrial prices

TABLE 7.1

TERMS OF TRADE BETWEEN AGRICULTURE AND INDUSTRY, 1944-67
(agricultural prices divided by manufactured goods prices)

Year	All agricultural products	Food products only	Internal v. external terms of trade
	(index: 1945-7 = 100)		
1944	81	83	59
1945	98	95	65
1946	95	93	104
1947	111	111	129
1948	131	124	150
1949	132	125	147
1950	130	117	104
1951	137	112	94
1952	147	135	107
1953	150	140	120
1954	134	123	91
1955	147	132	96
1956	142	129	100
1957	135	125	86
1958	128	116	80
1959	127	115	77
1960	145	127	98
1961	141	122	98
1962	153	135	123
1963	141	126	94
1964	138	126	98
1965	124	114	82
1966	141	130	91
1967	143	130	75

Notes: All estimates exclude coffee.
    The first two columns are based on series of wholesale prices excluding coffee, from *Conjuntura Econômica*. The first column is index no. 48 divided by no. 49; the second is index no. 57 divided by no. 49.
    The third column is equal to the first column divided by the external terms of trade. The latter was estimated by dividing *Conjuntura Econômica* index no. 84 by no. 130.

were unusually high relative to agricultural prices. Unlimited imports at an over-valued exchange rate in 1946 should have caused industrial prices to drop sharply relative to agricultural prices. Either this did not happen, or the indices did not pick it up. In 1947-8, with the imposition of strict rationing on imports of all manufactured consumer goods, industrial prices should have risen relative to agricultural prices; the index shows the opposite. As import substitution in industry proceeded throughout the period up to the early 1960s, behind varied but relatively high protection, one would expect a deterioration of agricultural prices relative to industrial prices; the index shows constant or slowly rising prices of agriculture relative to industry.

One element which helps to explain this anomalous behaviour is the incomplete coverage of the industrial price index.[1] Coverage is almost completely limited to standardized intermediate products; the only finished consumer goods covered are a few items such as shoes and textiles. As shown in Chapters 3 and 4, intermediate products tended to receive significant subsidies, but relatively low to moderate protection. The wholesale price series do not include a single finished consumer durable good: no cars, refrigerators, television sets, etc. These items received extremely high protection, and probably rose in price during the 1950s.[2]

Better indices would probably show somewhat more deterioration in agriculture's internal terms of trade during the 1950s. But another part of the picture is that industrial prices were probably unusually high, relative to agricultural prices, during the *entire* period for which the data are available (except perhaps for 1946). That is, agriculture's terms of trade may not have *deteriorated* very much since 1944—but they were already bad then.

Another way to look at the effect of policy on the internal terms of trade is to contrast the internal with the external terms of trade. Neutral policy would result in the two series being the same; discrimination against agriculture in the domestic market would cause agriculture's internal terms of trade to deteriorate relative to agriculture's external terms of trade.[3] The data for this analysis are far from ideal, and again one would not rely too strongly on

---

[1] The weights used during most of the post-war period are available in English in Werner Baer, *Industrialization and Economic Development in Brazil*, op. cit., pp. 304–5.

[2] The Fundação Getúlio Vargas does have price series for some of these products, on the retail level, in their basic data on consumer prices. But I was not able to form one single index which would give a complete and valid estimate of prices of all industrial products.

[3] Lack of appropriate data is a severe handicap here. The best data available on the external terms of trade for the period cover all imports, and all exports except coffee. However, almost all of Brazil's exports were primary products, and most of these were agricultural; on the import side, manufactures were between 60 and 90 per cent of all imports.

the results if contradictory evidence came to light. The results are shown in the third column of Table 7.1 above. They suggest that, *relative to world prices*, the internal terms of trade of Brazilian agriculture were unusually high in the late 1940s. Subsequently they have been fluctuating around an average slightly below the level of 1945–7. These results indicate that, while there may well have been discrimination against agriculture in the domestic market, that discrimination remained at a more or less constant level throughout the 1950s and early 1960s.

Comparing the food price index to the general agricultural price index shows that the sharpest rise, around 1947 and 1948, was less for food products than for other agricultural products, and that this difference was maintained throughout the rest of the period. This is consistent with the idea that the Government was concerned with keeping food prices down.[1]

Agricultural output and structural change

Agricultural output for the domestic market, in the most general terms, has been at a satisfactory level and has expanded at a

TABLE 7.2
AGRICULTURAL PRODUCTION FOR DOMESTIC CONSUMPTION
(physical output)

	Average annual increase (per cent per year)		
Period	Total	Food	Industrial raw materials
1945–7 to 1960–2	4·5	4·7	4·0
1960–2 to 1965–7	7·0	4·7	12·8

Source: *Conjuntura Econômica*, indices Nos. 38, 39, and 40.

satisfactory rate during the post-war period.[2] Performance is summarized in Table 7.2. Both *per capita* income and population were growing at about 3 per cent per year through 1962; food output increasing at 4·7 per cent per year seems roughly appropri-

---

[1] Other sources also testify to this. See, for example, E.C.L.A., 'Fifteen Years of Economic Policy in Brazil', *Economic Bulletin for Latin America*, November 1964, pp. 180–4.

[2] The adequacy of food production is attested to in R. Kahil, *Inflation and Economic Development in Brazil Since World War II*, unpublished doctoral thesis, St. Antony's College, Oxford University, 1966.

ate.[1] As we saw earlier, wholesale prices of food rose less rapidly than agricultural prices in general.[2]

The satisfactory performance of agricultural production in the face of continued discrimination, a very poor distribution and marketing system, and other problems is a result of several favourable factors. The most important is Brazil's ample endowment of arable land *per capita*. Virtually the entire increase in output during the post-war period—4·7 per cent per year for all products, from 1945–7 to 1965–7[3]—came from increased acreage. Output per acre, and output per man, were virtually stagnant.[4] Even though much agriculture in the north-east is based on poor land and poorer methods, expansion along the frontier in the west and centre-south has been sufficient and efficient enough to provide a satisfactory increase in total output.

In conclusion, Brazil would seem to have managed the agriculture–industry balance problem fairly well—as regards output. Many L.D.C.s have not done so well. Typically agriculture is squeezed too hard, whether through shifts in relative prices, social arrangements, or whatever; less favourable basic conditions (ratios of population to land, etc.) make expanding agricultural output more difficult; and the net result is that agricultural production becomes a constraint on development. There is no evidence that this has happened in Brazil.

The agriculture–industry balance in regard to the structure of employment and the growth of labour productivity is less satisfactory. As we shall see in Section II of this chapter, industry has not absorbed labour very rapidly. With an abundant supply of both labour and land, agricultural productivity has remained

---

[1] Rises in personal income were very concentrated; most of the labour force, especially in agriculture and services, had essentially constant disposable personal income. Even industrial wages rose only about 2–3 per cent per year until the early 1960s. Therefore an over-all income elasticity of demand for food of 0·57 does not seem too low. Moreover, imports of food products increased significantly during the period, because of wheat available at almost zero real cost under P.L. 480.

[2] *Retail* prices of food rose more rapidly, but this reflects Brazil's inadequate and generally monopolistic agricultural distribution and marketing system. See Gordon Smith, *Agricultural Marketing and Economic Development: A Brazilian Case Study*, unpublished Ph.D. dissertation, Harvard University, 1965; Baer, op. cit., pp. 153–5; E.P.E.A., *Diagnóstico Preliminar, Setor de Agricultura*, Ministry of Planning, Rio de Janeiro, 1966 (mimeo).

[3] *Conjuntura Econômica*, index No. 37.

[4] See E.P.E.A., op. cit.

essentially stagnant. Thus a large portion of Brazil's labour force has been virtually unaffected by development. This is a crucial social problem which is bad, has been getting worse, and could get still worse in the future. A direct and immediate bad effect of this on industry is that stagnant productivity in most of the labour force means slow growth of purchasing power, which in turn means a more limited market for industry. Brazil's large size makes this problem less acute and less apparent. But more widespread increases in labour productivity and a more even distribution of income would undoubtedly furnish a big boost to industrial production, as well as contribute to the more important goals of a more equitable, more stable, and more self-sustaining type of development.

II. THE STRUCTURE OF LABOUR PRODUCTIVITY IN THE BRAZILIAN ECONOMY

While industry produces at least 25 per cent of domestic income, it employs only 12 per cent of Brazil's employed labour force. Manufacturing produces between 24 per cent and 30 per cent of G.D.P.,[1] and employs only 9 per cent of the labour force. This means that labour productivity is much higher in these sectors than in the rest of the economy. In fact, the ratio of average labour productivity in manufacturing to average productivity in the entire economy is higher in Brazil than in any of the 50-odd countries for which data are given in *The Growth of World Industry, 1953–65*.[2]

This unique position of Brazil may in part be caused by differences in definitions in the censuses of the various countries. But much of the difference is real. In Brazil, while value added in manufacturing rose from 22 per cent of G.D.P. in 1949 to 30 per cent in 1959, employment in manufacturing remained constant at 9 per cent of the total. Here, with no problem of inconsistent definitions, it is clear that the average productivity of labour rose much faster in manufacturing than in the economy as a whole.[3]

---

[1] Twenty-four per cent would be consistent with the share of industry in national income; 30 per cent is the ratio of value added in manufacturing according to the Industrial Census, divided by G.D.P. All estimates for 1959.

[2] United Nations Statistical Office, 1967. ST/STAT/SER. P/4.

[3] This kind of problem is evidently a common one. See Werner Baer and Michel Hervé, 'Employment and Industrialization in Developing Countries', *Quar-*

It is hard to know how much of this difference is due to unusually high productivity in manufacturing, and how much to unusually low productivity in other sectors. International comparisons run up against the problem of the proper valuation of the domestic currency, which is in doubt for so many countries and especially for Brazil. The range of uncertainty as to the exchange rate appropriate for the comparison allows no clear answer. Both factors probably contribute: as noted above, much of Brazilian agriculture is characterized by an abundance of land and labour, and low use of fertilizers, modern machinery, etc. Labour productivity tends to be low and stagnant. On the other hand, Brazilian industry includes many processes which tend to be relatively capital-intensive, and subsidies to imports of capital equipment were a major factor in the industrialization of the 1950s.

This 'duality' between average labour productivity in manufacturing and in the rest of the economy was already strong at the start of the post-war period, and was exacerbated thereafter. Table 7.3 shows how almost all productivity increases were concentrated in manufacturing. In Table 7.3, the 'technological'

TABLE 7.3
COMPONENTS OF INCREASE IN LABOUR PRODUCTIVITY, 1949–59

Sector	Techno-logical	Structural
Agriculture	8%	4%
Manufacturing	20	−2
Mining, construction, electric power, transport, and communication	4	1
Commerce, services, and government	−4	1
TOTAL	28	4

Source: Taken from J. Bergsman and A. Candal, 'Industrialization: Past Success and Future Problems', in Howard S. Ellis (ed.), *The Economy of Brazil*, op. cit.

component is that part of the total increase which would have occurred if the structure of employment had remained constant; i.e. it is that part which is due only to growth in productivity within the sectors. The 'structural' component is approximately that part

terly *Journal of Economics*, February 1966. But the Brazilian situation seems to be among the most extreme.

of the total which is due only to changes in the structure of employment among sectors.

The total increase in the average productivity of labour in Brazil, between the census years 1949 and 1959, was (28 plus 4 or) 32 per cent. Of this, 20 per cent can be attributed to the increase of the average productivity of labour in manufacturing. Almost none of the total change was due to shifts of employment among sectors.

Shifting employment into manufacturing is an essential aspect of development through industrialization.[1] In Brazil, manufacturing's abnormally small share in employment relative to its share in output is a reflection of an abnormal difference between labour productivity in manufacturing and in the rest of the economy. This difference is partly caused by conditions causing low productivity of labour in the rest of the economy, and partly is itself a cause of that low productivity. The failure of manufacturing to absorb much labour ensures an abundant supply to the rest of the economy. This in turn reduces incentives to increase labour productivity in the rest of the economy, through more use of other factors such as tools, equipment, fertilizer, education, etc., etc. Most of Brazil's labour force is going to be in the primary and the service sectors for a long time in any case; one cannot be satisfied with Brazilian development unless the productivity of these workers grows. It will not grow—it has not grown significantly in the post-war period—unless it is induced to grow by more rapid absorption of labour into manufacturing.

In a wider sense, a shift of labour into industry is the means of achieving many of the benefits of industrialization. The better training, the more modern ideas, social and political structure, and other aspects of 'modernization' depend on modernizing the people as well as the structure of production. Just one example, but a crucial one, is the birth rate: effects of urban industrial life, exposure to rational planning, and control over nature are probably very important in limitation of births, and surely depend on absorption of labour by industry. Many of the 'external economies' of industrialization function through expanded industrial *employment*, rather than through expanded industrial production.

[1] Fei and Ranis make that shift the criterion for successful development in a labour surplus economy (*Development of the Labor Surplus Economy*, Richard D. Irwin, 1964). But one need believe neither that Brazil is a labour surplus economy, nor that the Fei–Ranis analysis is valid, to see that such a shift is at least one crucial aspect of development.

Yet another reason for wanting a shift of labour into industry relates to income distribution. The post-war period was characterized by rapid productivity gains by a small part of the labour force, leaving the rest stagnating. Reducing the increases in industry, and increasing it in the rest of the economy, would provide a basis for raising the income of the lowest-paid workers.[1] This not only seems more equitable, but also promises a more stable and healthier continued development.

Perhaps one of the reasons why highly productive sectors have not absorbed more labour is that Brazil's famous cheap labour is not cheap at all—but simply low priced. With half of the population unable to read or write, and another large group without the basic education needed even to start on-the-job training in modern industry, it may indeed be more economical to apply more and more physical capital to a small modernized labour force, rather than to absorb more and more new workers with less capital per worker. The best way to start to spread capital over more workers may be through education. Providing today's children with the abilities and the attitudes needed to work in modern activities will help to induce these activities to employ more of them.

A poorly educated and hence unproductive potential labour force is only one side of the problem. To induce industry to employ more labour—and less capital—some combination of increasing the potential productivity of labour *and* lowering its price relative to capital is needed. In Brazil, a large part of an extensive labour welfare programme appears as a cost to the employer. In addition, traditions such as *estabilidade* (no worker with ten years' seniority can be fired) may cost the employer and the consumer more than they benefit the worker. The cost of capital, on the other hand, has been kept rather low by tariff exemptions on imports of capital goods, subsidized financing to favoured sectors, etc. The businessman sees labour as relatively more expensive, and capital equipment as relatively cheaper, than the real costs of these factors to the economy.

It is possible to make a rough estimate of the effect of biases in the relative prices of capital and labour on the amount of labour employed. As an example of a policy which reduced the cost of

---

[1] The productivity increase would not guarantee the increase in income, but it would make it more likely.

capital, take S.U.M.O.C. instruction 113. In Chapter 4 it was estimated that this reduced the cost of capital goods (for eligible firms) by roughly 40 per cent. Removing this bias alone would have meant that the number of production workers employed in those firms might have increased by roughly 40 per cent.[1] If we also take into account that wages were considerably higher than the opportunity cost of labour (see Chapter 1), the combined effect of the two biases is much greater. Taking a conservative estimate that industrial wages were twice the opportunity cost of labour, the combined effect of removing the two biases in factor prices might have been to increase production workers employed by perhaps 130 per cent! These estimates are based on a production function which may overestimate the substitutability of capital for labour; the results nevertheless suggest that moving market prices closer to actual social opportunity costs might have caused a significant increase in the absorption of labour by manufacturing.

III. REGIONAL INEQUALITIES

Much has been written about the backwardness of the Brazilian north-east, and much more will be heard about it in the future. I wish here only to touch on one or two elements of regional inequalities which are especially relevant to the industrialization.

Table 7.4 shows the geographical structure of manufacturing as a whole. Over 90 per cent of manufacturing is in the eastern and southern regions; the state of São Paulo alone accounts for half of the total. On a *per capita* basis, the southern region has twice as much manufacturing as the national average; the state of São Paulo has three times as much. The north-east, which has over a quarter of the population of Brazil, has only 7 per cent of its manufacturing. On a *per capita* basis, the north-east has only one-fourth as much manufacturing as the national average, only 13 per cent as much as the south, and only 9 per cent as much as São Paulo!

Productivity also varies greatly. Referring to value added per

---

[1] Assuming a Cobb–Douglas production function, with the share of capital at 70 per cent. Another assumption involved is that output remains constant. This implies that some other promotional device, which is neutral in its effect on relative factor prices, is used instead of S.U.M.O.C. 113.

worker in 1959, five states were at less than one-third of the national average, and fifteen of the total of twenty-five states were below 75 per cent of the national average. The north-east has the lowest average productivity of any region: barely above half of the national average.

TABLE 7.4
GEOGRAPHIC DIFFERENCES IN MANUFACTURING, 1949 AND 1959

	Value added (per cent of national total)		Value added per inhabitant		Value added per worker	
			(per cent of national average)			
	1949	1959	1949	1959	1949	1959
Regions:						
North	1	1	19	30	57	91
North-east	5	7	29	22	52	56
East	26	31	81	75	95	95
South	67	61	192	192	114	108
Centre-west	1	1	18	17	92	81
	100	100				
Selected States:						
São Paulo	54	47	269	298	124	119
Guanabara	10	15	358	218	119	109

Source: Calculated from data in the Industrial and Demographic Censuses of 1950 and 1960. Mining is included.

These regional differences were already very great in 1949, and did not change very much in the ten following years.[1] Sample data for later years (up to 1965) indicate no significant changes; data for 1939 also give a similar picture.

Not only the total amount of manufacturing, but the product mix and the technology used differ radically in different parts of Brazil. Manufacturing in the more backward regions is more concentrated in traditional industries and uses more backward technology. (The concentration in traditional industries can be seen in the census data, which is not worth repeating here in detail. The technological backwardness can also be seen roughly in the census data; horsepower installed per worker, even within a sector on the two-digit level, tends to be less in the states with less industry.) The rest of this section will be devoted to a deeper analysis of technological differences among manufacturing in different parts of Brazil.

[1] The changes in the northern region reflect the establishment of a profitable and efficient manganese ore mining enterprise in Amapá.

M

Regional inequalities and externalities

Two kinds of regional inequalities in Brazilian manufacturing were described above: the amount of manufacturing is highly concentrated, and regions with relatively much manufacturing have relatively high productivity in manufacturing. This situation is by no means limited to Brazil; it is common throughout the world. Among countries, the concentration of manufacturing (and especially of high-productivity manufacturing) is the proximate cause of the notorious large and growing gap between the poor and the rich nations. Within a country, regional inequalities lead to concern about 'depressed areas'. The south-eastern United States, the north-west and west of France, and poor regions all over the world remain poor and backward; the north of England, the south of Italy, and the north-east of Brazil are still poor cousins even after decades of special programmes to bring them closer to the levels of the rest of their countries. A few programmes to 'revive depressed areas' have been moderately successful—for example, in the Tennessee Valley of the U.S.—but usually relatively backward areas remain relatively backward.

The reasons for the existence and the persistence of less-developed areas are extremely complex. One can find many economic and other factors which vary systematically with concentration of manufacturing and high productivity in manufacturing, but even with such results in hand it is hard to say what *causes* what. One factor which economists have long thought to be important is 'external economies'. What Meade called 'external economies' and what Scitovsky called 'technological external economies' is the dependence of the output of one firm, not only on the inputs which that firm uses, but also on the output or inputs used by other firms.[1] That is,

$$X_1 = f(K_1, L_1; X_2, K_2, L_2; X_3, \ldots)$$

where the subscripts distinguish different firms, and

X = value added,
K = capital used,
L = labour used.

[1] J. Meade, 'External Economies and Diseconomies in a Competitive Situation', *Economic Journal*, March 1952; T. Scitovsky, 'Two Concepts of External Economies', *Journal of Political Economy*, April 1954.

There is an analysis of Brazilian manufacturing which strongly suggests that external economies are very significant in Brazil. This analysis is an econometric study based on data from the industrial censuses of 1950 and 1960, performed by Carlos A. Rocca.[1] A summary of Rocca's methods and the results relevant here appear as Appendix 2 in this volume. What Rocca did is essentially the following: rather than deal with output, capital, and labour as in the equation above, he dealt with output per worker and capital per worker. He introduced, as an additional explanatory variable, the size of the firm (measured by number of workers). This is to take account separately of possible economies of scale, which are known to be important in many processes. His observations were the value added per worker, capital per worker, and average number of workers per plant within each 2-digit sector of Brazilian manufacturing, within each state, for each of the two census years. For each year and for each sector he made a regression on the observations for each of the twenty-one states. To see whether 'external economies' were important, he introduced as a third explanatory variable the total value added, by all manufacturing sectors combined, in the state. That is, for each sector and for each year:

$$\left(\frac{X}{L}\right)_i = f\left[\left(\frac{K}{L}\right)_i, (\bar{l})_i, (\textstyle\sum X)_i\right]$$

where the subscripts indicate the state, and

$\dfrac{X}{L}$ = value added per worker,

$\dfrac{K}{L}$ = capital per worker,

$\bar{l}$ = average number of workers per firm,

$\sum X$ = value added in all manufacturing sectors combined.

The results are striking. Capital per worker turns out to be a significant explanatory variable in virtually every sector, and economies of scale are significant in many. This is as expected. But the amount of manufacturing in all sectors combined is not

---

[1] Carlos A. Rocca, *Economias de Escala na Função Produção*, F.C.E.A., University of São Paulo, 1967 (mimeographed doctoral dissertation).

only significant in most sectors; it generally is roughly equal in importance to the combined effect of the other two explanatory variables. That is, the total amount of manufacturing in a state is just as important a determinant of the productivity of labour in that state, as are the combined effects of the amount of capital per worker and the scale of firms.

This means that the average firm in São Paulo or Guanabara is significantly more productive than a firm in the same sector, of the same size, and with the same amount of capital per worker, located in the north-east. As Rocca notes, it seems reasonable to assume that this is because states with a high degree of industrialization have a higher quality labour force, better or more reliable transport, energy, and other services, better or more readily available raw materials and intermediate goods inputs, and similar favourable elements which result in more efficient production.

Many of these factors which seem likely to be the causes of higher productivity are not within the usual narrower definitions of external economies. But it seems clear that many factors which make for higher productivity in manufacturing will be closely associated with the total amount of manufacturing in the area, *and that the causality will run in both directions*: manufacturing will tend to grow more rapidly where 'external economies' in our broader sense are stronger, and '*external economies' will be produced by a large amount of manufacturing*. This last is the important point here. Inequalities in amount and in productivity of manufacturing are maintained or aggravated because where industries exist, they *produce* a labour force which is skilled and adapted to the conditions of industrial work and this in turn attracts more industries; because for many industries it is important to locate near other industries which are suppliers and customers as well as near service and repair firms which can only exist where there are many customers; because in L.D.C.s industry is the main high-productivity sector, and this means a bigger tax base to pay for better infrastructure as well as politically powerful consumers to demand it.[1]

[1] In a recent article, Irma Adelman and Cynthia T. Morris have made a pioneering step in measuring this effect. ('An Econometric Model of Socio-Economic and Political Change in Underdeveloped Countries', *American Economic Review*, December 1968). They first use discriminant analysis to devise an index of economic development potential. This index in turn is used as the dependent variable in a regression analysis which selects other

It is unimportant whether we choose to call these effects 'external economies', or Hirschman-type pressures, or something else. The point is that industrialization itself induces efficiency and growth in industry. This is borne out by casual observations everywhere in the world as well as by Rocca's econometric study for Brazil. This 'vicious circle' in development can be either vicious or beneficial. It is vicious for the non-industrial country which does not have an exceptional advantage in some other activities. But it can be beneficial for the country which manages to create a large industry and also to take the other steps necessary to induce reasonable efficiency in that industry.

V. CONCLUSION

This rather diverse chapter does not lead to one unified set of conclusions. In this final section I want to emphasize two points.

1. The post-war industrialization in Brazil has maintained or aggravated two kinds of 'duality'. The first is in the sectoral structure of employment and productivity. Manufacturing employs an abnormally small (and constant, over the post-war period) percentage of the labour force. This reduces incentives to increase the productivity of labour in other sectors, and the result is that a small part of the total Brazilian labour force has experienced a rapid rise in productivity while the rest has been left in stagnation.

The second kind of duality is in the regional structure of manufacturing. Geographically, manufacturing is concentrated in a few states in the centre-south of Brazil. Moreover, labour

---

variables which explain (statistically) the value of the index. Adelman and Morris started with 39 economic, political, and social variables, and decided on the basis of their analysis that 18 were useful in explaining economic development potential. Of these, the 'change in degree of industrialization' was fifth in importance:

'The promotion of industrialization forms one of the keystones of practical development planning. In our model, a more rapid rate of industrialization increases capacity for economic growth by promoting the development of both the financial organization and the human resource base of the economy. The most important of these mechanisms functions through the impact of industrialization in bringing about improvements in financial institutions. This effect contributes 85 per cent to the total multiplier for the change in the degree of industrialization. The remaining 15 per cent is accounted for by the role of rising industrial demand for skilled labor in stimulating measures to increase the capacity of the education system.'

productivity in manufacturing is higher in these more highly industrialized areas. The backward parts of Brazil thus have relatively little manufacturing, and that little tends to be of a low-productivity nature.

2. The regional inequalities in the amount and the productivity of manufacturing in Brazil are common to other countries and to the world as a whole, and therefore to be expected. They are interesting primarily as a clear reminder that industrialization can breed efficiency which in turn breeds further industrialization, whereas backwardness usually breeds inefficiency which in turn makes progress more difficult.

PART IV

Conclusion

8

Strategies and Instruments for Industrialization

M Y purpose in this final chapter is to criticize the policies used to promote industrialization in the post-war period, to suggest what improvements might have been made in them, and to point out what appear to be important implications for goals and strategy in future economic policy.

There is a story about the famous American banker J. P. Morgan. Morgan was discussing a pet project with one of his legal advisers. The adviser told him that the project was illegal. 'Damn it,' replied Morgan, 'I don't pay you to tell me I can't do what I want to do. I pay you to tell me how to do it!' In the present story, the Brazilians are J. P. Morgan and I am the would-be adviser, the problem is economic rather than legal, and there is one more big difference: the Brazilians have already done much of it. I therefore have the benefit of hindsight, as well as that of not being personally involved.

Before entering into the critique, a review of the major findings of this study will be useful.

I. POLICIES AND THEIR RESULTS: A SUMMARY

Industrialization in Brazil prior to the first world war was limited in scope. Early prohibitions of all manufacturing, free trade policies until the mid-eighteenth century, and strong comparative advantage in many primary products combined to keep the economy based largely on agriculture, mining, and foreign trade. The power and outlook of feudal rural landlords and urban commercial interests were the results of these developments, and also became forces resisting moves in other directions. Nevertheless, there was some industrial activity, concentrated especially in textiles, and also in ferrous metals and products, shipbuilding, and food processing.

During the twentieth century a series of shocks in the external sector reduced the availability of imports. Domestic demand during these periods was either very high, or at least only moderately curtailed. The collapse of the market for Brazilian rubber, the first world war, the great depression of the 1930s, and the second world war were each responsible for a wave of import-substituting industrialization. By the end of the second world war Brazil already had a significant industrial sector, producing roughly 20 per cent of G.D.P. and with a broad scope and significant numbers of diverse activities.

In the post-war period, rapid industrialization was promoted by a number of policies, less deliberate at first but becoming quite deliberate under President Kubitschek in the late 1950s. In the area of commercial policy, three major characteristics can be seen. First, there was a wide gap between export and import exchange rates. This provided a strong incentive for domestic manufacture of import substitutes, and a strong disincentive to export anything at all. The results were what one would have predicted: domestic manufactures rapidly replaced imports in the domestic market, while exports of both traditional and manufactured goods stagnated.

Second, there was a great deal of inequality in the inter-industrial structure of protection. One dimension of this inequality is that raw materials and most capital goods received very low or negative protection, intermediate goods low to moderate protection, and finished consumer goods high protection. Complementing the effects of this aspect of commercial policy were Brazil's high apparent comparative advantage in many raw materials, iron and steel, and many capital goods; direct government investment, subsidies, domestic procurement requirements, and other special treatment to induce investment in production of many intermediate products; and the rapidly growing demand for both capital and intermediate goods which was induced by industrialization itself. The results were virtually complete import substitution in finished consumer goods, substantial progress in import substitution in intermediate and even capital goods, and (in rough terms) the reduction and concentration of imports to a relatively small number of raw materials, intermediate and capital goods of which domestic production is as yet either impossible or very costly. Here Brazil's experience differs from most other L.D.C.s. In Brazil the import-substituting industrialization went beyond the stage of consumer non-durables plus assembly of consumer durables, where most other L.D.C.s get 'stuck'.

Another dimension of the inequality in the structure of protection was that most of the industries in which Brazil was already self-sufficient at the end of the second world war received very high protection. These were mostly producers of non-durable consumer goods. A common result was deterioration of efficiency in these industries. The situation in the textile industry, which is the largest of these, was discussed in Chapter 6. Among the 'infants', on the other hand, durable consumer goods received high protection, while most producer goods received negative, low, or moderate protection. For durable consumer goods the high protection appears to be shielding a combination of high taxes, high costs which could have been avoided with less fragmentation and a little less complete import substitution, and some other high costs which may have been unavoidable in such industries in Brazil at the time. As we saw for the automotive industry, most of these high costs in consumer durables seem to have been avoidable. One conclusion from these facts is that removing *all* instances of very high protection could have cost Brazil very little of its industrialization and import substitution, and also could have produced great benefits by forcing older firms to improve their efficiency and by preventing the excess fragmentation of some new industries.

The third important characteristic of commercial policy was the combination of high protection for domestically available products, with low cost (both financial and administrative) of importing products which were not available domestically. In Brazil one does not see the situation (so common in some other L.D.C.s) where new industries have great difficulty in obtaining permission to import inputs even though the inputs are not available domestically, and where extra capacity is built simply to get enough import licences to operate a little more of the presently existing, largely idle plant. Once established, a Brazilian firm might have had to use some inferior or high-cost domestic inputs, but it did not stand idle because it could get neither the domestically produced input nor the licence to import it.

This concern for, or at least lack of harassment of manufacturing firms in Brazil was not limited to commercial policy. Especially for favoured infant industries (mostly intermediate goods plus the automotive industry) the administrative and legal environment was eased, often through 'Executive Groups' in which industry representatives worked intimately with high-level government officials from all the relevant ministries and other government agencies. In addition to the generally low level of administrative harassment, and the special administrative treatment for favoured new industries, there were outright financial subsidies and some-times direct public investment to promote progress in favoured new industries. Behind all the positive inducements to domestic manufacturing were the underdeveloped infrastructure, econ-omy, and society of Brazil. There is a whole set of factors which tend to make costs higher in Brazil than in advanced industrial countries. These are what I have called 'negative subsidies'. Several examples were discussed in Chapters 4 and 6: rate regulation prevented nominal utility rates from keeping up with inflation; the utility firms responded by cutting investment, and service deteriorated steadily. Inflation, together with the legal prohibition on adjustable nominal interest rates, completely eliminated the market for private loan capital of more than 180 days maturity. Inflation also reduced the ability to increase technological efficiency by increasing the difficulty of cost accounting, and decreased the motivation to increase techno-logical efficiency by making inventory management and financial management more important determinants of profits. In other areas of infrastructure, services in Brazil are not as good as in the countries Brazilian industry must compete with. This is true in physical infrastructure (notably public electric power, railroads, and coastal shipping) and also in education and in market organ-ization (the last notably in capital market regulation, and agricul-tural marketing services such as grading, credit, bonded ware-houses, etc.). In many ways Brazilian industry was and is less well served than industry in advanced countries. Brazilian costs are raised, rather than lowered, in relation to costs of competitors.

Looking at 'balances' in Chapter 7 led to the following conclu-sions: First, agricultural output for the domestic market was not unduly depressed by the promotion of industrialization. Here again the Brazilian experience was more successful than that of many other L.D.C.s. Second, the inter-sectoral structure of employment and labour productivity is drastically unbalanced. Manufacturing employs a small and constant share of the labour force, with rapidly growing productivity, while the rest of the economy is left with a large and rapidly growing labour force in which productivity is low and stagnant. This 'duality' is common to most L.D.C.s, but seems to be especially marked in Brazil. Policies tended to raise the private cost of labour, relative to the private cost of capital, and probably caused growth in manufacturing to be much more capital intensive, thus intensifying this imbalance. Third, the regional structure of the amount and the productivity of manufacturing is also extremely unbalanced. Most manufacturing is concentrated in the centre-south, and what little there is in other parts of the country shows very low productivity.

Further investigation of these regional differences in productivity showed that even for firms in the same sector, of the same size, and with the same amount of capital per worker, productivity varies greatly with location. The more industrialized the state in which the firm is located, the higher its efficiency—even after accounting for the other factors of scale and capital per worker. This is additional evidence for a commonly accepted view: industrialization breeds efficiency which in turn breeds more industrialization; backwardness breeds inefficiency which in turn makes progress more difficult.

II. EFFICIENT INTERVENTION FOR INDUSTRIALIZATION

General considerations

As stated in Chapter 1, the idea that industrialization is desirable, and even necessary, for the development of Brazil underlies this whole study. Furthermore, given Brazil's backwardness after the second world war (and still today), some promotional policies were and are necessary to achieve industrialization. The question is what sort of promotion was or would be best.

In Chapter 1 the reasons for intervention in international trade and industrialization in Brazil were discussed. First some 'static' reasons were mentioned. Monopoly power in international trade can be exploited by taxes on trade. Brazilian coffee is perhaps as good an example of this as any in the world today, but is probably the only example in the Brazilian case.

Several other reasons for intervention had to do with differences between domestic costs or values as perceived by private individuals, and as perceived by society—i.e. in the judgement of the Government. The appropriate intervention here would be either to remove the differences through domestic taxes or subsidies, or to provide better information, or to bypass the differences by direct public investment. One such case had to do with surplus labour: wages might be more than the alternative marginal product of labour. This distortion does appear to exist in Brazil.

Other reasons for intervention which were discussed were external economies, and large projects with long pay-out periods. Direct public investment is often the only practical solution in the latter case, and one important possible solution in the former. External economies usually involve infrastructure, in which public investment is generally the rule. As shown in Chapter 7 and Appendix 2, these external economies can also involve relations among manufacturing firms only, and appear to be very important determinants of industrial efficiency in Brazil. To the extent that optimal public investment in infrastructure does not induce enough investment in manufacturing to exhaust external economies, then further intervention is justified in manufacturing. This further intervention could be some mixture of better planning, direct public investment, and subsidies to private investors, the last two obviously only in areas which produce external economies.

Where does this leave us? There is no question that subsidies, where justified, are to be preferred to protection. This is not only on the grounds of the theory of international trade. The differences in dynamic effects on technological efficiency are perhaps even more important. Protection reduces incentives to increase technological efficiency. Foreign competition is reduced or excluded, and domestic competition seldom works very well in the smaller and less well-organized markets of L.D.C.s. The profit incentive would still result in minimizing costs if it were strong enough, but all too often owners and managers prefer a quiet life. This seems to have been the case in many Brazilian firms, with the inflation increasing the difficulty of controlling costs and at the same time increasing the ease of raising prices, while protection made high-cost operations possible in many sectors. Subsidies, on the other hand, can often be designed to increase technological efficiency: they can be made available for re-equipment, labour training, etc.

Once granted, protection is difficult to reduce; direct financial subsidies, however, are much more subject to review and to cutbacks. Protection could be designed to be temporary and could be reduced in regular, planned steps, but in fact this is seldom done. On the whole, then, protection is not as good an instrument as subsidies, because in the static sense it introduces a second distortion rather than eliminating the original, and also because it furnishes less incentive for improvements in technological efficiency over time.

Critique of policies

In fact, the policies actually followed were high protection, deficient infrastructure, and positive subsidies and other promotion of infant industries.

Most Brazilian governments have not been bashful about public investment, either in infrastructure or in manufacturing. But as I have argued, infrastructure on balance is deficient in Brazil. It is deficient both in quantity and in quality—in other words, both in amount of investment and efficiency of operation. The value that users of phone service, electric power service, etc., in Brazil receive for the taxes and fees that they pay is far below that in most advanced countries. The idea of government intervention in infrastructure is to provide services at lower real costs than would be possible if each industrial firm had to provide these services for themselves, or if private firms provided them. In fact, government interference with private firms in infrastructure, and deficient operation of public firms, has resulted in higher real costs of infrastructure services than in advanced countries, and in some cases in higher real costs than would have been likely in Brazil if the Government had not intervened.

The way protection was used leaves much to be desired. The highest protection—which was indeed very high—tended to be given to already well-established ('daddy') industries. There is no justification for this, and the results, as might have been expected, have often been stagnation or even deterioration in efficiency and in exports. Better policies would have included a real devaluation towards the free trade exchange rate, plus subsidies to exports of manufactures, and reductions in most or all of the highest tariffs, especially for 'daddy' industries. The results of these differences would have been the elimination or reduction of inefficiency in the 'daddy' industries, elimination or delay in the establishment of some of the most costly new import substituting industries, and more exports to pay for the increased imports which would therefore be necessary. In addition, an earlier start would have been made on switching the export mix towards products with higher income elasticities of demand.

It is possible to get a rough quantitative estimate of the cost of protection to Brazil. This cost consists of several elements. One is due to what economists call misallocation: producing the wrong outputs, or using the wrong inputs. Examples are using Brazilian coal in making steel—imported coal would be much more efficient —and producing synthetic rubber from alcohol made from sugarcane. These processes are inherently inefficient—the best managers and engineers in the world could not make them competitive with alternatives. A second element of the cost of protection is due to technological, engineering, or management inefficiency: not getting the most output for a given input, regardless of what those outputs or inputs might be. The high costs of the Brazilian textile industry are an example of this; this sector *could* be efficient in Brazil; it simply suffers from obsolete technology and incompetent management. We say that protection is responsible for these costs because, in the absence of protection, these inefficient activities would either disappear, or be forced to become competitive. Processes such as the coal and rubber production mentioned earlier would be driven out of existence by competing imports, and the textile industry would either cut its costs or similarly be driven out of business.

Appendix 4 is a rough analysis of these costs of protection.[1] The results can be summarized as follows: the cost of protection (as it existed in 1967) to Brazil was perhaps 8–10 per cent of G.N.P. Only a small part of this—less than 1 per cent of G.N.P.— was the result of misallocation. The rest consists of monopoly profits plus avoidable higher costs. This implies that moving to free trade in 1967 would have resulted in a saving amounting to only something less than 1 per cent of G.N.P., through substitu-

---

[1] As we have seen, protection in general implies taxing exports as well as imports. The costs of both are necessarily included in this analysis.

tion of more profitable export activities for less profitable import substituting activities. A further, larger saving and redistribution amounting to perhaps 8–10 per cent of G.N.P. would have resulted from cost reductions and the elimination of monopoly profits.[1]

In earlier years protection and export taxes were much higher than in 1967. Considering the average of the period 1954–64, the cost due only to misallocation amounted to at least 4 per cent of G.N.P., with the total cost rising to perhaps 10–20 per cent of G.N.P. The estimate of misallocation costs of 4 per cent implies that under free trade imports might have increased by anywhere from 25 per cent (elasticity assumptions of Appendix 3) to as much as 100 per cent (high estimates of the elasticities). Such a re-allocation would have had a great impact on domestic manufacturing, implying a direct effect of perhaps a 10–40 per cent reduction of domestic manufacturing, and indirect effects added to that.

These estimates are very rough, but serve as a quantitative statement of my conclusion that very high protection was not necessary to induce most of the import substitution that actually occurred in Brazil. Reduction of protection to, say, a maximum of 50 per cent for daddy industries and 100 per cent for infants, would have lowered average protection to somewhere around 30–60 per cent, and still permitted virtually all of the import substitution which occurred. What very high protection did accomplish was to permit significant deterioration of efficiency in many Brazilian firms which could have been competitive (or nearly so) under a better set of policies. The 'quiet life' effects of protection—permitting technological and managerial efficiency to deteriorate—seem to have been much more costly than the misallocation effects.[2]

'Quiet life' effects seem more important *per se* when we realize that economic development is a process taking place over time. A large part of growth in output—especially output *per capita*, which is an essential part of development—is caused by increases in technological efficiency. If protection reduces the search for

[1] The elimination of monopoly profits is a saving to the Brazilian consumer, but only a redistribution from the viewpoint of the entire economy.
[2] This may well be the case in most other countries as well. See Harvey Leibenstein, 'Allocative Efficiency *vs.* "X-Efficiency"', *American Economic Review*, June 1966.

N

better methods, better organization, better maintenance of equipment, and all the other elements of technological efficiency, the economy will suffer a permanent and increasing cost. This last effect seems to have been very significant in Brazil.[1]

We can conclude that Brazil would have been better off if infrastructure, including education, market organization, etc., had been better built and better operated; and if in addition direct subsidies to wage and other costs had been employed (as much as possible to pay for training, apprenticeship programmes, re-equipment, and other real-cost-reducing actions). To recommend such a programme as a *complete* substitute for protection, however, would be nonsense. The principal reason that such a programme would be economically justified in Brazil is the very reason why it cannot be done: Brazil is an infant economy; underdeveloped; poor in modern institutions and human resources. Where do we get the men to plan, to administer, and to operate these modern, efficient infrastructure activities? Where do we get the financial resources to pay for them? Where do we get the political push, even if the other resources were available? The plain fact is that a less-developed country such as Brazil cannot find the men to build and operate an efficient, modern infrastructure, including an education system and government regulatory agencies, etc., nor can it find the tax base and the political power to levy the taxes to pay for these things.

Protection, on the other hand, is much easier. It can be seen as the most economical instrument to foster industrialization, from the Government's point of view. It requires few people to design and operate, and increases revenue rather than expenses. By administrative fiat it makes up for high-cost and unreliable energy, high cost or unreliable transport, lack of middle-level manpower, telephones that don't work, and all the other difficulties of doing business in a less-developed country. It calls forth whatever entrepreneurial talent exists and permits it to function, although it does not induce it to function as efficiently as possible. I have seen industries functioning in Brazil in the face of lack of

[1] See Henry J. Bruton, 'Productivity Growth in Latin America', *American Economic Review*, December 1967. Bruton's logic is questionable on several grounds; but his observation that productivity growth was unusually slow in five Latin American countries (including Brazil) since the second world war, and his conclusion that lack of motivation was one major reason, probably have much validity.

everything—everything except a protected market and reasonably good raw material supply. The people who run these industries are conscious of their need for better services, and the existence of these industries does increase the pressure (à la Hirschman) for improvements in infrastructure. Protection may meet with political opposition in an agricultural country—as it did in Brazil for most of three centuries—but the cost is less direct and can be made to fall more on the common man. For these reasons, and perhaps others, it seems to be easier and even more attractive to government to allow high-cost domestic industries to exist by forbidding competing imports, rather than by subsidizing the domestic producers directly.[1]

This, it seems to me, is a gloomy conclusion, because of the many faults of protection. It is extremely unlikely that an L.D.C. will design its system of protection so as to minimize the inherent disincentives to efficiency. Old-established industries are likely to have the political power to get high protection, and may well prefer a quiet, protected life to one of competition. This is especially likely if the domestic market is a large one. Brazil's large domestic market has been both a help and a hindrance to progress. The larger scale of demand made a given amount of import substitution less uneconomical, and especially made possible the backwards vertical integration of Brazilian industry to intermediate and capital goods. But it also made most Brazilian manufacturers content with the domestic market.

Brazilian industry as it *now* stands is probably far better able to prosper and continue to expand without high protection, than it was fifteen or twenty years ago. The tariff reform of 1967 went a long way towards making Brazil a reasonably open economy. Adjustments will continue to be necessary, but I do not doubt that continued downward pressure on protection, if coupled with progress in infrastructure, market organization, etc., will be beneficial in the long run.[2]

[1] Cf. Albert O. Hirschman, 'The Political Economy of Import-Substituting Industrialization in Latin America', *Quarterly Journal of Economics*, February 1968, especially pp. 24–31.

[2] The most recent news from Brazil, relative to early 1969, indicates a rise in protection and in autarkic rhetoric.

III. GOALS AND STRATEGIES FOR THE FUTURE

The post-war industrialization in Brazil has been the major contributor to a significant increase in average *per capita* income, and a significant modernization. The criticisms made and the changes suggested in this study are in the nature of how to make a good thing better. This final section will be devoted to discussing some goals which should receive more emphasis than they did in the past, and some strategic considerations for policy formulation.

The structure of employment and labour productivity

In Chapter 7 it was shown that manufacturing's share in total employment has remained constant, and extremely low, while the share in total output increased rapidly and to a high level. Shifting employment into industry is an essential aspect of development through industrialization, and Brazil has not developed very well in this dimension.

There are several reasons for wanting to increase industry's share of employment. The first is to reduce the duality between industry and the rest of the economy. The less rapidly labour is absorbed by industry, the more labour will be available for agriculture and services, and the less will be the incentives to increase labour productivity in these latter sectors. Since the productivity of labour in industry tends to be higher than in other sectors in any case, a low rate of labour absorption by industry only aggravates a natural tendency towards this duality. One small part of the labour force experiences rapid productivity increases, while the rest is left behind.[1]

A second reason to increase industry's share of employment is that many of the 'external economies' of industrialization, and the modernization of the society, are the results of expanded employment, rather than output, in the industrial sector.

The way to induce greater absorption of labour in industry is to eliminate or reverse the biases which have reduced the private cost of capital equipment relative to the private cost of labour. Past policies such as S.U.M.O.C. 113 and the structure of pro-

[1] In technical terms, what is advocated is simply an allocation which would be nearer the social optimum. Because of the factors mentioned, this would involve a lower capital–labour ratio in industry, and hence lower productivity of labour in industry and higher productivity of labour in the rest of the economy. Total output would be greater, as well as more evenly distributed.

tection have tended to reduce the prices of machinery and equipment (at least for favoured users), and other policies such as *estabilidade*, shortfalls on government contributions to social security, and poor education have tended to increase the private cost of labour. Removing or even reversing these biases would be highly desirable. Subsidies to industry should either be biased towards reducing the private cost of labour, or at least be neutral as between labour and capital. Higher government contributions towards wage costs and better public education are examples of the first; income tax exemptions is an example of the second.

Export policy

Brazil's lack of interest in exporting is easy to understand. First of all, possibilities for trade *are* limited. Some expansion of exports of primary products is possible and would be profitable, but would probably not be sufficient for leading long-run development. As for manufactured exports, most countries discriminate against imports of manufactures, and of course Brazil faces some advanced competitors. A second reason is that domestic sales are much easier than exports, even in a neutral policy environment. This is especially true for industrial products, where export sales generally require setting up foreign offices, and often present difficulties of language, servicing, stocking of parts, etc., etc. Brazil's domestic market is a large one, and it is natural for Brazilian manufacturers to tend to be satisfied with it. A third reason is that a number of Brazil's new industrial firms are linked to parent companies in advanced countries which do not want the Brazilian firms to export.

No country has become an exporter of a large range of manufactures without first gaining experience in producing for its domestic market. But even this experience, once gained, does not in itself guarantee future export possibilities. To counteract the inherent attractiveness of the domestic market, policies must give inducements to exports—or at the very least be neutral. There must be inducements to industry to attain competitive costs, and no barriers to export sales for those that succeed. This has not been the case in Brazil. Policies have lessened the inducement to become competitive, and the over-valued export exchange rate has meant that Brazilian manufacturers had to be *more than competitive* in order to compete, and even then saw export profit margins which were only a fraction of domestic ones. Policies have increased the natural preference for the domestic market, and the self-confirming prophecy has been confirmed: exports will not be possible, therefore there is no sense in taking steps to encourage them, and therefore exports have not appeared.

It is not easy to estimate how rapidly Brazil could expand exports of manufactures. There is evidence that much more is possible than has been achieved; many industries have a few firms which are regular exporters. On the other hand, many of the problems are complex, and cannot be erased simply by changes in Brazil's commercial policy. In any case, Brazil *must* expand exports of manufactures. Imports as a share of G.D.P. cannot be continuously reduced, and therefore the export growth rate is a long-run constraint on the G.D.P. growth rate. While it is clear that Brazil could expand exports without changing the present product mix, it is doubtful that this expansion could continue at a rate which Brazil would regard as satisfactory for growth of G.D.P. A shift in the export mix to products with higher income elasticities of demand is needed, and this has got to include manufactures. This will not happen unless both manufacturers and government policy-makers reverse their inward orientation. The bias against export of manufactures, recently reduced, is still enormous; the incentives and the possibilities to reduce costs, recently increased, are still weak.

A shift towards a more export-promoting stance could benefit Brazilian consumers as well. Increased exports of primary products would probably imply higher domestic prices for food. But increased inducements to exports of manufactures could mean greater productivity, faster innovation, better quality control, and greater economies of scale for Brazilian industrial products.

Policies to reduce the bias against exporting would be quite easy to design. The first step would be a devaluation in real terms, to move the export exchange rate perhaps half-way from its 1967 level to the free trade rate. Drawbacks and other existing incentives to exports of manufactures should be continued, and new measures such as income tax write-offs, a bank to finance exports of manufactures, etc., should be considered. Selling manufactured products for export should be made at least as profitable as selling them domestically.

Current income or future growth

The most important reasons for intervention to promote industry are based on dynamic considerations, and involve sacrificing maximum allocative efficiency now in order to shift to a structure of production which will permit increased income later. It is true that there are some static reasons for intervention, and that intervention may have some positive effects on present income. But on balance I expect that optimum intervention would imply reducing present income. Balancing this cost against future benefits is anything but a trivial problem.

To reduce the sacrifice of current income, intervention should minimize the amount of non-competitive production which is permitted, and the degree of its non-competitiveness. If industrialization is to be promoted, why not set a uniform level of subsidy or protection, and let resources flow into the least inefficient branches of industry? This argument, often heard, has much to recommend it. My own judgement is that there probably should be a maximum level. The problem is that in order to be effective, this maximum may be far more than is required by many industries. The example of the Brazilian textile industry is very persuasive: it does not make sense to grant *more* protection than an industry needs. A ceiling on the strength of intervention is probably a good thing, but it is far from clear that the ceiling should be the floor as well.

A number of factors may make a uniform low level of intervention unproductive. Uncertainty is inherent in the problem: what one needs to do is to predict Brazil's future structure of comparative advantage. This is a little difficult! Not only Brazilian costs, but also competitors' costs are continuously changing, and one cannot know for sure which infants will grow up to be competitive, or when. There may be infants which will grow up quickly, but need relatively high protection or subsidies at the start. Paying too much attention to current costs may mean no progress. The importance of external economies also makes a less specialized development look more attractive, especially in a very large country. In addition to external economies in the economic sense, there are similar effects in the political sense. It is my impression that in Brazil the broad nature of the post-war industrialization made it easier to get the required political support.

Moreover, the more industry there is, the greater will be the pressure for improving infrastructure, thus lowering costs.

In the long run, the costs of not developing may be far greater than the costs of protecting a few inefficient new manufacturing processes. The combination of uncertainty and external economies may thus mean that fairly strong, fairly general promotion of new industry is the 'minimum regret' strategy: the cost of being wrong might well be least with a policy of widespread, strong protection or subsidy for new industrial activities.[1]

This policy also is easy to describe. Assuming that infrastructure, education, market organization, etc., are improved but continue to be somewhat 'underdeveloped' in Brazil, and also that outright subsidies to manufacturing will be limited, then some protection will still be required. The system might be designed as follows: all imports, without exception, would be subject to a minimum revenue tariff of 10 or 15 per cent. Manufactures which are already established in Brazil might have a tariff of 30 or 40 per cent, and new manufacturing activities might receive higher protection up to perhaps 70 or 80 per cent.[2] This last high tariff should be granted for a limited period only; say about five years. Tariffs on all manufactures should be periodically reviewed for products which could get along with less protection. Pleas to raise tariffs should be met with offers of assistance in reducing costs, such as re-equipment loans, better infrastructure, etc. Such a policy would increase imports only slightly, and would be consistent with the devaluation and other export-promotion policies suggested above. Whether such a policy could be administered as planned, and especially whether the excesses of protecting industries that don't need it (or that need it too much) could be avoided, is a big problem.

[1] This advice might be less good in other situations. One of the crucial determining factors is surely the size of the country. Where markets are smaller than in Brazil (as they are in most countries) more selectivity may be better. Moreover, some of the advantages of a 'big' industrialization probably depend on industry's share in G.N.P., rather than its absolute size. For example, the political pressure for better infrastructure, market organization, education, etc., is surely a question of share rather than absolute size. Thus, in a small country a more selective industrialization may still be 'big' enough to secure the same 'external economies' which in a very big country like Brazil may require a more complete industrialization.

[2] Product protection relative to the export exchange rate, assuming that the latter had been devalued as recommended above. Many observers have made suggestions for tariff reform along these lines.

Productivity and efficiency trends

Any process of development should aim for increasing productivity and for internationally competitive costs. There is nothing in infant industries or infant economies, imperfections in world markets, changing terms of trade, exploitation by advanced countries, patriotic or military considerations that alters the fact that it doesn't pay to produce for ever at higher costs than you can buy for. Brazilian policies have paid too little attention to future competitiveness, and the results show that too little has been achieved. This is most striking in those industries that were already well established at the start of the post-war period, where efficiency was allowed to stagnate or deteriorate behind high protection.

It is striking how frequently one encounters the idea that Brazil should not import anything that it can possibly produce domestically. The extra cost to the consumer is rarely considered. But Brazilian neglect of the goal of efficiency is not only important for the present; the greatest part of growth in output in all countries is due to productivity increases, and I believe it crucial that this goal receive higher priority in Brazil than it has in the past.

To the extent that possibilities for foreign trade are limited, it may pay for Brazil to produce anything and everything which is demanded domestically. But to the extent that trade is possible, there will be a net present cost to producing goods which could be imported for less. Changes in policy to increase the incentives and the ability to reduce such costs over time would be of great benefit to Brazil.

PART V

Appendices

Appendix 1
The Steel Industry
by WERNER BAER[1] (*Vanderbilt University*)

THIS appendix is divided into four parts. First, there is a brief description of the basic technological-economic facts of the steel industry (with special emphasis on the type of technological information relevant to the Brazilian industry); the following section will contain a review of the evolution of the industry; in the third section a review of government policies relevant to the industry, and finally an evaluation of the performance of the industry.

I. TECHNO-ECONOMIC FACTS ON STEEL

The making of final steel products involves four basic stages: the mining and treatment of raw materials, the reduction of iron ore into pig iron, the transformation of pig iron into steel, and the rolling of steel ingots into various steel shapes.[2]

A fully integrated mill includes all these stages (possibly excluding mining). The final products coming out of the rolling mill can be divided into two basic types: flat and non-flat products. The former includes such products as sheets, tin plate, etc.; i.e. products used in the automobile, shipbuilding, tin-canning, boiler-making, and many other industries. Non-flat products include bars, rods, rails, seamless tubes, heavy sections, etc. Many of the latter are associated with housing construction and road building.

In addition to fully integrated firms (specializing either in flats

---

[1] This appendix is based on Baer's forthcoming study: *The Development of the Brazilian Steel Industry*, Vanderbilt University Press. Bergsman assisted on some of the analysis in this appendix.

[2] One of the standard reference works for steel making is: United States Steel Corporation, *The Making, Shaping and Treating of Steel*, eighth edition, Pittsburgh: U.S. Steel Corporation, 1964.

or non-flats, or producing both types of products), one finds in Brazil many semi-integrated firms. These may be firms specializing in the production of just pig iron and pig-iron products, or firms making steel ingots from pig iron bought from outside or from scrap and rolling these ingots into shapes (some of these firms specialize in 'special steels'), or firms specializing only in rolling steel ingots bought from other firms into shapes.

Blast furnaces using charcoal rather than coke are still widespread in Brazil. In the mid-1960s about 40 per cent of the country's pig-iron production was still based on charcoal. Charcoal in Brazil comes mainly from natural forests or from eucalyptus plantations in Minas Gerais. It is relatively cheap owing to the low-wage rural labour employed and the abundance of land. The use of charcoal permits substantial capital savings, since costly coke ovens and ancillary units are not needed. The firm Belgo-Mineira, with an output of about 400,000 tons annually, is the world's largest integrated steel firm based on charcoal.[1]

The economist's traditional concern with capital- *versus* labour-intensive techniques is not too relevant in choosing steel technology, because of scale economies as well as for other reasons inherent in the technology. For example, the blast furnaces of large firms, producing 700 or more tons of pig iron per day, cannot rely on labour-intensive methods of charging the furnace. Given the large amounts of materials which have to be handled, the use of mechanized techniques is inevitable. Charcoal-using furnaces in Brazil have a greater degree of labour-absorption capacity, because of the labour-intensive methods in collecting wood and making charcoal.

The same situation holds for the steel shop. The choices in the rolling mills are even fewer and narrower. Older mills still use semi-automatic equipment; in smaller Brazilian mills one can still find workers pushing billets back and forth through rollers. However, this method cannot be used in the production of flat products.

---

[1] The future growth of charcoal-based steel production in Brazil is limited. With the vanishing natural wood supply close to the firms, and the possibility of the rise of labour costs and the costs of land which would have to be used for eucalyptus plantations, in the not-too-distant future the cost advantages of charcoal-based production may vanish. For firms with no plantations, the cost of charcoal is already increasing since the natural forests are farther and farther away from the mills.

The lack of the type of technological choice which is traditionally of interest to the economist, and the high capital intensity of the processes employed, do not mean that the steel industry has a small direct employment impact. Much labour is absorbed in a whole series of ancillary activities. Foundries making ingot moulds are usually an integral part of the firm and in Brazil the methods used are not overly automatic; maintenance workshops producing parts for all sections are labour-intensive in nature and larger in Brazil than in more advanced countries due to the difficulty of obtaining spare parts; the frequent relining of vessels and ladles with refractory bricks is by its nature labour-intensive. Thus, in 1964, with an output of over 3 million tons of ingot steel, the entire industry gave direct employment to more than 80,000 workers (not counting charcoal workers, office workers in headquarters and commercial branches of the firms, coal miners, etc.).

Brazil possesses most of the raw materials and other natural resources necessary for the manufacture of steel: iron ore, limestone, manganese, water, and a huge hydro-electric potential. The country has one of the world's largest iron-ore reserves. (Known reserves in 1966 amounted to more than 27 billion tons.) In quality these ores are among the best in the world, the iron content varying between 58 and 66 per cent.

Coal is the only important raw material which is in short supply. The only coal deposits in Brazil are of poor quality (owing to high ash content) and cannot be exclusively relied on for producing coke. The domestic coal which can be used has to go through expensive washing operations. Thus, since the introduction of coke-using blast furnaces in Brazil, the major imported current input has been coal.[1] Until the end of 1966, Brazilian mills using coke were forced by the Government to consume 40 per cent domestic coal in order to protect the domestic coal industry. This requirement is being relaxed, but the industry is still forced to use the same absolute amount of expensive domestic coal.

[1] In the decade from the mid-fifties to the mid-sixties Brazil has become a major iron ore exporter. The coal used by the steel industry is usually shipped in the empty returning ore vessels.

Investment costs and economies of scale

It is extremely difficult to predict the exact cost of a new integrated steel works. The initial cost estimates are usually prepared by a specialized engineering firm. These estimates are based on a variety of sources, some of which give exact information while others simply provide the engineers with an informed guess.

In less-developed countries, investment in an integrated steel mill usually involves complementary investments. For example, the erection of an integrated steel mill might require a substantial expansion of the regional power generating complex. It probably will involve substantial investments in the transport system which will serve the steel complex. The total complementary investments attributable to the steel mill are difficult to estimate. They might occur over a longer period of time. For example, some transport infrastructure might have to exist even prior to the beginning of the construction of the steel complex; the construction of such facilities, however, will also serve as a basis for other investment activities in the area. Other external investments might only be undertaken after the firm has reached a certain production capacity (e.g. the existing power supply might be adequate in the initial stage of a steel firm). In short, it would be difficult, and probably not too conclusive an exercise, to try to compute external investment costs and returns due strictly to the steel mill.

The original estimates of investment expenditures for steel mills usually turn out to be lower than the actual expenditures. Cost underestimation is even greater in a less developed country like Brazil. In the case of both Usiminas and Cosipa, the two newest mills, the construction period was longer than anticipated, which resulted in substantially higher costs. (Also, owing to the inflationary conditions in Brazil nominal costs in cruzeiros increased substantially above the original estimates.) For Usiminas, instead of the originally estimated cost of U.S.$238 million, actual costs were about U.S.$325 million.[1] Although the original cost estimate for Cosipa was U.S.$151·5 million (this excludes financial costs), the estimate before beginning construction was about U.S.$216

---

[1] Not included here are expenditures which Usiminas had to incur for building a city for its workers. The mill was located in an uninhabited area and thus substantial expenditures to build a city had to be incurred. The costs for this amounted to about U.S.$60 million.

million (which includes an additional U.S.$50 million for financial expenditures, e.g. interest on debt, etc.). The actual cost of Cosipa grew to about U.S.$299 million (excluding financial expenditures). The steep rise was mainly due to the very high construction costs for the mill; it was discovered only after work was begun that most of the terrain was swampy; this raised construction costs from an estimated U.S.$103 million to about U.S.$190 million!

One should be careful in trying to estimate from this information a capital–output ratio for the steel industry, or an accelerator-type relationship. Although Usiminas and Cosipa are producing at an annual rate of about 600,000 and 400,000 tons in 1966, their present rolling mill capacity is sufficient for 1·5 million tons. The expansion plans of Usiminas and Cosipa, costing U.S.$80 and U.S.$50–60 million respectively, will increase their actual productive capacity to 1 million tons each. Most of these sums will be spent to increase the capacity of sections other than the rolling mills. Most new integrated steel mills deliberately construct rolling capacity substantially greater than blast furnace and steel-shop capacities, because it is less expensive than to build up the rolling mill gradually. For example, in order to produce wide plates of over two-and-a-half metres, a mill of about one million ton capacity is necessary, even though at the time of installation of such a mill, there may be no market to use the plant fully. The blast furnace and steel-shop sections, on the other hand, can more easily be built up gradually.

The importance of economies of scale in an integrated steel plant can be understood by an examination of Tables A.1 and A.2. These were estimates made by the Economic Commission for Latin America for hypothetical Latin American plants. The cost of installed blast furnace capacity per ton of pig iron falls by about 35 per cent when comparing a blast furnace plant of 400 thousand and 1·5 million ton capacity; for an S.M. steel plant the cost of installed capacity per ton of steel ingot falls by 48 per cent; and for flat rolled products the cost of installed rolling mill capacity per ton falls by 42 per cent. These scale economies reduce cost of production per ton of pig iron, steel ingots, and flat-rolled products (again when increasing output from 400 thousand to 1·5 million tons) by 12·8, 16·5, and 28·7 per cent respectively. Economies of scale for non-flat rolling mills are not

O

TABLE A.1
ECONOMIES OF SCALE IN STEEL: INSTALLED PRODUCTION CAPACITY
(dollars of installed capacity per ton)

Section	Capacity in tons per year						
	100	200	400	500	800	1,000	1,500
Blast furnace: investment per ton of pig iron	94·73	86·07	75·00	69·33	57·53	52·60	48·33
Open hearth (S.M.) steel furnace: investment per ton of steel ingot	74·60	69·07	59·07	53·13	42·73	37·27	30·47
Flat products rolling mill: investment per ton	482·07	427·20	328·67	286·07	219·19	198·33	191·87
Total investment per ton of output	724·15	635·42	484·51	428·76	330·04	314·38	281·86
Per cent reduction		11·4	23·1	13·0	23·4	9·5	3·3

Note: These estimates were made using international equipment costs, which were increased by 20 per cent to take into account greater transport and assembly cost of equipment in Latin American countries as opposed to more industrialized countries.
Source: E.C.L.A., *La Economia Siderúrgica de America Latina*, February 1966 (mimeo).

TABLE A.2
ECONOMIES OF SCALE IN STEEL: HYPOTHETICAL PRODUCTION COSTS IN INTEGRATED FIRMS PRODUCING FLAT PRODUCTS
(dollars per ton)

Product	Annual capacity in thousands of tons						
	100	200	400	500	800	1,000	1,500
Pig iron (using 20 per cent sinter)	55·04	49·52	45·38	43·88	41·83	40·83	39·57
Steel ingot (S.M. with oxygen injection)	95·22	87·31	77·89	74·70	70·22	68·02	64·97
Flat rolled products	235·49	212·58	169·55	158·29	135·05	126·74	120·85

Source: Same as Table A.1.

quite as striking as economies in flat products; however, the capital cost per ton in these mills is also substantially lower (about one-third of the capital cost per ton in flat mills).

A glance at Table A.3 shows that by the mid-sixties only Volta

TABLE A.3
CAPACITY AND OUTPUT OF THE BRAZILIAN IRON AND STEEL INDUSTRY (in 1,000 tons)

A. Totals for Brazil

(a) *Pig iron*

	Output	Capacity	Output as per cent of 1965 capacity
1964	2,446		54
1965	2,259	4,541	50
1966	2,939		65

(b) *Steel ingot*

	Output	Capacity	Output as per cent of 1965 capacity
1964	3,044		60
1965	2,978	5,078	59
1966	3,775		74

(c) *Flat products*

	Output	Capacity	Output as per cent of 1965 capacity
1964	902		15
1965	1,019	5,927	17
1966	1,359		23

(d) *Non-flat products*

	Output	Capacity	Output as per cent of 1965 capacity
1964	1,207		43
1965	1,078	2,797	38
1966	1,317		47

B. Individual firms

	Output 1964	Output 1965	Output 1966	Capacity 1965	Output as per cent of 1965 capacity 1964	1965	1966
(a) *Pig iron*							
Volta Redonda	957	927	875	1,020	94	91	86
Cosipa		43	401	565		8	71
Usiminas	276	382	505	575	48	66	88
Belgo-Mineira	390	338	422	538	72	63	78
Mannesmann	170	122	80	280	57	44	29
Acesita	63	76	83	165	38	46	50
(b) *Steel ingot*							
Volta Redonda	1,218	1,256	1,248	1,400	87	90	89
Cosipa		30	431	625		5	69
Usiminas	276	383	529	634	43	60	83
Belgo-Mineira	421	409	475	450	93	91	105
Mannesmann	214	195	198	328	65	59	60
Acesita	82	91	103	120	68	76	86

TABLE A.3—*continued*

(c) *Plates*

	Output—1965	Capacity—1965
Volta Redonda	97	638
Cosipa	21	800
Usiminas	140	800

(d) *Hot rolled steel*

Volta Redonda	176	525
Cosipa	66	600
Usiminas	23	750
Acesita	27	43
Belgo-Mineira	61	105

Source: *Boletim IBS*, Instituto Brasileiro de Siderurgia; *Siderurgia-Metalurgia-Mineração*, Editora Banas, S.A., 1967; unpublished reports of Booz, Allen, and Hamilton to the B.N.D.E. and special study of Technometal for B.N.D.E.

Redonda had reached production levels where scale economies were reasonably well exploited. Of course, one cannot exactly apply the estimated scale economies of Tables A.1 and A.2 to individual Brazilian plants. The scale economies estimates were made for a flat products plant. Since Volta Redonda produces both flat and non-flat products, scale economies in its rolling mills were probably smaller than those indicated in Tables A.1 and A.2 for production levels of 1 million tons. However, Volta Redonda's expansion programme could expand its production to levels of 2·5 million in the mid-1970s and the levels of output of Cosipa and Usiminas, specializing in flat products, should pass the 1 million mark in the early seventies. Thus, by the next decade Brazil's largest mills should be producing at levels commensurate with taking advantage of scale economies.

The production level of Belgo-Mineira in Table A.3 should be analysed with proper qualifications. Although pig-iron production was only slightly above 400,000 tons, produced in two separate places, the pig iron was based on charcoal. It was already mentioned above that charcoal blast furnaces involve about half of the investment cost of coke-based blast furnaces. In addition, until the mid-sixties charcoal was cheaper than coke. Since pig-iron production at Belgo-Mineira is cheaper than at a coke-based plant and since pig iron is the main input into the steel furnace, the lower level scale economies in the steel shop of Belgo-Mineira were more than made up by the lower-priced input. At the rolling mill stage, Belgo-Mineira produces only a small amount of flat products[1] (mainly of the type which do not require the same scale as the products of Usiminas or Volta Redonda for economical production), and since the unit costs for non-flats are already quite satisfactory at levels of 300,000 to 400,000 tons, the mill is producing at a relatively satisfactory level.

Most other Brazilian steel firms produce non-flat products or special steels, where scale does not play the role it does in flat products. However, there can be no doubt that higher levels of production of finished rolled products at plants like Mannesmann and Acesita would substantially reduce the fixed cost per ton of output.

The expansion of the Brazilian steel industry during the 1950s and 1960s has probably deviated from the economic optimum by creating too many new firms rather than expanding old ones. The creation of two new mills, each producing less than 1 million tons per year in their initial stages, certainly cost more than one mill would have. Presently it appears that political pressures from the states of Guanabara and Bahia may result in one or even two additional mills being built before the currently existing mills are up to final optimal capacity.

It is interesting to compare the production levels and capacity estimates which are reproduced in Table A.3. As we have noted, when building an integrated steel mill, the initial production capacity of the rolling mills usually far exceeds the initial capacity of the blast furnace and steel-shop sections. The capacity figure for the blast furnaces should also be taken with some qualifications. A blast furnace is extremely flexible; through the use of beneficiated ores and/or injection of fuel oil, many blast furnaces have wound up producing substantially more than they originally were expected to produce. Another qualification to Table A.3 is the generally depressed state of the Brazilian economy during 1965–6.

It is interesting to note the decrease in the import content of investment projects in the steel industry in Brazil. The foreign cost of investments amounted to about 60–68 per cent of total expenditures in the 1950s, and dropped to a range of 25–39 per

[1] Belgo-Mineira uses a Steckel Mill, which is a hot reversing sheet mill adequate for the production of flat products on a small scale. Investment in such a mill is much lower than a regular flat products mill. The Belgo-Mineira Steckel Mill has an annual capacity of 120,000 tons.

cent in the steel investment plans for the late 1960s and early 1970s. This reflects the impact of the import substitution industrialization which made it possible for Brazil to rely to a greater extent on its own sources of supply. For example, the foreign cost of the blast furnace of Cosipa (built in the 1950s) amounted to over 80 per cent, while the plans for new blast furnaces at Volta Redonda to be built in the late sixties have a foreign cost component of only 35 per cent; the drop of foreign cost for the construction of the L.D. steel plant was from about 70 per cent to about 33 per cent; a substantial drop can also be seen in the foundry. The drop was less dramatic in the rolling mills, where most of the machinery still has to be imported; however, there is now a greater capacity in Brazil for producing medium-size rolling mill cylinders, various types of cranes, etc. Furthermore, there are now several Brazilian firms which are competent to act as general contractor to construct a mill.

II. A SHORT HISTORICAL SUMMARY OF STEELMAKING IN BRAZIL

Iron working activities in Brazil can be traced back to the middle of the sixteenth century. Forges operated at various times in the present state of São Paulo in the sixteenth and seventeenth centuries and a number of them operated in Minas Gerais at the time of the gold rush in the eighteenth century, producing utensils for the mines.[1] In the early nineteenth century, with the arrival of the Portuguese royal family in Brazil, official stimulus was given to establish iron smelting operations. Foreign experts were brought to Brazil to supervise the building and operation of a number of establishments which produced for the military, for diamond mining in Minas Gerais, and for farming. The activities of the early nineteenth century did not last and most establishments were closed as the century wore on.

Although iron production was never completely extinguished, it took place only in small shops. In 1864, 120 forges were reported in operation, producing about 1,550 tons annually. Scientific

---

[1] Until the nineteenth century the mercantilistic policies of the Portuguese government did not permit the establishment of any manufacturing operations in the Brazilian colonies; thus, all these early efforts were clandestine in nature.

interest in iron ore and iron and steel production was maintained throughout the century. In 1879 the School of Mines at Ouro Preto was founded for the training of geologists and metallurgical engineers. A little later the Escola Politécnica of São Paulo was started. The latter was of great importance in giving a rigorous engineering training and the opportunity of specializing in metallurgy. The Brazilian army has always shown a keen interest in metallurgy; it was always interested in industrial development and especially in the growth of iron and steel production. In order to remedy the scarcity of engineers and especially metallurgical engineers, the army founded in 1930 the Escola de Engenharia do Exército, which was to produce some of Brazil's finest metallurgical engineers. A large proportion of today's top men in the steel industry are graduates of this institute. Thus, although the first substantial spurt of steel production in Brazil did not occur until the fourth decade of the twentieth century, the country had for a long time viewed its future destiny as a large steel producer— hence the emphasis on the training of metallurgical engineers prior to the surge of demand for their services.

As Brazil entered the twentieth century, pig iron production had reached only 2,000 tons. Most of the production was used to make spare parts for railroads, and to service the machines and provide utensils for large coffee plantations and sugar mills. By the end of the first decade of the twentieth century, pig iron production had not grown much beyond that amount, while imports of rolled steel products averaged 272,500 tons in the period 1908–12. In 1924, the earliest date for which we have steel production statistics, total output was only 4,492 tons.

The growth of iron and steel production which did take place in the first three decades of the twentieth century was mainly based on the initiative of private entrepreneurs. In 1921 foreign capital and know-how entered the picture when the Belgian–Luxembourg A.R.B.E.D. group, at the invitation of the governor of Minas Gerais, absorbed a small steel shop and founded the firm Companhia Siderúrgica Belgo-Mineira. In the 1920s other small firms were founded, especially in the São Paulo area, producing steel and steel products destined for the manufacture of equipment for the sugar industry. Some of these firms constructed primitive rolling facilities to produce bars and rods for the construction industry.

In the mid-1930s Belgo-Mineira built its mill at Monlevade and by the end of that decade the steel industry had made substantial progress. Pig iron production reached 185,000 tons in 1940, and steel ingot production 141,200 tons. Brazil had stopped being an importer of pig iron and steel ingots. However, it still imported 70 per cent of the rolled products it consumed.

Throughout the 1930s there was a powerful movement within the Government to create a large-scale fully integrated steel mill based on coke[1] and as the decade wore on, President Getúlio Vargas became increasingly committed to build such a firm either by stimulating private enterprise (foreign and/or domestic) or by having a government firm enter the picture.[2] When the U.S. Steel Corporation decided not to build a plant, even though the report of its experts had made a favourable recommendation, the Government decided to build an integrated steel mill itself. After a period of negotiation, in which the Brazilians used the interest of the Germans in building a plant in Brazil as an implied threat, the U.S. Export–Import Bank agreed to finance the building of the steel works at Volta Redonda.[3] The plant was built in the period 1940–6 and due to war-time conditions the building took longer than originally expected. In April 1946 Volta Redonda began to produce coke and in June of that year the blast furnace and steel shop began to function. The rolling mills, however, were not finished until late 1947 and began to operate only in 1948. With the functioning of Volta Redonda, Brazil became the first Latin American country to have a fully integrated coke-based steel mill.

Throughout the thirties and forties smaller firms had been founded, many of a semi-integrated nature (i.e. firms producing steel using electric furnaces to melt down scrap); often these operations began as subsidiaries of firms producing various types

[1] Up to that time all fully integrated firms were based on charcoal, while semi-integrated firms used scrap, remelted in electric steel furnaces.

[2] Baer's forthcoming study will enter in much greater detail into the circumstances which led the Government to enter the picture. Also omitted in this narrative is the Farquhar controversy. Farquhar, an American entrepreneur, had a scheme for building a large firm exporting iron ore and a steel mill. The latter would use imported coal brought back by empty iron-ore boats. For political reasons, his scheme was never realized.

[3] Documentation for this episode can be obtained in *Foreign Relations of the United States, Diplomatic Papers, 1940*, Volume V, 'The American Republics', United States Government Printing Office, Washington, 1961, pp. 600–14.

of equipment which wanted to integrate backward. There were other examples of steel mills founded by private entrepreneurs but becoming government-owned firms due to their indebtedness. A good case in point is the fully integrated special steel firm Acesita, begun by private enterpreneurs but eventually passing into the control of its main creditor, the Bank of Brazil.

The industrial growth in the post-war period, and especially the emphasis in the fifties on vertical integration of Brazil's industry, led to the expansion of existing steel producing facilities and the creation of a number of new enterprises, both private and governmental. Volta Redonda, whose ingot capacity was 270,000 tons when it opened in 1946, went through successive expansions until its capacity in 1965 was approximately 1,400,000 ingot tons. Belgo-Mineira's successive expansions resulted in a capacity of 450,000 tons in 1965. Many of the smaller private firms, both semi-integrated and fully integrated, also expanded with the growth of the internal market. A number of new smaller firms made their appearance in the fifties. The largest of the new firms in the fifties was the German concern Mannesmann, which constructed a fully integrated mill specializing in the production of seamless tubes and various types of special steels.

During the fifties the erection of two new large integrated mills was conceived. The basic idea for the creation of these firms stemmed from private and state government interests. Usiminas was constructed by a Japanese steel consortium, which originally participated with a 40 per cent ownership. The Brazilian ownership was originally divided among the state of Minas Gerais, the B.N.D.E. (the government development bank), some other state-owned companies, and a smaller group of private interests. As the project's costs increased during construction beyond what was originally planned, the B.N.D.E. had to increase its contribution and gradually became the majority owner, Japanese interest shrinking to about 20 per cent. The Cosipa company was originally created by private interests. However, by the late fifties the government of the state of São Paulo and the B.N.D.E. had to enter the picture to get the project underway. Again the B.N.D.E. was obliged to acquire controlling interest in the company. Both Usiminas and Cosipa are fully integrated coke-based plants, specializing in flat products. Usiminas began operations in October 1962; Cosipa, which began operation of its rolling mills in December 1963 (rolling ingots from Volta Redonda), started to function as a fully integrated mill in early 1966.

The growth of Brazilian steel output

The growth of the iron and steel industry in absolute terms is summarized in Table A.4. The production and total apparent consumption of iron, steel ingots, and rolled steel products are shown for selected years and also the ratio of imports to apparent consumption. It would seem from the data that by the early thirties Brazil was completely self-sufficient in pig iron and that by the early fifties self-sufficiency in steel ingots had been achieved. This, however, would be an optical illusion. A detailed analysis of the imports of rolled steel products would show that a large proportion of these products were of a semi-finished nature, i.e. products which were destined for re-rolling operations in Brazil. The necessity for importing semi-finished steel products indicates that Brazil had not become completely self-sufficient in pig iron or steel ingot production. The process of import substitution in rolled steel products was even slower. Only with the full operation of Volta Redonda in the late forties did Brazil begin to rely on its own rolled products for almost 70 per cent of its needs. With the operation of Usiminas and Cosipa in the sixties, Brazil supplied itself with about 90 per cent of the steel products it needed.

Future growth prospects

In considering future demand, one should note that in the mid-1960s, Brazil's *per capita* steel consumption was still low. In 1964, Brazil's steel consumption was 44·2 kg *per capita*. This was below the Latin American average of 49·5. This discrepancy must be viewed in the light of Brazil's relatively high industrial production *per capita*. This comparison leads us to expect a relatively high future growth in steel consumption.

Projections for steel consumption in 1975 range from 7·4 to 12·7 million ingot tons. Five recently-made projections are shown in Table A.5.

By the mid-1960s, many projects had been developed to expand existing facilities and to build completely new plants. Volta Redonda had planned to expand from 1·4 to 3·5 million ingot tons; Cosipa from 625 thousand to 2 million; Usiminas from 634 thousand to 2 million, and Belgo-Mineira from 400 thousand to

TABLE A.4
BRAZILIAN PRODUCTION OF IRON AND STEEL
(tons per year)

Year	Pig iron			Steel ingot			Rolled steel products		
	Production	Apparent consumption	Imports as per cent of apparent consumption	Production	Apparent consumption	Imports as per cent of apparent consumption	Production	Apparent consumption	Imports as per cent of apparent consumption
1916	4,267								
1919	10,808								
1925	30,046	41,760	28·0	7,559	14,123	46·5	283	373,485	99·9
1930	35,305	37,258	5·2	20,985	24,766	15·3	25,895	259,224	90·0
1940	185,570	185,570	0·0	141,201	147,810	4·5	135,293	414,519	69·4
1945	259,909	259,909	0·0	205,935	233,474	11·8	165,805	465,639	67·5
1950	728,979	728,979	0·0	788,557	803,119	1·8	572,489	843,049	32·6
1960	1,749,848	1,749,848	0·0	1,843,019	1,843,019	0·0	1,712,289	2,128,331	20·4
1964	2,445,525	2,445,525	0·0	3,043,749	3,043,749	0·0	2,108,783	2,338,106	9·8
1965	2,258,529	2,258,529	0·0	2,978,122	2,978,122	0·0	2,096,815	2,308,860	9·1
1966	2,939,230	2,939,230	0·0	3,775,104	3,775,104	0·0	2,677,198		

Source: *A Economia Siderúrgica da America Latina: Monografia do Brasil*, E.C.L.A., Santiago, December 1964, mimeographed (prepared by Dr. M. Falção); *Boletim IBS*, Instituto Brasileiro de Siderúrgica; I.B.G.E., *O Brasil em Números*. Import data for iron and steel imports from Fundação Getúlio Vargas.

TABLE A.5
STEEL CONSUMPTION PROJECTIONS: BRAZIL: 1975

Date and source of study	Projection for 1975 (million ingot tons)
Apparent consumption, 1966	3·8
Consultec (1961)	9·2
Technometal (1963)	12·7
B.N.D.E. (1965)	7·9–9·7
Falção–C.E.P.A.L. (1964)	9·9–10·6
Booz–Allen–Hamilton (1967)	7·4

700 thousand. A recent study by Booz–Allen–Hamilton made the recommendations shown in Table A.6, which are generally regarded as conservative. None of these expansion plans take possible exports into account.

TABLE A.6
BOOZ–ALLEN EXPANSION RECOMMENDATIONS
(million tons)

Unit	1966 capacity	1975 recommendation
Volta Redonda	1·400	2·5
Cosipa	0·625	1·0
Usiminas	0·634	1·0
Belgo-Mineira	0·400	0·520
All others	1·218	1·926
	4·277	6·946

Source: Booz, Allen, Hamilton, op. cit.

III. GOVERNMENT POLICIES

Investment

About two-thirds of Brazil's steel capacity is in government-controlled firms. The Government's percentage of total capital investment in the industry is between 50 and 60 per cent. The companies controlled by the Government are C.S.N. (Volta Redonda), Cosipa, Usiminas, Ferro e Aço Vitoria, and Acesita. Even before any of these firms existed, however, Brazil already had 27 private firms producing iron and/or steel, with a production in 1945 of 260 thousand tons of pig iron and 206 thousand tons of steel ingot. As noted above, the Government built Volta Redonda in the 1940s only after foreign private interests were approached and had refused to participate. In Cosipa and Usiminas, in the

1950s, the Government started as a minority participant (through the B.N.D.E.) and assumed a controlling interest only as the private participants became unwilling or unable to finance the full costs of the projects. Government will probably continue to be important in future expansions and new mills.

Protection and prices

Official tariffs were not relevant to protection or pricing of steel in Brazil. Until 1961, C.S.N. and Acesita were the only entities allowed to import any basic steel products. These companies, controlled by the Government, set domestic prices independently of tariff considerations. C.S.N. was also the largest and strongest domestic producer, and was the price leader for most steel products. Since 1961, imports have been allowed only for products in short supply.

Until 1963, C.S.N. generally set prices high enough for it and most other companies to operate at a profit. Since 1963, the Government has kept a tight rein on steel price increases, keeping them generally behind the rate of inflation. Unfortunately I do not have reliable, consistent time series of prices for representative products in Brazil. I have one series for non-flat shapes, and shorter series for hot- and cold-rolled sheets. (The last two are probably underestimates.) These data, reproduced in Table A.7, should be compared with typical European prices of about \$135 per ton for non-flat shapes, \$145 for hot-rolled sheets, and \$160 for cold-rolled sheets (data for 1967). The comparison indicates that steel prices in Brazil during the early 1960s were up to roughly 25 per cent above European levels; since the Brazilian prices for flat products are known to be somewhat underestimated, I would say that Brazilian prices were roughly 25 per cent higher than European prices in that period.

Subsidies, positive and negative

Government policies affect costs in the steel industry in four major areas: capital equipment, iron ore, coal, and infrastructure.

Most of the capital equipment which has been imported from the construction of Volta Redonda (in the 1940s) to the present has received special treatment. In the case of Volta Redonda, taxes on imports of capital goods were not significant. Most of the imported equipment for Usiminas and Cosipa took advantage of S.U.M.O.C. Instruction 113. (See Chapter 4. Banas estimates the total value of machinery imported under S.U.M.O.C. 113 by the steel industry as $11 million; this seems likely to be an underestimate.) It is doubtful that any duties were paid on equipment imported for steel mills since such duties went into effect in 1957. Whether this should be regarded as a subsidy, or as an exemption from a tax, is open to question; various other industries received the same favourable treatment, still others did not.

TABLE A.7
WHOLESALE PRICES FOR STEEL IN BRAZIL
(dollars per ton)

Year	Non-flat products	Hot rolled sheets	Cold rolled sheets
1945	150	n.a.	n.a.
1946–53	151	n.a.	n.a.
1954–9	209	n.a.	n.a.
1960	185	178	242
1961	138	120	158
1962	149	141	196
1963	156	156	180
1964	169	148	197
1965	149	n.a.	n.a.
1966	111	n.a.	n.a.
1967	124	n.a.	n.a.

Note: Conversion to dollars for 1954–67 at the free trade exchange rate. (See Chapter 3.) For other years, the 1954 rate was projected backward by the general price index estimated by the Fundação Getúlio Vargas (index No. 2 of *Conjuntura Econômica*).

Sources: Basic data for non-flat products from a confidential source. Basic data for sheets from C.S.N. *Relatório da Diretoria* (annual reports). These last data are known to be underestimated in some years.

On the other hand, new steel firms (or existing firms which were expanding) were under considerable pressure to use domestic equipment to the extent it was available. Only since the mid-1950s has a significant amount of such equipment been available. However, a tour of the newest mill, Cosipa, reveals a large number of domestic travelling cranes, trucks and all sorts of material-handling equipment, foundry equipment, electrical equipment such as generators, motors, and transformers, and even some rolling mill parts and accessories.

Brazilian steel mills receive iron ore at the mill at a cost of about $3.00 per ton. The price of iron ore exported from Brazil, F.O.B., is about $8.50 per ton. The difference represents a reduction in the total cost of rolled products of about $5.00 per ton, or roughly 3 per cent of total cost. It is not clear that the opportunity cost of iron ore used in the mills should be taken as the export value, however. Brazilian iron ore reserves, as mentioned above, are enormous, and current exports are not limited by domestic use, except in the very short run. Only far in the future may exports be limited by current domestic use, but risk plus time discount factors would be very significant here, because of the large ratio of reserves to current use—known reserves would last for over 5,000 years at current rates of domestic use, or about 2,000 years at current rates of domestic use plus exports! On the other hand, the domestic price to the mills probably does not cover the full costs of labour, processing, and transport. I have not been able to estimate these costs. In any case the subsidy is a small part of the total cost of steel. In the calculations in Section IV iron ore costs have been calculated at a unit cost of $8.50 per ton.

As mentioned above, Brazilian steel mills are required to use a certain amount of domestic coal. This increases costs in three ways. The coal is more expensive per ton than imported coal, more of it is required per ton of pig iron produced, and its use reduces the production capacity of the blast furnace. I have three estimates of the quantitative effect of the use of domestic coal, all reasonably consistent. One is from Amaro Lanari, the President of Usiminas. The other two are from private consulting engineers. The 40 per cent requirement, in force until 1967, increased the cost of coke per ton of pig iron by 50–75 per cent, and also increased the capital cost per ton of pig iron by about 30 per cent. These factors combined increased the cost of rolled products by about 8–10 per cent.

A number of Brazilian mills were located far from existing towns and transport facilities. The steel firms themselves have borne the cost of constructing many of these facilities. Volta Redonda is the most striking example: its location between Rio and São Paulo, in the state of Rio de Janeiro, was chosen as a political compromise. The company builds and maintains all workers' housing, health services, extensive recreation facilities, schools, training programmes, local roads, water supply, etc. While some of these costs are the result of political considerations, others are simply unavoidable costs of progress in a country where infrastructure of all kinds is deficient. These costs did not have to be incurred in order to have the steel industry, and therefore they do not reflect adversely on the economic rationality of establishing a steel industry in Brazil.

The transport system serving the steel industry is deficient in many ways. The design of the railroad system was strongly influenced by the needs of farmers; routes meander around to pick up rural produce. For example, the distance from Monlevade (site of one of Belgo-Mineira's mills) to São Paulo is 1,100 kilometres by rail and 696 by road. More important, rail service is very poor. Most producers have relied heavily on highway transport, which I suspect is more costly than efficient rail transport would be in many cases. Where railroads have been used, many steel firms have been obliged to purchase their own rolling stock.

Use of domestic maritime transport is limited to bringing domestic coal from the mines in Santa Catarina. Its excessive costs and unreliable service make it undesirable.

IV. THE EFFICIENCY OF THE BRAZILIAN STEEL INDUSTRY

Labour productivity is not an important factor in steel costs. Among raw material costs, the most relevant indicator is the coke rate, i.e. the amount of coke consumed per ton of pig iron produced. Coke is the most important input into the blast furnace, amounting to about 70 per cent of the total cost of raw material inputs. Various techniques have been invented and more are still being developed to bring the coke rate down. Table A.8 contains the coke rates of some selected Brazilian and other Latin American firms. In examining the table, one should know that the most efficient blast furnaces are in Japan, where a coke rate of 450 kg per ton of pig iron has been attained. In the United States coke rates of 550–570 kg are presently the norm.

As explained above, coke-based steel firms are forced to use some domestic coal. Given the poor quality of this coal, its use has been prejudicial to productivity in blast furnaces. Technical studies have estimated that Brazilian coke rates could be brought down to levels of about 520–550 kg of coke per ton of pig iron if only imported coal were used.[1] That is, given the excellent qual-

---

[1] Amaro Lanari Junior, 'Consumo de Carvão Nacional na Siderurgia', in *Metalurgia*, Volume 21, No. 93, August 1965, p. 646. Another Brazilian steel expert has stated that according to his calculations, Brazilian firms could even bring their coke rates down to 500 kg.

ity of Brazil's iron ore and the techniques of production currently used in Brazil, the country could lower its coke rate to levels below that attained in the United States and many European countries. Table A.8 shows that Brazil already has a satisfactory coke rate when compared to other Latin American plants.[1] With

TABLE A.8
BLAST FURNACE PRODUCTIVITY
(consumption of raw materials in kilograms per ton of pig iron produced)

Mill	Date	Iron ore	Sinter	Coke
Brazil				
Volta Redonda	1960	1,416	101	815
	1964	911	635	656
Usiminas	1964	102	1,495	592
	1966	334	1,205	623
Chile				
Huachipato	1963	1,613		601
Argentina				
San Nicolas	1963	1,570		700
Mexico				
Monclova	1963	1,060		830

Sources: Calculated from materials made available directly by firms; for non-Brazilian firms, E.C.L.A., *La Economia Siderúrgica . . .*, op. cit.

a decline in the use of domestic coal and the injection of oil into blast furnaces, Brazil could easily be among the most efficient pig iron producers in the world. Since liquid pig iron is the major input into the steel furnace, a low coke rate obviously will make substantial reductions in the cost of steel ingot production, and this, in turn, produces substantial savings in the final product cost.

The most important cost input is capital costs. Reliable data on capital costs are very difficult to obtain, especially in Brazil where the inflation makes current values at different times non-comparable. Thus, while initial investment costs are sometimes available, the costs of expansions are not easily made comparable. However, some conclusions can be made from the information available.

Capital costs tend to be high in Brazil. For example, the capital–production ratio for Volta Redonda in 1963 implied by

[1] The coke rate in Indian steel mills in 1960 was approximately 900 kg per ton; see William A. Johnson, *The Steel Industry of India*, Harvard University Press, 1966, p. 206 fn.

P

the E.C.L.A. study cited earlier is over $500 per ton. The use of domestic coal contributes about $90 to this cost; removing this burden would reduce the capital–production ratio to about $425 per ton. Estimates of capital costs for Cosipa and Usiminas, the two newest mills, are around $400 per ton, at 1 million tons per year capacity.

In addition to major problems such as temporary undercapacity and domestic coal, many smaller inefficiencies and organizing deficiencies appear. These have the effect of reducing the output which a given mill actually produces and thus increasing the unit capital charge. In the early stages of the operation of Cosipa, for example, iron ore came by railroad and had to be transferred from standard-gauge cars to narrow-gauge cars in order to descend the steep hill next to the mill. In addition to increasing the cost of the ore, this caused the supply of iron ore to be an effective constraint on the capacity of the mill. Many such examples of silly problems which reduce the effective capacity of various mills at various times could be cited. Such situations are much less common in developed countries with longer histories of industrial operation, greater value placed on efficient organization and operations, and a larger supply of competent middle-level administrators, as well as better physical infrastructure. To develop these institutions, attitudes, skills, and facilities in a country such as Brazil requires time and experience.

Data on all production costs are of course crucial for an analysis of this kind. Table A.9 contains some of my own cost estimates for various types of Brazilian firms, and the cost estimates of E.C.L.A. for Volta Redonda and for a selected number of other Latin American firms.[1] Except for the cost of pig-iron production, Brazil has lower costs than other Latin American plants. One should note especially the low cost of pig-iron production of medium firms, since they all utilize charcoal. Estimates of capital charges in Table A.9 are adjusted to take into account temporary unbalanced capacity within the mill. That is, the estimates reflect costs as they will be when these imbalances are removed.

Other independent cost estimates are even lower than the ones

[1] A detailed description of how the estimates of costs were arrived at will appear in Baer's forthcoming study. Given the confidential nature of the information obtained from many firms, findings have been shown by type of firms, using averages for firms in each category.

TABLE A.9
COST ESTIMATES FOR BRAZILIAN AND OTHER LATIN AMERICAN IRON AND STEEL FIRMS
(U.S.$ per ton)ᵃ

	Direct estimates		E.C.L.A. estimates		
	Brazil	Brazil (Volta Redonda)	Argentina (San Nicolas)	Chile (Huachipato)	Mexico (Monclova)
Blast furnace					
Large integrated (coke-based)	48·49–50·32	40·50	56·72	45·96	43·11
Medium (charcoal-using)	34·49–38·93				
Steel furnace					
Large S.M.	67·36–71·85	71·75	85·37	73·91	71·23
Medium	65·35–71·03				
Large L.D.	68·85–73·44				
Medium L.D.	60·86–64·92				
Medium electric	64·95–72·75				
Rolling mills					
Large flat	120·63	156·24	180·99	187·46	172·67
Large non-flat	101·98	115·34		118·70	
Medium non-flat	103·77				
Medium flat	147·27				

ᵃ 'Large' or 'Medium' refers to large or medium integrated firms, except for medium electric steel furnace. When two numbers are cited in first column, they refer to cost ranges, i.e. the highest and the lowest cost estimated.
Sources: First column estimates based on information obtained from various steel firms. Capital charges are based on a total gross return to capital of only 9 per cent per year, and thus may be underestimated (E.C.L.A. estimates).

reproduced in Table A.9. For example, the estimates of a consulting firm for the Brazilian development bank (B.N.D.E.) and for the World Bank (I.B.R.D.) have costs of pig iron varying between U.S.$31.50 and 40.00 for large-scale integrated mills and costs as low as U.S.$23.60 for charcoal based pig iron. And a confidential report of one of the large integrated steel producers revealed a pig-iron cost of U.S.$44.38 in April 1966.

In a special report given by the president of Usiminas, it was stated that the basic operational cost conditions of Usiminas were better than those found in similar plants in the United States. The data presented were as in Table A.10.

TABLE A.10
COMPARATIVE COST STRUCTURE: BRAZIL AND U.S.A.
(in U.S.$ per ton—for first half of 1967)

Item	Usiminas	U.S.A.
Operational costs	89·86	105·95
(Production costs)	(81·53)	(98·71)
(Adm. and sales costs)	(8·33)	(7·24)
Financial costs	60·89	9·87
(Interest)	(40·56)	(1·32)
(Depreciation)	(20·33)	(8·55)
Taxes	22·93	7·89
(Income taxes)	—	(5·92)
(Other taxes)	(22·93)	(1·97)
Profit or loss	−48·60	7·90
Price of product	125·08	131·61

Source: *Estado do São Paulo*, 27 July 1967, p. 21. Based on talk by president of Usiminas, Amaro Lanari Junior.

Although Lanari is not an unbiased source, the numbers he presents appear to reflect the situation in 1967 accurately. At that time, money had been tight for about three years, and interest charges were high. Also, Usiminas had not yet attained balanced capacity in different operations, and temporary excess capacity in parts of the mill increased capital costs per unit of output. Third, the Government had been putting more and more pressure on the price of domestic steel, and in 1967 some Brazilian steel products actually were selling at or below European prices.

A similar analysis based on data collected by Booz, Allen, and Hamilton from 27 firms in ten countries shows a similar picture. (See Table A.11.) If we assume that the total cost in the U.S. is 20 per cent higher than in Europe, and in Brazil 30 per cent higher than in Europe, we can see more clearly just where Brazil's higher

TABLE A.11
TYPICAL COST BREAKDOWNS FOR STEEL FIRMS
(percentage distribution)

Item	Brazil	U.S.	Europe
Raw materials	31	37	44
Labour	10	35	18
Other production costs	22	14	17
TOTAL cost of production	(63)	(76)	(79)
Depreciation	7	5	5
Interest	11	1	4
TOTAL capital charges	(18)	(6)	(9)
Administration and sales	10	5	7
Sales and production taxes	9	3	5
TOTAL cost of sales	100	100	100

Source: 'Perspectivas da Participação Brasileira no Mercado Internacional de Aço', by Paulo Dias Veloso, July 1967 (unpublished).

costs come in. This is shown in Table A.12. Brazil is relatively efficient in direct labour and raw material costs. Financial charges and taxes are much higher in Brazil, as are administration and sales expenses and the unspecified 'other production costs'.

TABLE A.12
HYPOTHETICAL COMPARATIVE COSTS
(total cost for Europe = 100)

Item	Brazil	U.S.	Europe
Raw materials	40	44	44
Labour	13	42	18
Other production costs	29	17	17
TOTAL cost of production	(82)	(103)	(79)
Depreciation	9	6	5
Interest	14	1	4
TOTAL capital charges	(23)	(7)	(9)
Administration and sales	13	6	7
Sales and production taxes	12	4	5
TOTAL cost of sales	130	120	100

Source: Based on Table A.11.

In its study of the Latin American steel industry, E.C.L.A. tried to make some international price comparisons in order to get some idea of the relative efficiency of steel industries. In Table A.13 some of the E.C.L.A. estimates of dollar prices for steel products in various countries are shown. Although Brazil turns out in most cases to be the second lowest price producer in Latin America, these comparisons are suspect because in most cases Colombia, which is known to have one of the less efficient steel mills in Latin America, is the lowest price producer. Obviously one runs into the exchange rate problem—which is the correct one to use at which time? The variations one obtains when making conversions of prices in domestic currency into dollar prices are obvious when examining part (B) of Table A.13. Here Brazilian prices at various times have been converted using the prevailing official exchange rates, in lines A. One should note especially the prices in October 1965 and March 1967. The former was the month prior to a devaluation from Cr$1,850 to Cr$2,200 to the dollar and the latter was the month in which the cruzeiro was devalued from Cr$2,200 to Cr$2,700 to the dollar. In lines B the results using Bergsman's free trade exchange rate are shown. Table A.13 clearly reveals how sensitive prices are to the exchange rate one chooses and how close at times the Brazilian price comes to European prices. Part (C) of Table A.13 contains the price ranges found in October–November 1965 for some products by a special study group which obtained direct price information from firms. These prices are possibly a little on the low side, although they might contain special reductions offered to customers, but not listed, and they are prices at the mill rather than at the places of consumption.

These estimates are not very consistent. The problem with the third set, presented in part C of the Table, is probably the exchange rate. For the products analysed in parts A and B of the Table, Brazilian prices do not seem more than 30–50 per cent higher than European prices around 1964–5, and perhaps approach European prices at some phases of the inflation–real exchange rate cycles in 1965–7. The data in Table A.7, and knowledge of certain biases in it, indicated that Brazilian prices were 25–50 per cent higher than European prices. The truth is very probably that depending on the product and the exact time, Brazilian comparative prices actually did vary within this wide range of 0–50 per cent higher than European prices.

To summarize the analysis of costs so far, blast furnace productivity in Brazil could be competitive with any producer (except, perhaps, Japan) with the single step of removing the requirement

TABLE A.13
A. E.C.L.A. COMPARISON OF STEEL PRICES IN VARIOUS LATIN AMERICAN AND EUROPEAN COUNTRIES
(price in U.S.$ per ton, August 1965)

	Argentina	Brazil	Colombia	Chile	Mexico	Peru	Venezuela	W. Germany	Belgium	France
Reinforcing rods	238	139	122	164	154	206	148	108	99	104
Cold rolled sheets	287	243	165	298	208			158	153	149

Source: E.C.L.A., *La Economía Siderúrgica de America Latina*, February 1966, mimeographed, p. 170.

B. BRAZILIAN STEEL PRICES: ESTIMATES AT VARIOUS TIME PERIODS
(price in U.S.$ per ton)

	June 1964	October 1964	January 1965	October 1965	October 1966	March 1967
Round bars:						
A	230–270	190–230	190–220	130–150	n.a.	n.a.
B	165–190	135–165	130–155	90–105	n.a.	n.a.
Cold rolled sheets:						
A	250–310	220–280	210–270	n.a.	220–240	170–230
B	180–220	155–200	150–190	n.a.	175–190	150–200

Source: Calculated from prices listed in *Máquinas e Metais* of C.S.N.; in line A the exchange rate used was the prevailing official one; in line B the free trade rate was used. Price ranges represent the cheapest and the most expensive product in each category.

C. B.N.D.E.–WORLD BANK–BOOZ–ALLEN PRICE ESTIMATES FOR OCTOBER–NOVEMBER 1965
(price in U.S.$ per ton)

Concrete rod	89–127
Rolled bars	94–142
Cold rolled sheets	98–145

Source: Unpublished study for B.N.D.E. and World Bank by Booz–Allen. Prices were estimated for various firms—ranges represent cheapest and dearest prices. Rolled bars exclude bars of special steels.

that some domestic coal be used. The blast furnace represents about 40 per cent of the cost of rolled products in an efficient mill.

Productivity in Brazilian steel shops (which should represent about 30 per cent of total production costs) is already at competitive levels, given the technology used. That is, the two newest Brazilian mills, which are using the most modern process (L.D.), are not less efficient than similar shops in other countries. The same is true for Volta Redonda, which uses the older open-hearth process.

In the rolling mills Brazil's costs are higher than in efficient European, American, or Japanese firms. This is largely due to the present unbalanced capacity of the large Brazilian mills. As explained above, the blast furnace and steel shop capacity of Volta Redonda, Cosipa, and Usiminas is being expanded gradually over periods of up to twenty years. It was nevertheless more economical (or, in some cases, technically unavoidable) to build the rolling mills much nearer to ultimate capacity right from the start, because of the indivisible nature of much of the equipment.

In Table A.14 is an analysis of the costs of steel production at Volta Redonda in 1963. In this calculation, costs are taken from the national, rather than the private viewpoint. That is, the cost of iron ore is taken at the export price, rather than at the lower domestic price. The cost of coke is taken as if only imported coal were used, because the higher cost incurred by using domestic coal is a subsidy to the domestic coal industry from the nation's point of view. The value of the product was estimated by taking average prices for the products produced by Volta Redonda, in Japan, Germany, and the U.S. The analysis is in the form of calculating the exchange rate at which Volta Redonda is transforming cruzeiros (local costs) into dollars (net foreign exchange saved). The basic data are from the E.C.L.A. study cited above, adjusted as explained in the notes to the table.

The value of the product, as explained in the notes to the table, was conservatively estimated at $156 per ton. These calculations imply that the net cruzeiro cost was Cr$55,000 per ton, and the net foreign exchange saving was $82 per ton. Thus the equivalent exchange rate for Volta Redonda steel was Cr$670 per dollar. This can be compared with the average import rate including tariffs of 1,670, the estimated free trade rate of 830, and the average export rate (excluding coffee) of 553. This indicates

TABLE A.14
NATIONAL COSTS: VOLTA REDONDA: 1963

	Cost per ton of final product	
	Foreign exchange	*Local costs*
Item	(dollars)	(cruzeiros)
Blast furnace		
Iron ore	7.80	
Sinter	5.85	
Coke	16.00	
Other raw materials		−788
Direct labour		573
Indirect costs		2,380
Gross capital charge	7.55	2,200
Steel shop		
Additional raw material (mostly scrap)		12,342
Direct labour		1,514
Indirect costs		12,900
Gross capital charge	7.40	2,160
Rolling mill		
Additional raw material (mostly scrap)		−6,827
Direct labour		2,019
Indirect costs		7,150
Gross capital charge	29.50	8,660
Administration and sales		11,000
TOTAL cost of sales	74.10	55,000

Notes:
1. Iron ore: Physical requirement from E.C.L.A., op. cit. Price is average export price, F.O.B. Brazil, 1963 ($8.58/ton).
2. Sinter: Physical requirement from E.C.L.A., op. cit. Since iron ore represents something less than half of the cost of sinter, the price was raised by half as much as was the price of iron ore, as in 1 above.
3. Coke: The E.C.L.A. cost per unit of product was reduced by a factor of 0·685. This reflects a 25 per cent reduction in the coke rate and a 17 per cent reduction in the price of coal. It implies that domestic coal costs 75 per cent more than imported coal per ton of pig iron produced. Reduction in blast furnace capacity is not considered here.
4. Gross capital charges for blast furnaces: E.C.L.A. estimates were reduced by 32 per cent, to remove the effect of using 40 per cent domestic coal.
   The total effect of the adjustments for using 40 per cent domestic coal is to reduce the cost of pig iron by $9.50 per ton, or 20 per cent.
5. Gross capital charges, in general: I used the E.C.L.A. estimates, which are calculated as 15 per cent of total value of investment as estimated by E.C.L.A. Their estimate is only a very rough guess; unfortunately I was unable to obtain better estimates. As stated in the text, their estimate implies a capital–production

ratio of over $500 per ton of rolled products. In value terms this is over 3 to 1. Since the blast furnace and the steel shop of Volta Redonda were operating fairly near effective capacity, this estimate does not seem likely to be too low; however I must admit that this is certainly the weakest part of the data.

I divided the total capital charge into 70 per cent foreign exchange costs and 30 per cent domestic costs, which is the approximate breakdown suggested by C.S.N. personnel.

6. Administration and sales costs were estimated at approximately 10 per cent of total cost of sales. This figure is based on rough estimates from various Brazilian firms, including C.S.N.

7. All other costs are taken directly from the E.C.L.A. estimates.

8. Direct inquiry in 1967 at Volta Redonda yielded information on all costs except capital charges. The data were quite close to the E.C.L.A. figures.

9. The value of product, $156/ton, was estimated from the 1963 C.S.N. sales mixture and rough averages of 1967 prices in Germany, Japan, and the U.S. These prices were perhaps 10 per cent lower in 1967 than in 1963, so here my estimate is quite conservative. The basic data are as follows:

CALCULATION OF AVERAGE VALUE OF PRODUCT, C.S.N., 1963

Item	Per cent C.S.N. sales, 1963	1967 price, Germany–Japan–U.S.
Rails	2·1	$130
Other non-flat shapes	7·7	140
Heavy sheets	13·1	135
Hot rolled sheets	25·5	145
Cold rolled sheets	25·8	160
Galvanized plate	4·6	200
Tin plate	16·8	180
Average price per ton	95·6	$156

that the operation of Volta Redonda in 1963 was efficient in a comparative cost sense.

The same data can be used in a more conventional, rate of return analysis. If costs are converted at the estimated free trade rate for 1963 of Cr$830 per dollar, the results are as summarized in Table A.15: the return for the year was about 15 per cent. This is a healthy if unspectacular result.

This conclusion should be qualified in many ways. On the positive side, we should remember that Volta Redonda was the

TABLE A.15
RATE OF RETURN ON 1963 OPERATIONS, VOLTA REDONDA

Value of sales	U.S.$ 156
Operating costs	80 per ton
Gross profit	U.S.$ 76 per ton
Capital investment	U.S.$520 per ton
Rate of return	14·6%

Source: As Table A.14.

first large integrated coke-based steel mill built in Brazil. By 1963 it was already 17 years old, and its technology was already obsolete (especially in the steel shop).

On the other hand, various negative factors were not included in the analysis. Operation in early years may have been considerably less efficient than in 1963. No charges were made for special infrastructure costs such as workers' housing, local roads, etc., as described above. I believe such costs should be charged to a 'general costs of development' account rather than to the steel industry; others may disagree.

It appears that the two newest mills, Cosipa and Usiminas, will be more efficient than Volta Redonda when they reach 1 million tons per year capacity. (This is planned to happen by 1975 or earlier.) Their actual capital costs were each about $325 million for about 650,000 tons of ingot capacity (and 1·5 million tons in the rolling mills) and plans for expansion to 1 million tons call for additional investments of less than $70 million each. Thus their capital charges should be about 20 per cent lower than the E.C.L.A. estimates for Volta Redonda.

Based on this evidence, it seems reasonably clear that Brazil's steel industry is competitive in a comparative cost sense, without any recourse to external benefits, infant industry arguments, etc.

I will close with a word on exports. In the last four years (1964–7) Brazil has been exporting an average of about 320,000 tons of steel per year. This is almost 10 per cent of total output. The principal customer was Argentina, followed by the U.S. Again, the situation must be understood: the Brazilian economy was in a generally depressed state, and the export prices were below average cost at reasonable exchange rates. On the other hand, those costs included the cost of using domestic coal, lack of competitive financing of sales, and until 1966 very high taxes. The only thing that these exports prove is that Brazilian producers can dump steel just as producers of other countries do, especially when faced with slack domestic demand. Nevertheless, this is already something. Brazil's basic cost situation does not seem out of line with other countries generally thought to be efficient producers; with a little help from better infrastructure and reasonable regulations, and a little more learning, Brazilian steel could be generally competitive.

Appendix 2

Productivity in Brazilian Manufacturing

by CARLOS A. ROCCA (*University of São Paulo*)

I. INDUSTRIAL DEVELOPMENT AND PRODUCTIVITY

ONE of the points of great interest in the analysis of industrialization of developing economies is the determination of the factors which account for increases in the productivity of labour.

From this point of view the industrial growth of the Brazilian economy during the last 15 or 20 years is an interesting field of study. Although Brazil has maintained high tariff levels throughout the period, there are indications of substantial increases of the average productivity of labour in manufacturing. The diversification of the industrial structure, along with the introduction of new techniques of production, the increase of market size for industrial products, and the improvements in the quality of factors are some of the bases of such progress.

Unfortunately any effort at quantification of the relative importance of each of these factors in the explanation of the behaviour of productivity is extremely difficult due to the absence of time series data on the relevant variables. The problem becomes particularly serious because a substantial portion of productivity increments may be based on qualitative changes in the factors of production, technological change, and differentiation of the industrial structure.

However, some knowledge can be obtained from an inter-state comparison of productivity levels. The large productivity differentials observed among the various regions in the country offer a great range of variation of the factors which may determine these differences. In spite of the shortcomings of cross-section results for explanation of time trends, an inter-state analysis can offer at least some indication of the relative importance of each factor. In the present state of the available data, time series analysis can be done only for the economy as a whole (with national accounts data), and not for industry as a whole or by sectors.

One of the main characteristics of the industrialization in Brazil was a large geographic concentration in the centre-south region. Hence, the observed factor productivity levels in different states could reflect in some degree the differences introduced by the over-all differences in industrial growth among different regions.

The analysis was done on the basis of estimated production functions for each manufacturing sector. The sample used is stratified by size classes of establishments so as to permit the quantification of internal economies of scale. I add to the standard function which depends on inputs of capital and labour, another independent variable which represents the total amount of industrial production in each state. This variable accounts for the effect of factors related to the 'degree of industrialization' or to the size of the market for industrial products. This factor turns out to be among the important determinants of productivity. On the basis of the main features of the sample used, I believe that such a variable can account for the (combined) effects of the qualitative differences of the factors of production, managerial ability, technical knowledge, and degree of industrial specialization which in some general sense can be thought of as technological external economies at the level of the firm or even the industrial sectors.

In this way, rough measures are obtained of the relative importance of each of three factors (or sets of factors) on the observed differences in the average productivity of labour: namely, capital per worker, size of establishment (internal economies of scale) and the factors associated with the total amount of production in each state.

The third set of factors referred to above—the total amount of manufacturing activity in each state—is responsible for almost 50 per cent of the observed differences in labour productivity. Following in importance are capital per worker and scale of establishment. In other words, although capital per worker and scale are more or less important in different industries, the importance attributed to qualitative differences of the factors of production, managerial ability, technical knowledge, and other factors linked to the scale of the industry or market size is the most important factor in the explanation of differences of labour productivity in almost all sectors.

The plan of this Appendix is as follows. In Section II, the sources of data and their limitations are discussed. A summary of the methodological problems involved and the proposed solutions is given in Section III. The detailed empirical results are presented in Section IV. In the last section some implications of the results are discussed.

II. THE DATA AND THEIR LIMITATIONS

The empirical basis of this study was the general data on industrial activity supplied by the 1950 and 1960 censuses. That information is available for each sector of manufacturing and refers to establishments classified in groups by number of production workers. The class interval increases approximately according to a geometric series. This is very useful in our case, since the estimating procedure implies the logarithmic transformation of the variables.

For the 1950 census, the observations relative to establishments with less than two production workers employed were excluded from the computations. For the 1960 data, the first group included was the one having between one and four workers. The size classes excluded presented, between the two censuses, large differences in some variables when compared with the others. For instance, the variable representative of the amount of capital per worker took on, in these classes, values much higher than in any other classes. The same is true for the measure of average productivity of labour and any other variable which is normalized by the number of workers. Probably this is because the owner, partners, and family members in the production activity of these establishments are important as workers, but are not included as 'production workers'. This would result in the underestimation of production workers in those establishments. (Supposedly the criteria used by the Bureau of the Census would imply the inclusion of these categories as production workers, but I do not believe that this has in fact been done.)

Following is the list of variables used in this study:

VA_{ij} *Valor da Transformação Industrial* produced by establishments of a sector of manufacturing industries, in the ith state and classified on the jth size class of production workers employed. This is an approximation of value added and is the difference between the total value of production and the expenditure on raw materials, intermediate inputs, fuel and lubricants, electric power, and taxes.

The subscripts i and j used below have the same meaning:

CV_{ij} Horse-power installed.

O_{ij} Monthly average of production workers employed during the census years, 1949 and 1959.

VAT_i Value of industrial transformation produced in the ith state by all manufacturing establishments combined.

E_{ij} Number of establishments covered.

For the 1950 census the data were published for only seven manufacturing sectors, which represented an aggregation above the two-digit level of the standard industrial classification.[1] The 1960 census data have not been published as yet, but were obtained from the preliminary compilations of the I.B.G.E.[2] For that year, the data used have undergone only the first phase of review and, therefore, should be considered 'preliminary'.

III. METHODOLOGICAL PROBLEMS

In empirical studies of production functions, it is usually helpful to make some simplifying, though often restrictive, assumptions about the factors included in the function, their quality, and the existence of internal and external economies. In any case, it is obvious that some hypotheses must be made so as to formulate a model for estimation of parameters.

In cross-section studies, it is common to find inputs specified in terms of capital and labour only. The homogeneity of factors and the constancy of other elements which could affect production levels are usually assumed. The absence of internal and external economies is a very convenient simplifying assumption since, in that case, easier methods of estimation can be applied.

[1] I.B.G.E., Industrial Census of 1950.
[2] I am indebted to Professor G. Oscar Campiglia, President of *Instituto Brasileiro de Bibliografia e Documentação* and to Dr. Amaro de Costa Monteiro, from the *Serviço Nacional de Recenseamento*, who made those data available.

In this study, however, several of these effects are *estimated*, rather than assumed. The estimation of internal and external economies, the effects of changes in factor qualities, etc., are the very objectives of this study. A production function which permits the estimation of the required coefficients without the imposition of some of the very restrictive assumptions referred to in the preceding paragraph is therefore tested.

The existence of a production function, defined in terms of some inputs, is linked essentially to some state of technological knowledge which determines all possible combinations of inputs to produce each output. Managerial ability should be included, because superior management will result in larger outputs for the same quantity of inputs (technical efficiency) or better allocation of inputs (economic efficiency). In practical circumstances it may be possible to identify some factors which explain the differences in technological knowledge and managerial ability among the plants observed. For instance, there may be some barriers, geographical or otherwise, to the free diffusion of technological knowledge among industrial establishments. Managerial ability, associated with some kind of specialized training, also differs among firms. Even if one could assume the availability of the same technological knowledge to all firms, there might exist other restrictions to the application of the same techniques. For instance, the use of a number of techniques may be restricted to regions where there is a certain kind or degree of industrial development and thus certain needs for specific inputs could be satisfied from other firms or industries. Such inputs might be produced economically only in quantities which are greater than the demand of the individual user. It is common to assume complete and perfect diffusion of technological knowledge, even among countries, but in fact the conditions of the economy where the plant is located put limits on the range of alternative techniques which can actually be used.[1]

Other factors which may explain regional differences of productivity and which appear to be associated with the total amount of industry in the area can be thought of as technological external economies.[2] These economies often reflect indivisibilities in the

---

[1] For a recent discussion of this point see R. R. Nelson, 'International Productivity Differences', *American Economic Review*, December 1968.

[2] There are many classifications of external economies. For the present purpose

production of a number of services, public or not, which are used by the firm. The supply of many kinds of services, like transport and communications, technical research, etc., depends on the level of development of the economy or the amount of manufacturing.

Obviously, it is not always easy to distinguish the factors whose influence is directed to the production function from others which act on unit costs alone. Cheaper inputs of all kinds would fall in this latter category. These are the effects usually referred to as pecuniary external economies.

The possibility of participation in a large labour market which can supply qualified manpower without increasing costs (at least direct costs) is often cited as an example of external economies. Clearly, there is not a necessary link betweeen labour supply and external economies. Qualitative differences in labour inputs may be a problem of definition—better units of measurement of that factor—or, alternatively, a problem of inclusion of a new factor of production, namely, skilled labour. However, the absence of better information does not prevent the possibility that some relationship between quality of labour and the volume of industrial employment or production in each region exists.

Analogous considerations could apply to the level of managerial ability or entrepreneurship: the available amount of this input for establishments in many cases is correlated with the level of education or with the supply of better educated people. That relation may not exist in the case of some individual firms, when management requires very specialized knowledge, but probably exists for most firms taken as a whole.

Although in some cases one might expect the same relationship for the quality of capital equipment, there are a number of cases in which different patterns among states would be expected. Most important are factors which result in a different geographical distribution of the quality of inputs, derived from locational patterns of industry as affected by proximity of raw materials and other natural resources.

---

a very restrictive concept is not needed. For instance, the concept of techno-logical external economies as defined by Scitovsky in 'Two Concepts of External Economies', *Journal of Political Economy*, Vol. LXII, No. 2 (1954), pp. 143–51, would be appropriate. Another very useful concept is the 'atmo-sphere creating' external economies from Meade, 'External Economies and Diseconomies in a Competitive Situation', *Economic Journal*, LXII (March 1952), pp. 54–67.

Q

The joint effect of these factors on the production of each establishment does not seem to be negligible. On the other hand, it is clear that the inclusion of the variables representing these factors in the production function may create other problems since their effects might not be neutral. In other words, such factors may modify the marginal rate of substitution. In that case, the estimation problem would be analogous to the quantification of non-neutral technical progress.[1] At the same time, their exclusion will involve errors of specification. The simplest way of including these variables in the production function would be under a simplifying assumption about the neutrality of their effects, and thus introducing differences only in the constant term of the function. In that case, the problem is to find a variable or set of variables designed to represent the factors referred to above.

From the practical point of view the restrictions associated with the availability of data and estimation problems cannot be ignored. One of those problems is that these variables exhibit a very high degree of multicollinearity. The inclusion of a number of them in one function, which already presents high levels of inter-correlations among the basic explanatory variables, may result in an unduly high level of multicollinearity. In this case, in spite of the inclusion of all possible variables to represent those factors (if the data were available), one still could not measure their separate effects.

In the present case census data relates to some quantitative aspects of various manufacturing industries, including size classes of establishments for different states.[2] There is not much useful information on the quality of labour, at least not in the needed detail.[3] Nor is there available reasonably sophisticated data on the age distribution of capital.

On the basis of these considerations, it was decided to include a single variable to account for 'other factors', namely, the value added by all manufacturing industries in each state. The factors

---

[1] On this, see Murray Brown, *On the Theory and Measurement of Technological Change*, Cambridge University Press, 1966.

[2] That is, the classification by groups according to number of production workers.

[3] The available information at the time of making this study did not permit the construction of a detailed series of the quality of labour. Recently, however, the *Serviço Nacional de Recenseamento* has published some information on the composition of manpower for the year 1960. See the Census of Population, for 1960, published in 1968.

represented by such a variable are, clearly, not identical to the list of all the elements noted above. Nevertheless, the postulated relationship between the total amount of production and the 'other factors' may help in the interpretation of the results.

For instance, the said variable indicates both the volume of industrial production in each state and the relative level of development of the state. Second, since the sample is stratified by size classes for every sector, there is no risk of spurious correlation (where the real cause is internal economies of scale) except in cases where the volume of production is very small and the industrial structure too specialized. Since the measure of production is value added per firm in every size class, the use of specific size or level of development variables for every industry could otherwise raise the problem of spurious correlation.

Of course the use of the variable of total value added in each state does not allow discrimination among all factors influencing the situation. From the theoretical viewpoint, it would be better to use such a variable to account for the more general factors, while at the same time using separate indices for the quality of the factors of production, entrepreneurial and administrative ability, and so on. However there are no data available to construct those indices.

The classification of regions used in the sample, which follows the political division into states, is of course arbitrary. The separation into homogeneous regions would have to allow for a great number of factors and one would have to take into consideration particular ways through which the external factors spread their influence. This is beyond the scope of the present research; only the division into states was used.

The discussion above suggests a production function of the form:[1]

$$x_{0j} = f(x_{1j}, x_{2j}) \cdot g(A) \qquad (1)$$

which relates the production in the firm j to the amount of factors, x_{1j} and x_{2j}, used in it, and to the amount of all other factors linked to the total volume of production and represented by $g(A)$ above.

---

[1] A function similar to this was suggested by M. Frankel, 'The Production Function in Allocation and Growth: A Synthesis', *American Economic Review*, Vol. LII, No. 5 (1962), pp. 995–1022. Marshall has already suggested that production in each firm depends on the total production in the industry; see Alfred Marshall, *Principles of Economics*, Book V, Chapter 11.

In so far as $g(A)$ stands for the net effect of external economies and diseconomies, and other factors, and assuming

$$\frac{\partial x_{0j}}{\partial g(A)} \cdot \frac{\partial g(A)}{\partial A} > 0$$

one can think of a family of production functions, each of them being at a higher level, the higher the value of $g(A)$.

Whatever the interpretation given to the factors allowed for in the function $g(A)$, it is important to note that they are neutral as to the marginal rate of substitution between the factors included explicitly in the function f. If technological external economies and the other factors are related to the volume of the total industrial production in each state, putting $g(A)$ in the function is an attempt to account for their effects. In a broad way specification (1) can be interpreted as a relation between the volume of the factors used in their respective units of measure at a certain quality level associated with a certain level of external economies and other factors. The variable 'A' introduces economies derived from the size and development of industry as a whole in the region in which the firm is located. In this way the variable is made to test the net effect of all other factors, such as technical knowledge, quality and quantity of the services provided by overhead capital, entrepreneurial knowledge, etc., in so far as these are linked in the sample to the total volume of production.

In the present research value added has been used as a measure of the level of production. This measure may cause the variable which accounts for other factors to account also for price differentials.

Finally one should mention that the existence of heterogeneous processes of production in the sample of a given industry brings in a further difficulty in attempting to separate internal and external economies. If some of the effects of the size of the market accounted for by the volume of industrial production are due to diversification and specialization among firms, the classification of firms into size groups is inadequate for investigating scale economies. The relevant variable would not be the size of the *firm*, since it can use several production processes, but the scale in which each *process* is used, in so far as the market allows for it. If we proceed along this line we cannot avoid falling into the difficulties of defining a process or a plant. If we did do this, however, the variable which accounts for external economies might also be accounting for a part of the internal economies.

IV. PRODUCTION FUNCTION ESTIMATES

The production function model in which the assumption of constant returns to scale is not included reduces considerably the specification alternatives and the forms of estimation of the parameters involved. The estimation of a model which allows non-constant returns to scale precludes the application of many of the current methods, especially those based on factor shares. With the constraint imposed by the available data in this case, there are only two functional forms which can be tested: the Cobb–Douglas and the C.E.S. functions.

The Cobb–Douglas function was selected on the basis of two considerations. First, I tested a C.E.S. function. The estimates obtained did not allow rejecting the hypothesis that the elasticity of substitution equals unity in most cases.[1] Second, the usual procedures for the estimation of the C.E.S. function require the use of data concerning factor shares which are available only in crude approximations, due to the differences between the concept of 'value of industrial transformation' and that of 'value added'. The estimates of the capital share on the basis of the existing information are made from the difference between the value of industrial transformation and the wage bill, which forces the inclusion of the differences referred to above in this estimate. Hence, the results achieved according to the existing data indicate an unusually large share of capital in the 'value added'.

The Cobb–Douglas function was estimated for each one of the manufacturing sectors studied, on the basis of a sample stratified by the number of workers per establishment. There are ten size classes, of which only nine were used, as explained earlier. The model is given by:

$$\frac{VA_{ij}}{E_{ij}} = a_0 \left(\frac{CV_{ij}}{E_{ij}}\right)^{n_1} \left(\frac{O_{ij}}{E_{ij}}\right)^{a_2} VAT_i^{a_3} u_{ij} \qquad (2)$$

where the subscript 'i' indicates the state and 'j' the size class of the establishment; u_{ij} is the random component, which is assumed

---

[1] The estimates for the elasticity of substitution were obtained from the appropriate generalized C.E.S. function, with the inclusion of VAT. In the majority of cases we cannot reject the hypothesis of unitary elasticity of substitution.

to satisfy the needed hypotheses for the application of least squares and confidence tests.

It is convenient to note that this specification assumes that all establishments of any given size have the same production function in all states. The variable represented by VAT_i will stand for those factors which change from state to state and are related to the volume of industrial production of the state or to the size of the market supplied by each state's industry.

The above production function may be viewed as long-run in character, allowing for an approximately continuous change in all factors. The variables were adjusted to represent the 'typical' unit of production of each size category in different states and for every one of the manufacturing sectors. In this sense, this production function resembles very much the one defined in microeconomic analysis, having been estimated at the lowest level of aggregation allowed by the available information.

Although the data are available on the relevant variables for each size group, the procedure employed assumes a single production function for all classes. Obviously, this procedure implies that the parameters do not change with the size of the productive unit. A test of that assumption could be developed at least in two ways: first, preliminary estimation of production functions for every size category and comparison of the resulting coefficients; second, the introduction of slope-shifting dummy variables in the models in order to allow for differences in coefficients of the production function from size class to size class.

The first alternative would present the advantage of requiring a small number of variables each time. However, besides the computational difficulty associated with the comparison of the various multiple regression coefficients, the multicollinearity did not permit estimates from whose comparisons significant differences among the parameters could be inferred. The largest number of observations, for any manufacturing sector, was 21 (the number of states); for many sectors there were only ten observations. The high degree of inter-correlation, especially between the variables representing capital and labour, introduced an excessively high multicollinearity problem. In most cases the results completely lost any significance.

The second alternative, using dummies for every size category, became very difficult in this case. In order to adequately test this hypothesis, it would be necessary to introduce at least three dummy variables for each size group, corresponding respectively to the differences in the constant terms and in the labour and capital coefficients. Furthermore, one might put in another for the VAT coefficient. In most cases, this procedure would correspond to the estimation of a regression function with more than thirty variables. Apart from computational difficulties, this procedure would be impossible in many cases because of the relatively small number of observations. However, production functions were estimated with dummies for the constant terms, with the restriction of unitary elasticity of scale. The results, which are not presented here,[1] are consistent with tests of constant returns to scale presented later on in the text. For the sectors which show evidence of increasing returns to scale the dummy coefficients present a steady increase as the size increases, and vice versa.

Numerical results

In Table A.16 are the results from the 1950 census. Immediately below each estimate are the corresponding standard errors. For interpretation purposes, the estimates which differ from zero at the 10 per cent level are indicated by 'a' and those at the 5 per cent level by 'b'. The estimates with no indication are not significantly different from zero at the 10 per cent level.

Although one cannot forget the restrictions imposed on the results by the use of single equation methods, it can be said that the results achieved are reasonably good. From the strictly statistical point of view, the quality of fit is rather good, and the coefficients found are, in most cases, highly significant.

The analysis of the simple correlation coefficients calculated for the explanatory variables may provide some useful information with regard to the multicollinearity problem. These coefficients are given in Table A.17. The multicollinearity is essentially a consequence of a high degree of correlation between the variables representing capital and labour. The levels of correlation observed between VAT and the other variables are considerably lower and their influence on the variance of the estimates is small. In this case, the attainment of significant coefficients is due only to the

---

[1] For detailed estimates, see the author's *Economias de Escala na Função Produção*, mimeographed doctoral dissertation, Faculdade de Ciencias Econômicas e Administrativas da Universidade de São Paulo, São Paulo, 1967.

TABLE A.16
PRODUCTION FUNCTION ESTIMATES, SPECIFICATION (2): DATA FOR
1950

Sector	Constant	Coefficients of the variables			R^2
		$\dfrac{CV_{ij}}{E_{ij}}$	$\dfrac{O_{ij}}{E_{ij}}$	VAT_i	
Non-metallic mineral products	0·20249	0·169[b] (·047)	0·909[b] (0·068)	0·161[b] (0·028)	0·953
Metallurgy, machinery, electrical machinery, and transportation equipment	0·51327	0·162[b] (0·070)	0·895[b] (0·085)	0·138[b] (0·026)	0·975
Wood products and furniture	0·42672	0·262[b] (0·063)	0·817[b] (0·061)	0·131[b] (0·019)	0·960
Chemicals and pharmaceuticals	0·52583	−0·003 (0·052)	0·985[b] (0·071)	0·192[b] (0·032)	0·918
Textiles	0·32353	0·141[a] (0·079)	0·756[b] (0·074)	0·202[b] (0·026)	0·955
Clothing	0·19666	0·106[b] (0·030)	0·878[b] (0·047)	0·195[b] (0·022)	0·971
Food products, beverages, and tobacco	0·43874	0·554[b] (0·077)	0·481[b] (0·087)	0·145[b] (0·033)	0·923

[a] Significant at the 10 per cent level.
[b] Significant at the 5 per cent level.
The 'constant' is the decimal logarithm of the constant term.

high explanatory power presented by the variables included in the function (high R^2) and to the relatively large number of observations.

The available data for 1960 allowed the estimation of production functions for 20 sectors defined in the census. The analysis was

TABLE A.17
DATA FOR 1950: SIMPLE CORRELATION COEFFICIENTS

Sector	Correlation between the variables[a]		
	r_{12}	r_{13}	r_{23}
Non-metallic mineral products	0·896	0·500	0·345
Metallurgy, machinery, electrical machinery, transportation equipment	0·966	0·399	0·334
Wood products and furniture	0·913	0·170	0·221
Chemicals and pharmaceuticals	0·871	0·281	0·325
Textiles	0·958	0·131	0·175
Clothing	0·862	0·449	0·366
Food products, beverages, and tobacco	0·933	0·418	0·327

[a] The definition of the variables is: $x_1 = CV/E$
$$x_2 = O/E$$
$$x_3 = VAT$$

limited to the manufacturing sectors, excluding the sector 'Miscellaneous' (*Diversas*). The estimated coefficients and their standard errors are presented in Table A.18. The results seem to be inferior to those for 1950 data. In six cases the coefficients for capital are not significant even at the 10 per cent level. Apart from other problems, it should be recalled that the data used consist of preliminary results taken from the 1960 Census, and thus may be modified at a later stage. On the other hand, the period of time covered by the census coincides, in this case, with the rapid expansion of important sections of a number of sectors,

TABLE A.18
PRODUCTION FUNCTION ESTIMATES, STRATIFIED SAMPLE, SPECIFICATION (2), 1960 DATA

		Coefficients of variables			
Sector	Constant	CV/E	O/E	VAT	R^2
Non-metallic mineral products	1·504	0·237 [b] (0·034)	0·858 [b] (0·055)	0·127 [b] (0·028)	0·961
Metallurgy	1·649	0·124 [a] (0·067)	0·948 [b] (0·080)	0·137 [b] (0·034)	0·953
Machinery	1·107	−0·009 (0·075)	0·999 [b] (0·076)	0·287 [b] (0·026)	0·972
Electrical equipment	1·587	0·028 (0·097)	1·048 [b] (0·099)	0·180 [b] (0·065)	0·947
Transportation equipment	1·299	0·096 (0·063)	0·952 [b] (0·064)	0·218 [b] (0·031)	0·961
Wood products	1·623	0·216 [a] (0·111)	0·887 [b] (0·100)	0·100 [b] (0·040)	0·866
Furniture	1·604	0·141 [b] (0·047)	0·874 [b] (0·054)	0·133 [b] (0·026)	0·950
Paper and products	2·000	−0·009 (0·072)	1·098 [b] (0·104)	0·082 (0·057)	0·917
Rubber products	2·440	0·095 (0·091)	0·878 [b] (0·121)	0·054 (0·060)	0·853
Leather products	1·872	0·110 [b] (0·040)	0·950 [b] (0·058)	0·076 [b] (0·029)	0·940
Chemicals	1·303	0·430 [b] (0·109)	0·560 [b] (0·127)	0·254 [b] (0·053)	0·807
Pharmaceuticals	1·105	0·136 [b] (0·045)	0·956 [b] (0·050)	0·322 [b] (0·051)	0·948
Perfumes, soaps, etc.	2·004	0·066 (0·088)	0·956 [b] (0·124)	0·157 [b] (0·062)	0·831
Plastics	1·640	0·521 [b] (0·130)	0·583 [b] (0·143)	0·112 (0·087)	0·953
Textiles	1·877	0·595 [b] (0·088)	0·305 [b] (0·088)	0·107 [b] (0·045)	0·824
Clothing	1·881	0·140 [b] (0·030)	0·886 [b] (0·041)	0·090 [b] (0·023)	0·973
Food products	1·841	0·224 [b] (0·039)	0·763 [b] (0·040)	0·224 [b] (0·039)	0·935
Beverages	1·204	0·115 [b] (0·054)	0·975 [b] (0·075)	0·263 [b] (0·038)	0·937
Tobacco	2·510	0·364 [b] (0·081)	0·734 [b] (0·102)	−0·021 (0·072)	0·908
Printing and publishing	1·757	0·294 [b] (0·082)	0·680 [b] (0·083)	0·147 [b] (0·039)	0·899

[a] Significant at the 10 per cent level.
[b] Significant at the 5 per cent level.
The 'constant' is the decimal logarithm of the constant term.

particularly those associated with transportation equipment and machinery, in which it is reasonable to assume rather low levels of utilization of physical capacity. Recalling that the variable used for capital is approximately proportional to the 'stock', and that the situation noted above was particularly important in the more developed states, that fact might affect the results, i.e. the coefficient of capital may be biased.

As has already been pointed out in the analysis made in the previous part, the *VAT* variable—although not able to provide for a precise discrimination of the factors represented by it, including those defined as external economies—allows for the explicit introduction in the function of the influence of some variables such as entrepreneurial ability, technological differences, and quality of factors, which would otherwise be assigned to the other factors explicitly included. If the sectors presented in the table above were listed according to the order of magnitudes of the coefficients yielded by *VAT*, we would see a relationship between the value of that coefficient and the technical characteristics of the production processes involved. The industries with higher coefficients, such as pharmaceuticals, machinery, chemicals, and transportation equipment, for instance, are those in which it is agreed upon that the technological level and the quality of labour and capital are particularly important determinants of productivity. It is interesting to note in the same context that the effects introduced by *VAT* are not significant for the plastics industry. Plastics is a relatively new industry in Brazil, concentrated in the more developed states. The factors mentioned above would not, in the sample used, have shown a large enough range for their effect to be observed.

V. DIFFERENCES OF AVERAGE LABOUR PRODUCTIVITY

Having presented the general results obtained from the estimation of the production functions, I shall, in this section, discuss a procedure which can facilitate the approximate determination of the relative importance of a few of the factors on the regional differences in industrial productivity. The procedure used here to test the hypothesis of economies of scale and, at the same time, to determine the relative importance of the other factors discussed above, is based on a modification of specification (2) above. We can divide by the average number of workers per establishment (O/E) and write:

$$\frac{VA_{ij}}{O_{ij}} = a_0 \left(\frac{CV_{ij}}{O_{ij}}\right)^{a_1} \left(\frac{O_{ij}}{E_{ij}}\right)^{(a_1 + a_2 - 1)} VAT^{a_3} u_{ij} \qquad (3)$$

In this expression, the average productivity of labour, measured by VA/O is a function of three components: the amount of capital (in the unit chosen) per worker, the establishment size measured by the number of workers employed, and the total amount of industrial production in the state where the corresponding establishment is located. It is easy to demonstrate that the same results are obtained from specifications (2) and (3), in terms of the estimated coefficients. The coefficients presented for specification (2) could be obtained from the coefficients estimated from the above expression, the only difference being the error of approximation.

Table A.19 contains the results obtained for 1950 data. Note that the test of the null hypothesis of the true coefficient of O/E in expression (3) is identical to the test of the hypothesis of constant returns to scale. There is evidence of economies of scale in three of the seven sectors included. In the textile industry, diseconomies of scale are suggested.[1] The results for the 1960 Census show

TABLE A.19
TESTING FOR ECONOMIES OF SCALE: 1950 CENSUS

Sector	Constant	Coefficients of variables			R^2
		$\dfrac{CV_{ij}}{O_{ij}}$	$\dfrac{O_{ij}}{E_{ij}}$	VAT_i	
Non-metallic mineral products	0·202	0·169[b] (0·047)	0·078[b] (0·034)	0·161[b] (0·028)	0·608
Metallurgy, machinery, electrical equipment, transportation equipment	0·513	0·162[b] (0·070)	0·058[b] (0·025)	0·138[b] (0·026)	0·538
Wood products and furniture	0·426	0·262[b] (0·063)	0·080[b] (0·026)	0·131[b] (0·019)	0·466
Chemicals and pharmaceuticals	0·525	−0·003[b] (0·052)	−0·017 (0·037)	0·192[b] (0·032)	0·309
Textiles	0·323	0·141[b] (0·079)	−0·101[b] (0·022)	0·202[b] (0·026)	0·461
Clothing	0·196	0·106[b] (0·030)	−0·014 (0·027)	0·195[b] (0·022)	0·668
Food products, beverages, and tobacco	0·438	0·544[b] (0·077)	0·035 (0·033)	0·145[b] (0·033)	0·505

[b] Significant at the 5 per cent level.
The 'constant' is the decimal logarithm of the constant term.

[1] There are some reasons to believe that the results were affected by the omission of a quality index for capital.

analogous indications on the size of the estimated scale elasticity. These results are presented in Table A.20.

TABLE A.20
TESTING FOR ECONOMIES OF SCALE: 1960 CENSUS

Sector	Constant	Coefficients of variables			
		$\dfrac{CV_{ij}}{O_{ij}}$	$\dfrac{O_{ij}}{E_{ij}}$	VAT_i	R^a
Non-metallic mineral products	1·504	0·237 [b] (0·034)	0·096 [b] (0·029)	0·127 [b] (0·028)	0·658
Metallurgy	1·649	0·124 [b] (0·067)	0·072 [b] (0·027)	0·137 [b] (0·034)	0·337
Machinery	1·107	−0·009 [b] (0·075)	−0·010 (0·025)	0·287 [b] (0·026)	0·674
Electrical equipment	1·587	0·028 [b] (0·097)	0·077 [a] (0·039)	0·180 [b] (0·065)	0·265
Transportation equipment	1·299	0·096 [b] (0·063)	0·049 [a] (0·029)	0·218 [b] (0·031)	0·530
Wood products	1·623	0·216 [b] (0·111)	0·193 [b] (0·050)	0·100 [b] (0·040)	0·146
Furniture	1·604	0·141 [b] (0·047)	0·015 (0·028)	0·133 [b] (0·026)	0·366
Paper and products	2·000	−0·009 [b] (0·072)	0·088 [b] (0·048)	0·082 [b] (0·057)	0·118
Rubber products	2·440	0·095 [b] (0·091)	−0·025 (0·065)	0·054 [b] (0·060)	0·320
Leather products	1·872	0·110 [b] (0·040)	0·060 (0·032)	0·076 [b] (0·029)	0·229
Chemicals	1·303	0·430 [b] (0·109)	0·008 (0·055)	0·254 [b] (0·053)	0·279
Pharmaceuticals	1·105	0·136 [b] (0·095)	0·093 [a] (0·046)	0·322 [b] (0·051)	0·604
Perfumes, soaps, etc.	2·004	0·066 [b] (0·088)	0·023 (0·069)	0·157 [b] (0·062)	0·123
Plastics	1·640	0·521 [b] (0·130)	0·104 [b] (0·050)	0·112 [b] (0·087)	0·475
Textiles	1·877	0·595 [b] (0·088)	−0·098 [b] (0·037)	0·107 [b] (0·045)	0·332
Clothing	1·881	0·140 [b] (0·030)	0·027 (0·022)	0·090 [b] (0·023)	0·490
Food products	1·841	0·224 [b] (0·039)	−0·011 (0·023)	0·224 [b] (0·039)	0·376
Beverages	1·204	0·115 [b] (0·054)	0·090 [b] (0·039)	0·263 [b] (0·038)	0·545
Tobacco	2·510	0·364 [b] (0·081)	0·099 [a] (0·058)	−0·021 [b] (0·072)	0·378
Printing and publishing	1·757	0·294 [b] (0·082)	−0·024 (0·041)	0·147 [b] (0·039)	0·296

[a] Significant at the 10 per cent level.
[b] Significant at the 5 per cent level.
The 'constant' is the decimal logarithm of the constant term.

From the point of view of economies of scale, it is possible to reject the hypothesis of constant returns to scale at the 5 per cent level in six of the sectors, and at the 10 per cent level in another five sectors. In the remaining nine cases, the hypothesis is not rejected at the 10 per cent level. The coefficient of VAT is significant in the majority of cases.

The adjusted function can be interpreted in the following

manner: it gives the level of the average productivity of labour as a function of the amount of capital and scale of establishments (in the units of measurement employed here) for given levels of quality and other factors included in *VAT*. The variations attributed to this last variable could be associated with quality differentials of the inputs, management, technological knowledge, industrial diversification, and other factors which, in the sample, are correlated with *VAT* and which could be broadly classified as technological external economies.

The calculation of the relative importance of each factor (or factor set) on the basis of the estimated coefficients is not an easy matter in this case, due to the characteristics of the estimated function. The relative importance will depend on the coefficient and the range of the corresponding variable. An approximate measure of the relative importance can be constructed in three steps: First, compute the estimated formula for the lower limit of the variables included; second, take the same calculation for all variables, except for one which is put at its upper limit; third, the difference between the value obtained in the second step and in the first is considered an approximation of the individual effect of that variable. The sum of the individual contributions obtained will be the total against which each individual contribution will be compared.

For instance, consider the estimated function for non-metallic mineral products in 1960. The range of state averages of each variable is the following:

capital per worker	0·15 to	5·00
workers per establishment	2 to	14
total value added	1,000 to	296,000

It is relevant to note that there is not necessarily one particular establishment which simultaneously presents the values referred to above. For instance, in this case the lower limits of the capital and scale variables are the averages observed in Piaui State, while the upper limits refer to the State of Rio de Janeiro. With respect to total value added in manufacturing, the lower limit is from Piaui but the upper limit refers to the State of São Paulo.

The value of the estimated function at the lower and upper limits of the variables is 46·6 and 327·3 respectively. The proportion of this difference which could be attributed to each factor in this case is:

capital per worker	30 per cent
economies of scale	11 per cent
other factors (*VAT*)	59 per cent

When we consider the range of the variables among the size classes of establishments, the relative importance of scale increases very much as indicated below. In this case, the range of the size variable is from 2 to 1,800 workers per establishment, and the importance of the three explanatory variables is:

capital per worker	21 per cent
economies of scale	37 per cent
other factors (*VAT*)	42 per cent

Similar calculations made for a number of other industries show substantial differences on the relative importance of each factor. The results are presented in Table A.21 where only the ranges of state averages were considered. As noted earlier, state averages narrow the range of capital per worker and size of establishment and reduce the relative importance attributed to these factors on the productivity differentials.

In approximate terms, one could say that in the majority of sectors considered, the factors which are associated with the volume of manufacturing activity in each state account for a substantial part of the observed differences in the average productivity of

TABLE A.21

APPROXIMATE IMPORTANCE OF EACH FACTOR ON REGIONAL
PRODUCTIVITY DIFFERENCES

Sector	Capital per worker CV/O	Economies of scale O/E	Other factors VAT
	(*per cent of total for each sector*)		
Non-metallic mineral products	47·0	8·1	44·9
Metallurgy	36·0	11·7	52·3
Electrical equipment	1·5	12·9	85·6
Transportation equipment	9·2	6·1	84·7
Wood products	31·0	23·0	46·0
Furniture	30·5	1·5	68·0
Leather products	33·7	18·0	48·3
Chemicals	23·3	0·5	76·2
Pharmaceuticals	10·6	3·7	85·7
Perfumes, soaps, etc.	13·7	2·8	83·5
Plastics	68·5	8·4	23·1
Clothing	56·2	3·0	40·8
Beverages	8·1	6·2	85·7

Based on range of state averages.

labour. The coexistence of large differentials of productivity inside the same economy suggests a low degree of integration in the national market. From the economic policy point of view, the results could be important for regional development or international economic integration projects, and even for an evaluation of export possibilities of underdeveloped countries.

VI. FINAL COMMENTS

The estimates of production functions made in the previous sections give substantial importance to factors other than capital intensity and scale of establishment in the explanation of industrial productivity differences among states. The factors which we can expect to be correlated with VAT are mainly those related to quality differences, external economies, and also industrial specialization. In this respect the results are not much different from the time series and cross-section estimates available for other countries; in particular, those for the United States.[1] In general, these studies find strong indications of the great importance of the catch-all concept 'technological progress', which probably includes in some degree the factors accounted for here by the variable VAT.

An interesting question could be raised from the above results concerning the interpretation of the factors accounted by total industrial value added (VAT): to what extent are those factors actually a result of the amount of industrial production in the state, *per se*, or to what extent are they only *associated* with this value, in the sample. Unfortunately, I cannot give a complete answer as yet. Better knowledge of the determinants of regional differences of industrial productivity in Brazilian manufacturing will become available only through the inclusion of quality variables in the production function. However, apart from some factors dependent on location *per se*, it seems reasonable to accept the existence of some relationship between a number of those other factors and the total amount of industrial production or the size of the market for industrial products. For instance, better infrastructure, spread of know-how, skilled labour, and better supply of intermediate goods are very often results of a high degree of industrialization.

[1] See, for instance, R. M. Solow, 'Technical Change and the Aggregate Production Function', *Review of Economics and Statistics*, August 1957, 39, 312–20; R. R. Nelson, 'Aggregate Production Functions', *American Economic Review*, September 1964.

Appendix 3
Methodology and Sources for Chapter 3

I. BASIC DATA: SOURCES AND TREATMENT

1. Tariff rates were taken from Abilio Corrêa, Lahire Nobre, and J. C. Magalhães: *Tarifa das Alfândegas*, Rio de Janeiro (in looseleaf form which is kept up to date).

2. The premium for goods in the special category as of June 1966 was taken to be 100 per cent. This rate was approximately constant at this level throughout 1966 (data from Central Bank).

3. In calculating the average product tariff for each of the 24 sectors, tariffs on individual items were weighted by the sum of imports and domestic production of those items in the year 1958. (Data on imports from S.E.E.F., *Estatística do Comércio Exterior do Brasil*, 1958, Ministério da Fazenda, Rio de Janeiro; on domestic production from I.B.G.E., *Produção Industrial Brasileira, 1958*, Rio de Janeiro.) In forming the weights, domestic production values were deflated by 1966 tariffs, to make them appropriate to add to import values.

4. To average the 24-sector results, the sum of imports plus gross value of domestic production was used to average product protection, and domestic value added was used to average effective protection. These weights were constructed from 1964 data, which was the latest available.

As explained below in paragraph 5(*b*), the estimate of effective protection for the perfumes sector seems too high. This causes the average of effective protection to be too high. Another method of averaging, discussed in Section II of this Appendix, yields much lower results. I have adopted what seems to be a reasonable solution; in the text I cite the averages excluding the perfumes sector. This is an unimportant problem; the absolute level of this average is not particularly important. What is important are its changes over time, and the sectoral structure which makes it up.

5. The structure of inputs for these 24 sectors was given by an

input–output table for 1959, compiled and kindly made available by Willy van Rijckeghem. The table has since been published as *Relações Interindustriais no Brasil*, Cadernos I.P.E.A. No 2, I.P.E.A., Ministério do Planejamento, Rio de Janeiro, December 1967. The data in the van Rijckeghem table were modified as follows:

(*a*) All flows were put at producer prices by deducting trade and transport margins, both from inputs and from outputs. Excise taxes were also deducted from inputs. (Output values were already net of excise taxes.)

(*b*) The value of the coefficients at world prices was estimated by multiplying the observed value by the ratio of 1966 tariffs on the product and on the input:

$$(a_{ij}, \text{world}) = (a_{ij}, \text{observed}) \left(\frac{1 + t_j}{1 + t_i} \right) \qquad (1)$$

I do not put much faith in this assumption, but could find no better way to make the adjustment. The results seem sensible in all cases except the perfumes sector. In this sector value added, calculated as a residual after the adjustment, appeared very small. This implies that the tradable inputs used by the industry cost almost as much (at free trade prices) as the output is worth (also at free trade prices), and that value added could have been 66 times as much as in a free trade situation. This is inefficiency indeed! It is possible that there exist in Brazil some processes for which this is true. But there is no reason to believe that this entire sector, on the average, is so inefficient. The explanation that the adjustment according to equation (1) above was not accurate seems much more likely to be nearer the truth.

6. Port charges and across-the-board surcharges were added to the tariffs. These were 12 per cent *ad valorem* plus 1 per cent of the tariff for both years; 13 per cent was used. Excise taxes levied on domestic production, but not on imports, were deducted from the product tariff in calculating the effective tariff. Thus the estimates measure the net effect of tariffs on imports and excise taxes on domestic production. The level of these domestic excise taxes for 1966 was estimated from data in the E.P.E.A., *Diagnostic of Public Finance*. A rough average for the states of São Paulo, Rio de Janeiro, Guanabara, and Minas Gerais, including a rough guess at the extent of cascading, was used. (The tax in 1966 was

R

levied on total value of sales at each sale.) This estimate was 7 per cent. For 1967 a rough average for the same states was used, which was 10 per cent.

7. Estimates of actual price ratios, or other adjusted figures, were used instead of tariffs in three cases, as follows:

(a) For most export products, domestic prices generally are different from export prices. They are often higher than the export price times the export exchange rate. On the other hand, these products all have a legal tariff, and the domestic prices are usually much lower than the import price plus the tariff.

This problem was handled as follows: Major regular exports (except coffee) were assigned a zero tariff relative to the basic import exchange rate. (This was virtually equal to the export rate in 1966 and 1967.) This adjustment to zero tariff was made for a large number of products, mostly in the wood products, food products, tobacco, and three primary sectors. For coffee, the actual ratio of price to the producer to world price was used. This gave a 'tariff' for coffee of −60 per cent for 1966 and −47 per cent for 1967.

Even after this adjustment, there remain a number of other products, especially in the primary sectors, for which world prices transformed by the basic import exchange rate plus the tariff overstate the cruzeiro price in the export market. Moreover, there are at least a few products for which the world prices transformed by the basic import exchange rate plus the tariff overstate the cruzeiro price in the domestic market. This last is most notable in the primary animal products sector.

These dual prices are, incidentally, the reason why virtually all sectors are shown to have positive protection relative to the free trade exchange rate. Domestic prices are higher than export prices for many products.

(b) Capital goods were divided between imports or domestic production. The tariffs on imported capital goods were calculated as the ratio of actual tariff collections to actual value of imports (data from the Ministry of Finance). For domestically produced capital goods, which are mostly simpler types than those imported and are somewhat protected by the Law of Similars, it was assumed that no exemptions were available and the tariffs as published were used. These adjustments applied to the metallurgy and the three machinery sectors.

There is a major problem in accounting for the effect of variations in tariff exemptions on imported capital goods *as the exemptions vary by sector of destination*. The quantitative data needed to take this into account are not available. Thus the effects of what was probably a very important feature of commercial policy's effect on resource allocation, the different costs of capital equipment to different using industries, have not been included in the tariff calculations. A rough feel for the importance of these exemptions can be had from Chapter 4.

(c) For particular standardized products where either restrictions or exemptions were important, an estimate of the ratio of domestic ex-factory prices to C.I.F. prices was made. This was done for the following products: soda ash, caustic soda, eight different petroleum products, natural rubber, various kinds of automotive tyres and tubes, aluminium, lead, tin, copper and zinc ingots, coal, various steel products, fertilizer, and cement. Most of these prices are set administratively, either by government agencies, government-controlled corporations, or in close consultation with the Government. Prices are adjusted (to the inflation) irregularly, and often not in conjunction with devaluations. In many cases the data seemed to be internally inconsistent, and I had to use my best judgement, forming averages of internal prices for several months if data were available and if this seemed to give a more reasonable estimate of the implicit tariff. In a few cases (notably cement and tin) I was not able to get reasonable price comparisons, and therefore made an estimate of the price effect of the official tariff plus any restrictions or exemptions. Adjustment for quality was necessary only in the case of coal, where an estimate of blast furnace productivity was used as the index of quality.

8. For those domestic similars which were not covered by the adjustments listed above, the treatment was the following: for 1966, the 100 per cent special category premium plus the (high) tariffs on these products were used. For 1967, when the special category had been abolished, the provision of the Brazilian regulations that no protection would be given if the domestic price exceeds the C.I.F. price plus the tariff was accepted, and thus the tariff alone was used. This may have overestimated the actual price increases allowed by protection to most similars in 1966, and underestimated it for many similars in 1967.

9. Value added in the Brazilian input–output table includes depreciation.

II. METHODOLOGY FOR FURTHER CALCULATIONS

Table 3.2

The calculation of the nominal exchange rate, including protection, for imports is rather complicated. The detailed analysis of tariffs and other protective devices for 1966 and for 1967 gives estimates of average protection for those years. I did not have the time or other resources to do this for each preceding year, and therefore adopted a way to approximate the result.

Two quantitative analyses of the variation in protection from 1953 on were available. These were the work of Clark and Weisskoff and of Morley, cited in Chapter 3. The Clark–Weisskoff (C–W) results were used for this purpose because they were based on a fixed set of weights: tariffs on individual products in each year were weighted by 1962 imports. (Morley's method attempts to approximate each year's imports as weights for that year's tariffs.) Two problems remained: first, the C–W estimates were based on import weights, while for my purposes total supply weights were needed. The C–W annual estimates of tariffs and other protection were therefore multiplied by the ratio of my average for 1967 to the C–W average for 1967. This amounted to increasing the C–W estimates for each year by 76 per cent. The second problem is that the C–W estimates do not include adjustments for advance deposits and surcharges during 1961–5. Before making the 76 per cent adjustment mentioned above, I therefore added the E.P.E.A. estimate of the effect of these advance deposits and surcharges to the C–W estimates for 1961–5. This procedure is shown in Table A.22 below. One additional problem arose: the change from 1966 to 1967 was different in the C–W results and in my results. For the purposes of Table 3.2 I chose to project my April 1967 results backward according to the C–W series. Therefore the average tariff I present for 1966 in Tables 3.2 and 3.4 does not agree with my averages in Tables 3.3 and 3.5.

Redundancy

Redundancy means that domestic prices are not as high as import prices plus protection. It means that, in terms of equation (1) in Chapter 3:

$$t > \frac{X}{P} - 1 \qquad\qquad (2)$$

The measures presented in Chapter 3 are estimates of the maximum protection which the actual system, as legally constituted and as actually administered, allows. The problem of redundancy might be serious where tariffs are high and products are not standardized—consumer goods. Since in Brazil there is very little trade in consumer goods, there is even more reason to suspect redundancy.

TABLE A.22
CALCULATIONS FOR COLUMN 3, TABLE 3.2

Year	1	2	3	4	5	6
1954	28%		28%	49%	41·80	62·30
1955	25		25	44	63·80	91·90
1956	35		35	62	73·80	173·00
1957	93		93	163	65·60	173·00
1958	9		9	16	149·00	173·00
1959	25		25	44	202·00	291·00
1960	25		25	44	223·00	321·00
1961	62	11%	73	128	268·00	611·00
1962	68	27	95	167	390·00	1,040·00
1963	75	33	108	190	575·00	1,670·00
1964	58	18	76	134	1,284·00	3,000·00
1965	52	9	61	107	1,899·00	3,930·00
1966	39		39	69	2,220·00	3,750·00
1967[a]	21		21	37	2,730·00	3,730·00

[a] Refers only to period after devaluation (in February) and tariff reform at end of March.

Column 1: C–W tariff plus premia, Tables B-4a and 1b, op. cit.

     2: Adjustment for advance deposits, surcharges, etc. Source: E.P.E.A., *Comércio Internacional*, op. cit.

     3: Sum of Column (1) and Column (2).

     4: Column (3), adjusted so that the value for 1967 is 37 per cent.

     5: The 'basic' import exchange rate in cruzeiros per dollar, including premia for 1st category (1954–7) or general category (1957–61). Source: E.P.E.A., ibid.

     6: The 'basic' exchange rate multiplied by (Column (4) plus unity) Equals Column (3), Table 3.2.

In a continuous, rapid inflation, with only occasional adjustments in the exchange rate, the precise meaning of redundancy is not clear. If a tariff is such that the domestic price equals the world price just before a devaluation—and therefore there is redundancy at all other parts of the inflation–devaluation cycle—

is there zero redundancy? Should redundancy be defined as some sort of average, perhaps at the mid-point between devaluations? This would imply that 'zero redundancy' would permit imports half of the time. Added to the problem of definition are the problems of measurement. The commodities are not standardized; prices vary among parts of Brazil and among exporting countries.

The question of redundancy is a real one, and an interesting one, even if definition is ambiguous and measurement difficult. I have not been able to make valid price comparisons for enough consumer goods to satisfy myself enough to present numerical estimates for the relevant sectors. There is, however, enough information to draw some general conclusions.

As shown in Table 3.4, real import rates fell sharply in 1966 and 1967. Imports of consumer goods have risen sharply: in 1967 automobiles were being imported at the rate of roughly 1,000 per month; previously imports averaged 340 per year. The dollar value of imports of manufactured consumer non-durables grew 23 per cent in 1966 and 44 per cent in 1967, and appears to be growing rapidly in early 1968.[1] Clark concludes that 'about a third of the large import increase in 1966 was attributable to import liberalization, the remainder being due to the sharp recovery of gross investment'.[2] These rising imports, together with some crude price comparisons at the retail level made in February 1968, suggest that there was very little, if any redundancy before the devaluation at the end of 1967—the point of minimum redundancy in recent years. In fact, many consumer goods were being imported at that time. My measures for 1966, at the middle of the period between devaluations, probably include significant redundancy for consumer goods.

Redundancy is more of a problem in calculating *effective* protection; tariffs on inputs should certainly be non-redundant. In the present case I believe this problem to be unimportant, since price comparisons and other methods have been used to adjust the tariffs on many of the important producer goods. I doubt that any significant redundancy remains in our tariffs on producer goods. This same kind of problem does exist, however, as an aggregation problem: many producer goods are in the same

[1] S.E.E.F., Ministry of Finance, *Mensário Estatístico* and unpublished worksheets. Protection for these goods rose sharply in early 1969.
[2] Clark, op. cit., p. i.

sectors as consumer goods, and for some sectors the average tariff for the sector overstates the tariff on those products of the sector used as inputs to manufacturing.

In summary, the estimates of both product and effective protection for February 1967 contain little or no redundancy. The estimates for June 1966 probably contain some redundancy, especially in finished consumer goods sectors, for both product and effective protection. In all cases, the estimates should be taken as the maximum protection which commercial policy permits; in some cases domestic competition or other factors may reduce the actual prices or margin available for value added.

Non-tradable inputs

The theory of effective protection, in its simplest form, is based on a division of all inputs into one of two classes: tradable and value added. Effective protection is the protection to value added afforded by product protection on the product and on the tradable inputs. However, a third class of inputs exist which are neither tradable nor value added. These are domestic services such as transportation, electric power, etc. There have been different proposals about how to treat these inputs. Some treat them as tradable inputs with a zero tariff; others prefer to incorporate them into the using manufacturing sectors. In this latter treatment, first suggested by Corden in the paper cited in Chapter 3, these 'non-tradable' inputs are broken down into value added and tradable components, and the components are then combined with the same tradable inputs and value added in the using manufacturing sectors. This latter method has been chosen here, essentially for the reasons suggested by Corden. This method always gives lower estimates of effective protection than the former. I have also made estimates with the former method; the results are presented in Bergsman and Malan, 'The Structure of Protection in Brazil', in Bela Balassa *et. al.*, *The Structure of Protection in Developing Countries*, Johns Hopkins Press, to appear.

Estimation of the free trade exchange rate

This is an inherently hypothetical analysis. I have had to use a lot of judgement for many of the necessary assumptions; the most I claim for the results is that they seem at least as reasonable as any others, and that they allow estimates of the effects of commercial policy on incentives which are much closer to the truth than I could achieve by ignoring this question.

The first step is to estimate the price elasticities of supply and demand for exports and imports. It seems reasonable to assume that the elasticity of supply of imports is infinite. There are two estimates of the elasticity of demand for imports: these are approximately -0.4 and -0.6.[1] Both these estimates are 'partial' in the sense that they do not include effects of price changes on import substitution or on domestic income. As stated in Chapter 3, this seems more appropriate than a 'total' estimate, and a value of -0.5 was therefore adopted.

There is, if anything, even more uncertainty regarding exports. None of Brazil's non-coffee exports account for more than 10 per cent of either total Brazil non-coffee exports or total world exports of the commodity involved.[2] For these exports, the elasticity of demand is thus on the order of 20 times the total world elasticity. If the latter is, say, about one-third, the Brazilian elasticity would be about 7. In the event of an actual devaluation, minor exports would probably expand much more, because of the large number of products which are an even smaller percentage of world trade. It seems reasonable to estimate the demand elasticity as at least 7; actually anything up to infinity implies very similar results, as will be shown below.

There are estimates of the domestic elasticity of supply of a few export products, as around 0.8 to 1.3.[3] The elasticity of them all taken together would probably be less. The share of exports in total production of these commodities varies widely; an average would be 0.5 or less. A reasonable estimate of the supply elasticity for exports would be, then, around 1 or 2.

The data are consistent with the assumptions of unitary supply

[1] See Clark and Weisskoff, op. cit., Clark, op. cit., and Morley, op. cit.

[2] For those products which have the highest percentages, the figures are as follows:

	Share in	
Product	World exports	Brazil non-coffee exports
Cacau	10%	5%
Bananas	6	1
Cotton	5	11
Sugar	3	8

[3] See Antonio Delfim Netto et al., Agricultura e Desenvolvimento no Brasil, Estudos Anpes No. 5, 1967.

and infinite demand elasticities for non-coffee exports. The former assumption could be contradicted by a regression of the quantum on the (real) domestic price. Such a regression gives an estimated elasticity of 0·98. The latter assumption could be contradicted by a regression of the quantum on the foreign price. Such a regression does not show a significant relationship; this is consistent with an unshifting, infinitely elastic demand curve. The absence of a relation between the quantum and the world price can also be seen in a regression of the quantum on the (real) exchange rate. This regression gives the same elasticity (1·03) with respect to the exchange rate as the first equation's estimate with respect to the exchange rate times the foreign price.[1] I do not pretend that these results give reliable estimates of either of the elasticities. They do show that the quantity and the price of non-coffee exports did behave almost exactly as they would have if my set of assumptions had been true.

If the actual exchange rate is defined as the average rate (including subsidies) for non-coffee exports, then subsidies and export taxes are zero. With assumptions of infinite elasticities of demand for exports and supply of imports, the percentage devaluation needed to compensate for a removal of tariffs is given by:[2]

$$\frac{r' - r}{r} = \frac{t\left(\frac{M}{X}\right)\left(\frac{e_M}{e_X}\right)}{\left(\frac{M}{X}\right)\left(\frac{e_M}{e_X}\right) - (1 + t)} \tag{3}$$

[1] The results are as follows:

$$\log Q = 0\cdot44 + 0\cdot98 \log (rp) \qquad R^2 = 0\cdot39$$
$$ (1\cdot30) \quad (0\cdot28)$$
$$\log Q = 0\cdot14 + 1\cdot03 \log r \qquad R^2 = 0\cdot67$$
$$ (0\cdot78) \quad (0\cdot17)$$

where Q = quantum of non-coffee exports (*Conjuntura Econômica*, index No. 70).
r = average export exchange rate for products other than coffee, deflated by the domestic wholesale price index. (See Table 3.4, Chapter 3.)
p = average dollar price of non-coffee exports (*Conjuntura Econômica*, index No. 84).
Data cover 1946–66. Both elasticities are significantly different from zero at the 0·005 level. The regression of Q on p gives an R^2 of 0·11, which implies that the elasticity is not significantly different from zero at the 0·05 level.

[2]
$$\frac{\Delta X}{X} = e_X \frac{(r' - r)}{r}$$
$$\frac{\Delta M}{M} = e_M \frac{(r' - (1 + t)r)}{(1 + t)r}$$
Setting $\Delta X = \Delta M$ gives the result in the text.

where: r' = free trade exchange rate
r = actual export rate (both in cruzeiros per dollar)
t = tariffs
M = value of imports
X = value of exports
e_M = elasticity of demand for imports
e_X = elasticity of supply of exports

If the assumption of infinite elasticity of demand for exports is dropped, the formula looks just like (3) except that the definition of e_X is now:[1]

$$e_{X'} = \frac{e_{SX}(e_{DX}+1)}{e_{DX} - e_{SX}} \qquad (4)$$

where e_{SX}, e_{DX} = elasticities of supply of and demand for exports.

Before selecting the set of assumptions to calculate the free trade rate for each year, it is worthwhile to explore the effect of variation in the assumptions for the single year 1967. This is shown in Table A.23.

TABLE A.23
DIFFERENT PARAMETERS AND IMPLIED PERCENTAGE DEVALUATION

Estimate number	Parameter estimates			Percentage devaluation $\frac{(r' - r)}{r}$
	e_{DX}	e_{SX}	e_M	
1	−7	2	−0·5	14%
2	−7	1	−0·5	19
3	−∞	1	−0·5	14
4	−7	2	−2·0	27
5	−∞	1	−2·0	29

The first three sets of assumptions seem to cover the reasonable range. These give results quite close to each other. For the reader who believes that a 'total' elasticity of demand for imports should have been used, that parameter has been arbitrarily set at −2 for

[1] This follows from:

$$\frac{\Delta Q}{Q} = e_{SX}\frac{\Delta(pr)}{pr} = e_{DX}\frac{\Delta p}{p} \qquad (5)$$

where Q = quantum of exports
p = foreign price of exports

From (5) we can derive the change in exports at foreign prices as:

$$\frac{\Delta X}{X} = e_{X'}\left(\frac{r' - r}{r}\right)$$

where $e_{X'}$ is as defined by (4).

estimates 4 and 5. This does make quite a difference. Estimate number 3 seems quite reasonable, and offers the added advantage of easy arithmetic. Therefore the third set of parameter estimates was used for each year during 1954–67.

Effective protection for capital goods, intermediate goods, and finished consumer goods in 1966

As explained earlier, this is very difficult to do with any precision because the Brazilian census (and input–output table) lumps more than one of these categories within single sectors. The results presented here are very rough, and should be taken only as indicating the orders of magnitude of the relative levels of protection.

The first step in making the estimates was to aggregate the input–output table and re-aggregate the product tariffs, and then to calculate effective protection in the usual manner. The proper methods of aggregation of both the input–output table and the product tariffs present some problems. I aggregated the input–output table in a way which reflects a narrow definition of intermediate goods, designed to exclude some sectors where import substitution was relatively complete by 1949. The aggregation was as follows:

'Capital goods':

> Machinery
> Electrical equipment $\left.\right\}$ half
> Transport equipment

'Intermediate goods':

> Non-metallic mineral products
> Metallurgy
> Wood products
> Paper and products
> Rubber products
> Chemicals

'Finished consumer goods':

> Electrical equipment $\left.\right\}$ half
> Transport equipment
> Furniture

Leather products
Pharmaceuticals
Perfumes, soaps, etc.
Plastics
Textiles
Clothing
Food products
Beverages
Tobacco

The basic criterion for the aggregation was to get a representative input structure for each of the three categories.

In estimating the average product tariffs, I used the data underlying Table 3.7. The same gross value of product weights were used for aggregation. I also modified a few input tariffs, where the particular input was important and where there was an obvious large difference between the average tariff on outputs of a sector and the average tariff on inputs from that sector into another sector.

Effective protection was then calculated, according to the 'Corden' method. The results were shown in the second column of Table 3.8. (The averages were rounded off to remove some of the misleading apparent precision.)

Both the structure of inputs and the average product protection which have been used to make these estimates are not at all precise. The results do, however, seem reasonable. To check further on this, I have made two comparisons. First, the effective protection for each of the sectors included under 'Intermediate goods' was averaged, using value added weights. The result is 35 per cent. Second, the results for the three categories were averaged and compared to the average of the twenty-one manufacturing sectors. Using the same (value added) weights in each case, the average for the three grand categories is 117 per cent. This seems quite reasonable when compared with the twenty-sector average (excluding perfumes) of 98 per cent, and the twenty-one-sector average of 180 per cent.

A different measure of effective protection

In many studies of effective protection, the results showed that a number of highly protected sectors had 'negative value added at world prices'. This is the extreme case of what happened with the perfumes sector in my calculations. The formula for effective protection does not give reasonable results in such cases. In an attempt to get reasonable estimates for some concept, a new measure, u, was defined as 'the percentage of domestic value added due to protection':

$$u \equiv \frac{\left(\begin{array}{c}\text{Domestic value added,} \\ \text{with protection}\end{array}\right) - \left(\begin{array}{c}\text{Value added at} \\ \text{world prices}\end{array}\right)}{(\text{Domestic value added, with protection})}$$

This measure, having the *domestic* value added as its denominator, does not give apparently unreasonable values when the estimate of value added at world prices is small or negative. The u measure bears a simple relation to effective production, z:

$$u = \frac{z}{z+1}$$

Measures of u, derived from effective protection as shown in Table 3.5, are shown here in Table A.24.

It is possible to convert averages of u back to z, and compare these with the z averages. This is interesting because of the problems with the z averages due to the high z of the perfumes sector. The results are:

AVERAGE EFFECTIVE PROTECTION
('z')

	June 1966			*April 1967*		
	With perfumes	*Without perfumes*	*Converted from u*	*With perfumes*	*Without perfumes*	*Converted from u*
All sectors	122%	72%	47%	55%	31%	22%
Manufacturing	180	98	69	91	52	45

This might be taken as an indication that the average effective protection, excluding the perfumes sector, is not an inappropriate average to use.

Taxes on goods actually imported

Morley's estimates of the total cost of actual imports,[1] relative to my estimated free trade exchange rate, are as shown in Table A.25. These data were calculated simply by dividing the effective total cost of imports in cruzeiros per dollar, as estimated by Morley,

[1] Morley, *op. cit.*

TABLE A.24
ESTIMATES OF 'u'
(derived from Table 3.5)

Sector	June 1966	April 1967
Primary vegetable products	7%	−5%
Primary animal products	52	2
Mining	0	−1
Non-metallic mineral products	32	18
Metallurgy	20	16
Machinery	11	14
Electrical equipment	60	42
Transport equipment	50	35
Wood products	13	9
Furniture	63	49
Paper and products	42	28
Rubber products	47	47
Leather products	42	38
Chemicals	21	20
Pharmaceuticals	9	15
Perfumes, soaps, etc.	99	97
Plastics	55	28
Textiles	74	57
Clothing	71	53
Food products	32	19
Beverages	77	58
Tobacco	69	49
Printing and publishing	48	32
Miscellaneous	45	34
Average, all sectors	32	18
Average, manufacturing	41	31

by my estimate of the free trade exchange rate, and subtracting unity. The actual taxes paid, as reported by the Ministry of Finance, are shown in Table A.26.

The total effective cost of imports was quite a bit higher than it would have been at the basic import exchange rate, especially before 1961. But that cost was never much higher than it would have been at the free trade exchange rate.

TABLE A.25
TAXES, ETC., ON ACTUAL IMPORTS
(relative to the free trade situation)

Year	Consumer goods				Processed intermediate goods		Capital goods, for:			
	Non-durable	Durable	Fuels	Wheat	Metallic	Non-metallic	Construction	Agriculture	Industry	Transport
1954	-4%	19%	-24%	-34%	-2%	-3%	-11%	-19%	-13%	21%
1955	-14	26	-18	-54	-1	-12	-21	-19	-19	-11
1956	-14	35	-31	-56	5	-9	-17	-11	-16	-9
1957	-17	20	-36	-36	-16	-30	-30	-30	-31	-22
1958	44	112	19	-33	39	35	23	1	-2	-2
1959	35	81	12	-38	30	12	-1	-5	-21	-34
1960	19	58	-13	-52	6	-2	-13	-15	-31	-29
1961	11	28	-11	-37	-17	-15	-24	-33	-31	-33
1962	4	21	-13	-35	-20	-7	-6	-24	-18	-7
1963	9	27	-16	-33	-19	-4	-6	-21	-15	-9
1964	1	16	-20	-35	-27	-14	-15	-34	-22	-24
1965	4	23	-2	-25	-13	-3	-1	-16	-13	-10
average:										
1954-6	-11	27	-24	-48	1	-8	-16	-16	-16	0
1958-64	18	49	-6	-38	-1	1	-6	-19	-20	-20
1954-64	7	40	-14	-40	-2	-4	-11	-19	-20	-14

Source: Calculated from Morley, op. cit.

TABLE A.26
TAXES, ETC., ACTUALLY COLLECTED ON IMPORTS

Year	Import taxes (1)	Profit on auctions (2) (Cr$ billions)	Total (3)	Imports C.I.F. (4)	Taxes, etc., as per cent of imports (5) (per cent)	Effective cost of imports (6) (Cr$ billions)	Imports C.I.F. (7) (U.S.$ millions)	Effective exchange rate (8) (Cr$/$)	Taxes, etc., relative to the free trade situation (9) (per cent)
1954	2·3	12·2	14·5	55·2	26	69·7	1,633	42	11
1955	2·2	7·1	9·3	60·2	15	69·5	1,307	53	−8
1956	2·0	18·5	20·5	71·6	29	92·1	1,234	74	4
1957	2·8	12·6	15·4	86·5	18	101·9	1,489	68	−16
1958	12·9	35·9	48·8	103·3	47	152·0	1,353	112	18
1959	19·1	47·4	66·5	161·3	41	228·0	1,375	165	3
1960	22·0	52·4	74·4	201·2	37	275·0	1,462	188	−11
1961	35·7		35·7	299·4	12	335·0	1,460	229	−35
1962	58·4		58·4	511·7	11	570·0	1,475	386	−30
1963	86·8		86·8	782·2	11	869·0	1,487	584	−30
1964	124·4		124·4	1,242·9	10	1,367·0	1,264	1,080	−37
1965	303·0		303·0	1,929·6	16	2,233·0	1,096	2,040	−18
average:									
1954–6					23				2
1958–64					23				−17

Sources:
Columns 1, 2: E.P.E.A., *Finanças Públicas*, op. cit.
Column 3: Sum of columns 1 and 2.
Columns 4, 7: E.P.E.A., *Comércio Internacional*, op. cit.
Column 5: Column 3 as a percentage of column 4.
Column 6: Column 3 plus column 4.
Column 8: Column 6 divided by column 7.
Column 9: Percentage by which column 8 exceeds the free trade exchange rate (column 1, Table 3.4).

Appendix 4
The Cost of Protection

PROTECTION may have both benefits and costs. The benefits presumably come from changes in the structure of production, induced by protection, which increase future growth. Costs arise from misallocation of resources, and from reduced incentives for technological progress, quality improvements, etc. In this Appendix the costs of protection in a static sense will be estimated.

I. FRAMEWORK OF ANALYSIS

The static cost of protection can be viewed as a result of the gap between the import and export exchange rates. Moving to a free trade situation increases both imports and exports; the domestic cost of the first additional dollar of exports is $1.00 less the highest export tax, but the domestic value of the first additional dollar's worth of imports is $1.00 plus the highest import tax.[1] Further increases in imports and exports are progressively less valuable, as the trading of the most profitable exports for the least profitable import substitutes is progressively exhausted. As a first approximation, one could assume that taxes decrease linearly from the highest to zero. In that case, the total cost of protection would be the area of a triangle, with the base equal to the sum of the highest import and export taxes, and the altitude equal to the value of the increase in imports or exports.[2] This can be seen from the sketch in Figure A.1.

The analysis of the structure of protection in Brazil presented

---

[1] This basic idea was suggested by Arnold Harberger in 'Using the Resources at Hand more Effectively', *American Economic Review, Proceedings*, May 1959.

[2] As we have seen earlier, taxing imports implies also taxing exports. The 'cost of protection' necessarily includes the effect of both.

in Chapter 3 can be used instead of the linear approximation. This leads to equation (1):

$$\text{cost} = \sum_i rt_{m,i}\Delta M_i + \sum rt_{x,j}\Delta X_j \qquad (1)$$

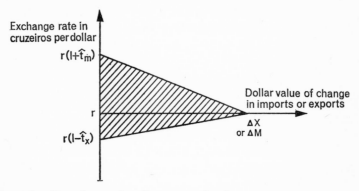

Figure A.1. Cost of protection: linear approximation

r = free trade exchange rate
$\hat{t}_m, \hat{t}_x$ = highest taxes on imports and exports, relative to r
$\Delta M = \Delta X$ = increase in dollar value of exports (or imports) resulting from moving to free trade

Where $t_{m,\,i}$; $t_{x,\,j}$ = taxes on imports (exports), sector $i(j)$. Since export taxes were essentially the same for all commodities (other than coffee, which is not considered here), equation (1) can be simplified as:

$$\text{cost} = \sum_i r(t_{m,i} + t_x)\Delta M_i \qquad (2)$$

In order to use the data actually available, we define a new variable, ΔF_i, as the value in domestic currency units, in the protected situation, of domestic production which in a free trade situation would be replaced by imports. This implies that:

$$\Delta F_i = (r)\,(\Delta M_i)\,(1 + t_{m,i}) \qquad (3)$$

Substituting (3) in (2), and dividing by G.N.P., gives the final result:

$$\frac{\text{cost}}{\text{G.N.P.}} = \sum_i \left(\frac{t_{m,i} + t_x}{1 + t_{m,i}}\right)\left(\frac{\Delta F_i}{\text{G.N.P.}}\right) \qquad (4)$$

An analogous formula results from considering value added and effective protection, rather than value of product and product protection:

$$\frac{\text{cost}}{\text{G.N.P.}} = \sum_j \left(\frac{z_{m,j} + z_x}{1 + z_{m,j}} \right) \left(\frac{\Delta V_j}{\text{G.N.P.}} \right) \tag{5}$$

where $z_{m,j}$; z_x = effective protection against imports, or tax on exports, sector (i.e. process) j.

ΔV_j = domestic value added in process j, in the protected situation, which would disappear with the removal of taxes on trade.

II. RESULTS FOR BRAZIL, 1967

Given the estimates of protection from Chapter 3, the only problem in applying either equation (4) or equation (5) is to estimate the 'weights' ΔF_i or ΔV_j. One way would be to assume that any sector with positive average protection would disappear entirely upon removal of taxes on trade. This extreme assumption gives an upper bound estimate of the cost of protection. Using the data for 1967, the results are 11·8 per cent of G.N.P. for equation (4), and 12·5 per cent for equation (5).

These results are too high, however, because of the way the weights were estimated. The 24-sector aggregation hides a lot of variation, and in a sector with positive average protection, many commodities may have zero or negative protection.[1] An examination of tariffs on individual items shows this to be true, especially for sectors where average protection is low, such as:

Sector	Product protection	$\dfrac{\Delta F_i}{G.N.P.}$
Primary animal products	2%	4·1%
Wood products	7	0·1
Food products	10	10·7

Detailed sampling of the thousands of individual tariffs used to make up the 24-sector aggregates shows that products which have zero or negative protection, but are included in sectors with positive protection on the average, account for some 20–30 per

---

[1] The opposite may also be true: sectors with non-positive average protection may include commodities with positive protection. There are two sectors with non-positive protection—primary vegetable products and mining—but only a few commodities in these sectors receive significant positive protection.

There is also a compensating error: if commodities with negative protection are removed from the weights, they should also be removed from the protection. Thus the proper t_m on the remaining ΔF would be higher, and the fraction $\left(\dfrac{t_{m,i} + t_x}{1 + t_{m,i}} \right)$ in equation (4) would be larger.

cent of the cost of protection as estimated above. This reduces the estimate to between 8 and 10 per cent of G.N.P.

What are the possible sources of this 'cost'? High prices permitted by protection may be the result of any combination of several factors:

1. Allocative inefficiency: the process is at an inherent comparative disadvantage in Brazil.

2. Avoidable high costs: the process *could* be competitive in Brazil, but management prefers a 'quiet life' which protection and lack of competitive behaviour in domestic markets permit.

3. Monopoly profits, similarly permitted by protection and lack of price competition in domestic markets.

For those products where high prices under protection are due to allocative inefficiency, a move to free trade would cause replacement by imports. But where the high prices are shielding avoidable high costs or monopoly profits, the expected result of moving to free trade would be to force reduction in costs or profits, rather than to replace domestic production by imports.

It would be interesting to estimate the relative importance of each of these three elements. Unfortunately, I have been able to estimate only the first, and hence indirectly the sum of the second and third. The estimate of the amount of domestic production which would actually be replaced by imports in a move to free trade in Brazil will give us an estimate of how much of the 'cost of protection' is due to allocative inefficiency. The remainder of the 8–10 per cent of G.N.P. we can then attribute to avoidable high costs or monopoly profits.[1]

Since the extent of the actual displacement of import substitutes is exactly what we don't know, let us try instead to estimate the export expansion which might result from a move to free trade. This will be equal to the import expansion, because of the need to maintain balance of payments equilibrium.

The results of Appendix 3 can be used to estimate the possible export expansion. We need to know the supply and demand elasticities for exports, and the percentage devaluation. As explained in Appendix 3, infinite demand and unitary supply elasticities seem a reasonable pair of estimates. (The effects of others will be analysed below.) These estimates, combined with

[1] Monopoly profits are, of course, only a re-distribution from the point of view of the entire economy.

estimates of infinite elasticity of supply and 0·5 elasticity of demand for imports, imply a devaluation of 14 per cent from the export exchange rate to reach a free trade equilibrium in 1967. This in turn implies an expansion of non-coffee exports of the same percentage, and of all exports and therefore of all imports of roughly 7 per cent. Assuming that the domestic production which would be replaced by imports would be that enjoying the highest protection, the cost of protection due to allocative inefficiency would be under 0·6 per cent of G.N.P.

The elasticity parameters used to derive the estimate of allocative inefficiency of 0·6 per cent of G.N.P. may be open to some question. It turns out, however, that the result for this analysis is not very sensitive to the choice of these elasticities. This is because of the interaction between the elasticities, and the tariffs and export taxes relative to the free trade equilibrium exchange rate. If the estimate of the elasticity of demand for imports goes up, for example, the estimate of the free trade exchange rate also goes up (i.e. a greater devaluation is needed to maintain balance of payments equilibrium after removing tariffs and export taxes), and the tariffs relative to the free trade rate go down. I have arbitrarily changed the parameters to an elasticity of demand for imports of 5·0 and an elasticity of supply of exports of 2·0, both separately and in combination. I then re-estimated the equilibrium free trade exchange rate, and the tariffs and export taxes relative to it. The resulting cost of allocative inefficiency remains less than 1 per cent of G.N.P. in all cases. Changing the parameters can almost double the estimate of allocative inefficiency, but even the higher estimate is very small compared with the total 'cost of protection'.

The difference between 8–10 per cent of G.N.P., and less than 1 per cent of G.N.P., is so large that the reader may still wonder about the estimates. To get an upper limit to the cost of allocative inefficiency which I feel no one can argue with, consider the following: Assume that devaluation to a free trade equilibrium required raising the exchange rate all the way to the former average import exchange rate including tariffs. In 1967 this would have amounted to a 38 per cent devaluation of the export exchange rate. How much might exports have expanded? For our purposes here, we can make the generous estimate of infinitely elastic demand and a supply elasticity of two. Thus the 38 per cent devaluation might expand non-coffee exports by as much as, say, 80 per cent. Non-coffee exports were roughly half the total; therefore, the expansion in total exports would be about 40 per cent. This is surely an overestimate of the actual expansion which might take place in a move to free trade equilibrium.

This overestimate of export expansion (in response to a devaluation all the way to the average import exchange rate including protection) can now be used as an upper bound on the *import* expansion which would result from a move to a free trade equilibrium. This gives us an upper-limit ΔM. To calculate the cost of protection implied by these assumptions we also need average import and export taxes. Again overestimating, let us take import taxes for the entire amount replaced to be 100 per cent, which was the maximum protection on any single product in 1967 (relative to the export exchange rate) and export taxes as zero (by definition). This gives a cost due to allocative inefficiency of 3·2 per cent of G.N.P.

Even this succession of assumptions leading to overestimates cannot raise the cost due to allocative inefficiency to over about 3 per cent of G.N.P. This means that, at the very least, avoidable high costs plus monopoly profits amounted to 5–7 per cent of G.N.P. in 1967. The more reasonable estimates reported above put the importance of allocative inefficiency at less than 1 per cent of G.N.P., and avoidable high costs plus monopoly profits as between 8 and 10 per cent of G.N.P.

This makes sense if we look at the economy sector by sector. There are a number of sectors enjoying and exploiting positive average protection, but in which there is reason to believe that Brazil *could* be competitive for most products of the sector, in the domestic market, even in a free trade situation. A conservative listing of such sectors is as follows:

Primary animal products	Textiles
Non-metallic mineral products	Clothing
Wood products	Food products
Furniture	Beverages
Leather products	Tobacco

The 'cost of protection' in these sectors alone, from equation (4) and not correcting for products with non-positive protection, is 8 per cent of G.N.P. If two-thirds of this represents monopoly profits plus avoidable high costs, then such 'costs' in these ten sectors alone would amount to 5 per cent of G.N.P.

These high estimates of monopoly profits plus avoidable higher costs indicate a considerable lack of competitive behaviour in the Brazilian domestic market. My experience during one and a half years with the industry department of the research office of the Ministry of Planning in Rio allowed me to verify this. In sector after sector, cost studies show very wide ranges in costs among firms producing the same or similar products. Not all Brazilian managers are exploiters of the 'quiet life' or monopolistic profits. Some firms in many different sectors compete successfully in export markets, and cost studies show that in most sectors there are some firms which are efficient when compared to similar firms in advanced industrial countries. But in general these efficient firms are not aggressive in enlarging their share of the domestic market through price competition. They are apparently content to take high percentage profits, permitting their less efficient competitors to enjoy a quiet life.

The best-documented instances of avoidable higher costs are in the textile industry. Some of this evidence was reviewed in Chapter 6. Objective evidence that there are no inherent reasons why the Brazilian textile industry should be inefficient—and on the average it is one of the most inefficient in Latin America, according to E.C.L.A.—is that at the same time the study cited in Chapter 6 was made, fully 10 per cent of the production of the Brazilian textile industry was being exported.

It should be noted that in earlier years the cost of protection was far greater. During 1954–64, the devaluation to reach free trade would have been anywhere from 45 per cent (elasticity estimates as in Appendix 3) to perhaps 100 per cent (assuming much higher elasticities). The effect of such a devaluation might have been as much as a doubling of imports; if all these were substitutes for industrial import substitutes, the direct effect alone would have been to decrease the size of the industrial sector by perhaps 10–40 per cent. Indirect effects, both through a conventional multiplier effect and also through the removal of the psychological inducements of protection would probably have caused a serious diminution of Brazil's industrialization.[1]

[1] By psychological inducements I mean, for example, that a businessman may not invest unless he knows he can get, say, 100 per cent protection. But after

III. CONCLUSIONS

The numerical analysis presented above is admittedly somewhat imprecise. But the difference in the size of the results permit solid conclusions to be drawn nevertheless. First, the total 'cost of protection' in Brazil is high—roughly between 8 and 10 per cent of G.N.P. even with the low protection of 1967. Second, of this total 'cost', less than 1 per cent of G.N.P. is due to misallocation in the usual economic sense. The rest consists of monopoly profits plus avoidable higher costs. Removal of taxes on trade in Brazil in 1967 would have resulted in a saving of only something less than 1 per cent of G.N.P. by substitution of profitable exports for inherently uneconomic import substitution activities. A further saving and redistribution amounting to perhaps 8–10 per cent of G.N.P. could have resulted from cost reductions and elimination of monopoly profits, which currently exist only by grace of Brazil's protective commercial policy.

---

investing he may find he *needs* only, say, 40 per cent after one or two years of operation and only, say, 20 per cent after five years.

List of Works Cited

I. OFFICIAL PUBLICATIONS
(1) INTERNATIONAL

INTERNATIONAL MONETARY FUND

Annual Report on Exchange Restrictions (various years beginning 1950).

UNITED NATIONS

A Study of Industrial Growth, 63.II.B.2 (New York, 1963).

Economic Commission for Latin America

A Economia Siderúrgica de America Latina: Monografia do Brasil (Santiago, December 1964, mimeo. prepared by Dr. M. Falcão).
La Economia Siderúrgica de America Latina (February 1966, mimeo.).
La Exportación en el Mercado Mundial: Una Perspectiva para el Desarollo de la Industria Textil Latin-Americana, ST/ECLA/Conf. 23/L.43 (March 1966, mimeo.).
'Fifteen Years of Economic Policy in Brazil', *Economic Bulletin for Latin America* (November 1964).
'The Growth and Decline of Import Substitution in Brazil', *Economic Bulletin for Latin America* (March 1964).
The Textile Industry in Latin America: II: Brazil, E/CN.12/623 (October 1963).

Statistical Office

The Growth of World Industry, 1953–65, ST/STAT/SER. P/4 (1697).
S

(2) NATIONAL

BRAZIL

Banco Nacional para Desenvolvimento Economica
XIII Exposicãô Sôbre O Programa de Reaparelhamento Econômico (1964).

Central Bank of Brazil
Bulletins

Escritório de Pesquisa Econômica Aplicada
Diagnóstico Preliminar, Educação, Ministry of Planning (Rio de Janeiro, June 1966).
Diagnóstico Preliminar, Energia Elétrica, Ministry of Planning (Rio de Janeiro, 1967).
Diagnóstico Preliminar, Finanças Públicas, Ministry of Planning (Rio de Janeiro, December 1965, mimeo.).
Diagnóstico Preliminar, Indústria Mecânica e Elétrica, Ministry of Planning (Rio de Janeiro, 1966).
Diagnóstico Preliminar da Indústria Têxtil, Ministry of Planning (Rio de Janeiro, January 1967, mimeo.).
Diagnóstico Preliminar, Setor de Agricultura, Ministry of Planning (Rio de Janeiro, 1966, mimeo.).
Diagnóstico Preliminar, Setor de Comércio Internacional, Ministry of Planning (Rio de Janeiro, March 1967, mimeo.).
Plano Decenal, Tomo V, Vol. 2, *Indústria Mecânica e Elétrica,* Ministry of Planning (Rio de Janeiro, 1967).

Fundação Getúlio Vargas
A Indústria de Alimentos no Brasil (1966, mimeo.).

Instituto Brasileiro de Geografia e Estatística (I.B.G.E.)

Anuário Estatístico (Rio de Janeiro, 1963).
Industrial Census of 1940, 1950, and 1960.
Indústrias de Transformação Dados Gerais—1963/64 (April 1966 for 1964).
Números Indices Annuais dos Preços e das Quantidades no Comércio Exterior e de Cabotagem.
O Brasil em Números.
Registro Industrial for 1955, 1958, and 1962.

Instituto Brasileiro de Siderúrgica
Boletim IBS

Ministry of Finance
Mensário Estatístico

UNITED STATES

Foreign Relations of the United States, Diplomatic Papers, 1940, Volume
V, *The American Republics* (United States Government Printing
Office, Washington 1961).

II. BOOKS, ARTICLES, AND SERIAL
PUBLICATIONS

Adelman, Irma and Morris, Cynthia T. 'An Econometric Model of
Socio-Economic and Political Change in Underdeveloped Coun-
tries', *American Economic Review* (December 1968).
Arrow, Kenneth J. 'The Economic Implications of Learning by Doing',
Review of Economic Studies (June 1962).
Associação Nacional dos Fabricantes de Veículos Automotores (An-
favea), *Indústria Automobilística Brasileira* (1966).
Baer, Werner. *Industrialization and Economic Development in Brazil*
(Richard D. Irwin, 1965).
 The Development of the Brazilian Steel Industry (Vanderbilt Uni-
versity Press, forthcoming).
Baer, Werner and Hervé, Michel. 'Employment and Industrialization
in Developing Countries', *Quarterly Journal of Economics* (Febru-
ary 1966).
Balassa, Bela. 'Tariff Protection in Industrial Countries: An Evalua-
tion', *Journal of Political Economy* (December 1965).
Balassa, Bela and Schydlowsky, Daniel M. 'Effective Tariffs, Domestic
Cost of Foreign Exchange, and the Equilibrium Exchange Rate',
Journal of Political Economy (May–June 1968).
Baranson, Jack. *Automotive Industries in Developing Countries,* Report
EC-162, International Bank for Reconstruction and Development
(Washington, D.C. 31 May 1968).
Barber, C. L. 'Canadian Tariff Policy', *Canadian Journal of Economics
and Political Science* (November 1955).
Bergsman, Joel and Candal, Arthur. 'Industrialization: Past Success and
Future Problems', in Howard S. Ellis (ed.), *The Economy of
Brazil* (University of California Press, 1969).
Bhagwati, Jagdish and Ramaswami, V. K. 'Domestic Distortions,
Tariffs, and the Theory of Optimum Subsidy', *Journal of Political
Economy* (February 1963).
Bhagwati, J. N. and Desai, P. *India: Planning for Industrialization.
Industrialization and Trade Policies since 1951* (Oxford University
Press for O.E.C.D., London, 1970).

Booz, Allen, and Hamilton, unpublished reports to the Banco Nacional para Desenvolvimento Econômica.

Brown, Murray. *On the Theory and Measurement of Technological Change* (Cambridge University Press, 1966).

Bruton, Henry J. 'Productivity Growth in Latin America', *American Economic Review* (December 1967).

Chenery, Hollis B. 'Comparative Advantage and Development Policy', *American Economic Review* (March 1957).

'Patterns of Industrial Growth', *American Economic Review* (September 1960).

Clark, Paul. *Brazilian Import Liberalization* (September 1967, mimeo.).

Clark, Paul and Weisskoff, Richard. *Import Demands and Import Policies in Brazil* (February 1967, mimeo.).

Compania Siderúrgica Nacional, *Máquinas e Metais. Relatória da Directoria* (annual reports).

Conjunctura Ecônomica (Rio de Janeiro).

Corden, W. M. 'The Structure of a Tariff System and the Effective Protection Rate', *Journal of Political Economy* (June 1966).

Delfim Netto, Antonio *et al. Agricultura e Desenvolvimento no Brasil*, Estudos Anpes No. 5 (1967).

Diaz, Carlos. 'On the Import Intensity of Import Substitution', *Kyklos*, Vol. XVIII, No. 3 (1965).

Editôra Banas. *O Capital Estrangeiro no Brasil*, 3rd edn. (São Paulo, June 1961).

Ellis, Alfredo Junior. *A Evolução da Economia Paulista e Suas Causas* (Companhia Editôria Nacional, São Paulo, 1937).

Fei, John C. H. and Ranis, Gustav. *Development of the Labor Surplus Economy* (Richard D. Irwin, 1964).

Frankel, M. 'The Production Function in Allocation and Growth: A Synthesis', *American Economic Review*, Vol. LII, No. 5 (1962).

Furtado, Celso. *The Economic Growth of Brazil* (University of California Press, 1963).

Gordon, Lincoln and Grommers, Engebert. *United States Manufacturing Investment in Brazil* (Harvard University Press, 1962).

Harberger, Arnold. 'Using the Resources at Hand More Effectively', *American Economic Review, Proceedings* (May 1959).

Harbison, Frederick and Myers, Charles A. *Education, Manpower, and Economic Growth* (McGraw-Hill, 1964).

Herring, Hubert. *A History of Latin America*, 3rd edn. (Alfred A. Knopf, 1968).

Hirschman, Albert O. 'The Political Economy of Import-Substituting Industrialization in Latin America', *Quarterly Journal of Economics* (February 1968).

The Strategy of Economic Development (Yale University Press, 1958).

Huddle, Donald L. 'Balanço de Pagamentos e Contrôle de Câmbio no Brasil', *Revista Brasileira de Economia* (March 1964).

'Balanço de Pagamentos e Contrôle de Câmbio no Brasil: Eficácia, Bem-Estar e Desenvolvimento Econômico, *Revista Brasileira de Economia* (June 1964).

Johnson, Harry G. 'Trade Preferences and Developing Countries', *Lloyds Bank Review* (July 1966).

Johnson, Leland J. 'Problems of Import Substitution: The Chilean Automobile Industry', *Economic Development and Cultural Change* (January 1967).

Johnson, William A. *The Steel Industry of India* (Harvard University Press, 1966).

Kafka, Alexander. 'The Brazilian Exchange Auction System', *Review of Economics and Statistics* (August 1956).

Kahil, R. *Inflation and Economic Development in Brazil Since World War II* (unpublished doctoral thesis, Oxford University, 1966).

Klein and Saks, *O Problema de Alimentação no Brasil* (Rio de Janeiro, 1954).

Kuznets, Simon, Moore, Wilbert E., and Spengler, Joseph J. (eds.), *Economic Growth: Brazil, India, Japan* (Duke University Press, 1959).

Lanari, Amaro Junior. 'Consumo de Carvão Nacional na Siderurgia', *Metalurgia*, Volume 21, No. 93 (August 1965).

Leff, Nathaniel H. 'Export Stagnation and Autarkic Development in Brazil, 1947–1962', *Quarterly Journal of Economics* (May 1967).

The Brazilian Capital Goods Industry 1929–1964 (Harvard University Press, 1968).

Leibenstein, Harvey. 'Allocative Efficiency vs "X-Efficiency" ', *American Economic Review* (June 1966).

Lewis, W. Arthur. 'Economic Development with Unlimited Supplies of Labor', *Manchester School* (May 1954).

Loeb, G. F. *Industrialization and Balanced Growth: With Special Reference to Brazil* (Groningen, Holland, 1957).

Marshall, Alfred. *Principles of Economics*, Book V, Chapter 11.

Meade, J. 'External Economies and Diseconomies in a Competitive Situation', *Economic Journal*, LXII (March 1952).

Morley, Samuel A. 'Import Demand and Import Substitution in Brazil' to appear in Howard S. Ellis (ed.), *The Economy of Brazil* (University of California Press, 1969).

Morley, Samuel A., and Smith, Gordon, 'On the Measurement of Import Substitution', *American Economic Review*, to appear.

Nelson, R. R. 'Aggregate Production Functions', *American Economic Review* (September 1964).

'International Productivity Differences', *American Economic Review* (December 1968).

Nurkse, Ragnar. *Problems of Capital Formation in Underdeveloped Countries* (Oxford University Press, 1953).

Revista Brasileira de Economia (Rio de Janeiro, March 1962 and June 1964).

Rocca, Carlos A. *Economias de Escala na Função Produção* (mimeographed doctoral dissertation, Faculdade de Ciéncias Econômicas e Administrativas da Universidade de São Paulo, São Paulo, 1967).

Rosenstein-Rodan, P. N. 'Problems of Industrialization of Eastern and South-Eastern Europe', *Economic Journal* (September 1943).

San Francisco Chronicle (30 August 1968).

Scitovsky, Tibor. 'Two Concepts of External Economies', *Journal of Political Economy*, Vol. LXII, No. 2 (April 1954).

Simonsen, Mário Henrique. 'Inflation and the Money and Capital Markets in Brazil' to appear in Howard S. Ellis (ed.), *The Economy of Brazil* (University of California Press, 1969).

Simonsen, Roberto. *História Econômica do Brasil* (Companhia Editôria Nacional, São Paulo, 1962).

Skidmore, Thomas E. *Politics in Brazil* (Oxford University Press, 1967).

Smith, Gordon. *Agricultural Marketing and Economic Development: A Brazilian Case Study* (unpublished Ph.D. dissertation, Harvard University, 1965).

Solow, R. M. 'Technical Change and the Aggregate Production Function', *Review of Economics and Statistics* (August 1957).

Stein, Stanley J. 'Brazilian Cotton Textile Industry, 1850–1950' in Simon Kuznets, Wilbert E. Moore, and Joseph J. Spengler (eds.), *Economic Growth: Brazil, India, Japan* (Duke University Press, 1959).

Tendler, Judith. *Electric Power in Brazil* (Harvard University Press, 1968).

Travis, William P. 'The Effective Rate of Protection and the Question of Labor Protection in the United States', *Journal of Political Economy* (May–June 1968).

United States Steel Corporation. *The Making, Shaping and Treating of Steel*, 8th edn. (Pittsburgh, 1964).

Veloso, Paulo Dias. *Perspectivas da Participação Brasileira no Mercado Internacional de Aço* (July 1967, mimeo.).

Vieira, Dorival Teixeira. 'The Industrialization of Brazil' in T. Lynn Smith and Alexander Marchant (eds.), *Brazil: Portrait of Half a Continent* (The Dryden Press, 1951).

Villela, Anníbal. 'As Empresas do Governo Federal e Sua Importância na Economia Nacional—1956/1960', *Revista Brasileira de Economia* (March 1962).

Index